THE SOURCES FOR THE LIFE OF
S. FRANCIS OF ASSISI

THE
SOURCES FOR THE LIFE OF
S. FRANCIS OF ASSISI

BY

JOHN R. H. MOORMAN, B.D.

Emmanuel College, Cambridge
Rector of Fallowfield, Manchester

WITH A FOREWORD BY

A. G. LITTLE, D.Litt., Litt.D., F.B.A.

MANCHESTER UNIVERSITY PRESS
1940

67-82048

Republished in 1966 by
Gregg Press Limited,
1 Westmead, Farnborough, Hants., England.
Printed in England.

FOREWORD

THE publication of Sabatier's *Speculum Perfectionis* in 1898 gave a new direction to Franciscan studies. Sabatier himself was misled by an erroneous date—which turned out to be a mere scribal error—and this warped his judgment and vitiated his immediate conclusions. He told me once that it did not much matter if his date were proved wrong, the essentials would remain. And in a sense this is true. He had proved the importance of much primitive material which had hitherto been neglected, and an active search was now begun for the sources which lay behind the *Speculum Perfectionis* and the *Second Life* by Celano. Many discoveries were made, the most important being those by Father Lemmens, Father Delorme and myself.[1] I have for long hoped that some younger scholar, equipped with full knowledge and unconnected with the controversies and prejudices of the past, would make a fresh survey of all the available materials and establish their origins and relations to each other and their relative values. This is what Mr. Moorman has done, with knowledge, industry and insight. I look forward to his book being examined in detail by Franciscan scholars and subjected to the severest tests, and feel confident that it will emerge from the ordeal substantially unharmed.

In another section of his book Mr. Moorman deals with the vexed problem of the *Legend of the Three Companions* and its relation to the *First Life* of Celano. This has been the subject of much controversy, the principal protagonists being Sabatier and Father van Ortroy. I have worked at the question a good deal from time to time, and though convinced that van Ortroy was wrong have never been quite satisfied with Sabatier's arguments and have had to leave the puzzle unsolved—saying that " the problem could probably be definitely solved from the existing materials by an acute and unprejudiced critic ". Now Mr. Moorman comes along with the startling theory " that the *Legenda* represents the earlier tradition and *Celano* the copy ". This is an entirely new and original idea (though Sabatier seems at one time to have approached near it) and Mr. Moorman works it out in detail in a piece of historical criticism which would have delighted that most

---

[1] I may mention that the MS. generally known in recent Franciscan publications as *MS. Little* is no longer in my possession, but has found a permanent home in the Bodleian Library, where its reference number is now MS. Lat. th. d. 23.

brilliant of critics, the late Professor Burkitt, to whose inspiration Mr. Moorman evidently owes much. A new idea like this has to be subjected to a rigorous examination before it can be accepted, but at first sight it does seem to me to meet many of the difficulties presented by the *Leg. 3 Soc.* and it may well prove to be the true solution and a discovery of first-rate importance.

I warmly commend Mr. Moorman's scholarly book to all who are interested in S. Francis and Franciscan history. Present conditions are unpropitious to any immediate success, but it is of lasting value and will influence Franciscan studies for many years to come.

A. G. LITTLE.

PREFACE

THE Sources for the Life of S. Francis have long provided an interesting study. Forty or fifty years ago learned periodicals in most European countries were opening their columns to now one now another theory put forward by the scholars of the day. With an eagerness which is characteristic of the expert, the problems of the inter-relationship of the *Speculum Perfectionis, Celano* and the *Legend of the Three Companions* were thrashed out to the point where it would seem impossible for anything new to be said.

It might, therefore, be regarded as almost an impertinence to offer a new solution of the problems, but my reasons for doing so are these. The first is that, since the great battles were fought out, at least one really important discovery has been made, the *Legenda Antiqua* found by Father Delorme in the Public Library at Perugia in 1921; and the second, that the whole investigation was given a new lease of life by the brilliant thesis which Burkitt contributed to the volume of *Essays in Commemoration* in 1926. These two facts seemed to make it desirable that a new and comprehensive study of the sources should be made.

In launching my theories on the world I have to thank two friends of an older generation, Dr. A. G. Little and Dr. G. G. Coulton, both of whom have been ungrudging in their advice and encouragement and whose erudition has saved me from many pitfalls. In expressing my thanks to them I am only adding to the debt which everyone who ventures into the realms of Franciscan history owes to these eminent scholars. I should like also to thank Dr. E. Rosenthal for his assistance, my wife for much help given in many ways, and Mr. McKechnie of the Manchester University Press for the pains which he has taken to see this book through the press in these inauspicious days.

JOHN R. H. MOORMAN.

FALLOWFIELD,
  November, 1940.

CONTENTS

BIBLIOGRAPHY

I. *Texts*

Beati Patris Francisci Assisiatis Opuscula, ed. Wadding, Antwerp, 1623, and frequently reprinted, e.g. by J. J. von der Burg, Cologne, 1849.

Opuscula Sancti Patris Francisci, ed. Leonardus Lemmens in *Bibliotheca Franciscana Ascetica Medii Aevi*, I, Quaracchi, 1904.

The Writings of Saint Francis, translations by "A Religious of the Order", London, about 1890 ; Paschal Robinson, Philadelphia, 1906 ; and C. de la Warr, London, n.d. (This is most untrustworthy.)

Thomas de Celano : Sancti Francisci Assisiensis Vita et Miracula, ed. Edouard d'Alencon, Rome, 1906.

Vita I et II S. Francisci auctore T. de Celano in *Analecta Franciscana*, X, i and ii, Quaracchi, 1926.

S. Francis according to Thomas of Celano, ed. H. G. Rosedale, London, 1904. (Very inaccurate.)

The Lives of S. Francis by Thomas of Celano, translated by A. G. Ferrers Howell, London, 1908.

Speculum Perfectionis, ed. Paul Sabatier, Paris, 1898.

Speculum Perfectionis, ed. Paul Sabatier in *B.S.F.S.*, XIII and XVII, 1928 and 1931.

The Mirror of Perfection, translations by Sebastian Evans, London, 1898 ; Robert Steele, London, 1903 ; and C. de la Warr, London, 1902.

Legenda Trium Sociorum, ed. Faloci-Pulignani in *Misc. Franc.*, VII, 1898.

La Leggenda di S. Francesco da Tre Suoi Compagni, ed. Marcellino da Civezza e Teofilo Domenichelli, Rome, 1899.

The Legend of S. Francis by the Three Companions, translated by E. Gurney Salter, London, 1902.

Legenda Antiqua S. Francisci, ed. Ferdinand Delorme in *A.F.H.*, XV, 1922.

La " Legenda Antiqua Sancti Francisci ", ed. F. Delorme in " *La France Franciscaine* ", Paris, 1926.

Documenta Antiqua Franciscana, three parts ed. Leonardus Lemmens, Quaracchi, 1901–2.

Julianus de Spira : *Vita S. Francisci* in *An. Boll.*, Vol. XXI (1902), ed. F. van Ortroy.

Julianus de Spira : *Vita S. Francisci* in *An. F.*, X, iv, 1, 1936.

Julianus de Spira : *Officium Rhythmicum S. Francisci* in *An. F.*, X, iv, 1, 1936.

Henricus Abrincensis (Henry of Avranches) : *Legenda Versificata* in *An. F.*, X, iv, 2, 1936.

S. Bonaventura : *Legendae Duae de Vita S. Francisci*, ed. Quaracchi Fathers, reprinted from the edition in Vol. VIII of the *Opera Omnia S. Bonaventurae*, Quaracchi, 1898.

Bonaventura's Life of S. Francis, translations by Miss Lockhart, London, 1867, and another, London, 1904.

Actus Beati Francisci et Sociorum Eius, ed. Paul Sabatier in *Collection d'Études et de Documents sur l'Histoire religieuse et littéraire du Moyen Age*, IV, Paris, 1902.

Fioretti di San Francesco, ed. L. Amoni, Rome, 1889.

The Little Flowers of S. Francis, translations by Manning (1863), Arnold (1898), Heywood (1906) and Okey (1919).

Testimonia Minora Saeculi XIII, ed. L. Lemmens, Quaracchi, 1926.

Tractatus de Indulgentia, ed. Paul Sabatier in *Collection d'Études*, II, Paris, 1900.

S. Francisci Legendae Veteris Fragmenta Quaedam, ed. Paul Sabatier in *Opuscules*, fasc. iii, 1902.

Sacrum Commercium : The Converse of Francis and his Sons with Holy Poverty, Latin and English versions ed. by Canon Rawnsley, London, 1904.

The Lady Poverty, translation of the *Sacrum Commercium* by Montgomery Carmichael, London, n.d.

La Leggenda Latina di San Francesco secondo l'Anonimo Perugino, ed. F. van Ortroy. *Misc. Franc.*, IX, 1902.

Liber de Laudibus S. Francisci, Bernard of Bessa, *An. F.*, III, 1897.

A. G. Little : *Description of a Franciscan MS.*, in *Collectanea Franciscana*, I (*B.S.F.S.*), 1914, and in *Opuscules*, fasc. xvii, Paris, 1914–19.

Chronica XXIV Generalium, in *An. F.*, III, 1897.

Chronica N. Glassberger in *An. F.*, II, 1887.

Salimbene da Parma : *Chronica* in *Monumenta Germaniae Historica* (*Scriptorum*), XXXII, ed. Holder Egger, Hanover, 1905–8.

G. G. Coulton : *From S. Francis to Dante*, 2nd edition, London, 1904.

Angelo Clareno : *Historia VII Tribulationum* in *A.L.K.G.*, II, ed. F. Ehrle, 1885.

Angelo Clareno : *Le Due Prime Tribolazioni*, ed. F. Tocco in *Rendiconti della Reale Accademia dei Lincei*, Rome, 1908.

Angelo Clareno : *Expositio Regulae*, ed. Livarius Oliger, Quaracchi, 1912.

Verba Fr. Conradi de Offida in *Opuscules*, ed. P. Sabatier, fasc. vi, 1903.

Eccleston : *De Adventu Fratrum Minorum in Angliam*, ed. A. G. Little in *Collection d'Études*, etc., VII, Paris, 1909.

Eccleston : *The Coming of the Friars*, translations by Father Cuthbert, London, 1903, and E. Gurney Salter, London, 1926.

Jordano da Jano ; *Chronica*, ed. H. Boehmer in *Collection d'Études*, etc., VI, Paris, 1908.

The Chronicle of Brother Jordan, translated by E. Gurney Salter, London, 1926.

Bartholomew of Pisa : *Liber de Conformitate* in *An. F.*, IV and V, 1906 and 1912.

II. *Studies of Texts*

Adrichem, D. van : *De Prima Editione Actuum* in *A.F.H.*, XXI, 1928.

Beaufreton, Maurice : *S. François d'Assise, Étude des Sources*, Paris, 1923.

Bihl, Michael : *Disquisitiones Celanenses. A.F.H.*, XX and XXI, 1927 and 1928.
De Legenda Versificata S. Francisci. A.F.H., XXII, 1929.
La Questione Francescana riveduta dal Signor Professore M. Barbi alla luce dell' opera dei Tre Compagni, in *Studi Francescani*, Florence, 1935.

Boehmer, H. : *Analekten zur Geschichte des Franciscus von Assisi*, Tübingen, 1904.

Bracaloni, Leone : *Il Cantico di Frate Sole*, Todi, 1925.

Bughetti, Benvenuto : *Ricostruzione di due capitoli aggiunti ai Fioretti. A.F.H.*, XIII, 1920.
Alcune Idee fondamentali sui Fioretti in *A.F.H.*, XIX, 1926.

Burkitt, F. C. : *The Oldest MS. of S. Francis's Writings* in *Revue Bénédictine*, 1922.
A Study of the Sources of the Life of S. Francis in *Essays in Commemoration*, London, 1926.
S. Francis and some of his Biographers in *Franciscan Essays*, II (*B.S.F.S.*), 1932.
Scripta Leonis and the Speculum Perfectionis in *Miscellanea Francesco Ehrle*, III, Rome, 1924.
La Légende de Pérouse et S. Isidore 1/73 in *Revue d'Histoire Franciscaine*, II, 4, Paris, 1925.

Coulton, G. G. : *The Story of S. Francis* in *The Beginnings of Christianity*, Vol. II, London, 1922.

Cuthbert, Father : *Saint Francis of Assisi*, Appendix ii, London, 1912.

Ehrle, Franz: *Osservazioni sulle più antiche storie* in *Misc. Franc.*, I, 1886.

Faloci-Pulignani, Michele: *Gli Autografi di San Francesco* in *Misc. Franc.*, VI, 1891.

Testo latino dei Fioretti in *Misc. Franc.*, VII, 1892.

Gardner, Edmund : *The Little Flowers of Saint Francis* in *Essays in Commemoration*, 1926.

Goetz, Walther : *Die Quellen zur Geschichte des Franciscus von Assisi*, Gotha, 1904.

Jörgensen, J. : *A Study of the Sources* in *S. Francis of Assisi*, English tr., London, 1912.

Little, A. G. : *A Guide to Franciscan Studies*, London, 1920.

Sources of the History of S. Francis in *E.H.R.*, 1902.

Some Recently Discovered Franciscan Documents and their Relations to the Second Life by Celano and the Speculum Perfectionis, London (British Academy), 1926.

Description du MS. Canon. Misc. 525 in *Opuscules*, fasc. v, 1903.

Mandonnet, P. : *Fr. Leo, storico di San Francesco* in *Misc. Franc.*, VII, 1899.

Manzoni, L. : *Studi sui Fioretti* in *Misc. Franc.*, III and IV, 1888–9.

Minocchi, Salvatore : *La Leggenda di Tre Compagni* in *Archivio Storico Italiano*, Rome, 1899–1900.

Müller, Karl : *Die Anfänge des Minoritenordens*, Freiburg, 1885.

Ortroy, F. van : *Legenda Trium Sociorum* in *Anal. Boll.*, XIX, 1900.

Bonaventura et Tractatus de Miraculis in *Anal. Boll.*, XVIII, 1899.

Sabatier, Paul : *Étude des Sources* in his *Vie de Saint François*, Paris, 1894.

Nouveaux travaux sur les Documents in *Opuscules*, fasc. vii, Paris, 1903.

Examen de quelques travaux récents in *Opuscules*, fasc. x, 1904.

L'incipit et le premier chapitre du Speculum Perfectionis in *Opuscules*, fasc. xvi, 1910.

Description du MS. Franciscain de Leignitz in *Opuscules*, fasc. ii, 1901.

Description du Speculum Vitae in *Opuscules*, fasc. vi, 1903.

Examen des récits concernant les visites de Jacqueline de Settesoli à S. François in *Opuscules*, fasc. xv, 1910.

Tractatus de Miraculis in *Misc. Franc.*, VI, 1897.

La Légende des Trois Compagnons in *Revue Historique*, 1901.

Études inedites sur S. François, ed. Arnold Goffin, Paris, 1932.

La Première Partie de la Vie de S. François in *Studi Medievali*, Turin, n.d.

Seton, Walter : *An unusual MS. version of the Testamentum S. Francisci* in *A.F.H.*, XX, 1927.

Suyskens, Constantius : *Prolegomena* in *Acta Sanctorum*, October, Vol. II, 1768.

Tamassia, Nino : *S. Francis and his Legend*, translated by Lonsdale Ragg, London, 1910.

III. History of the Order

Beaufreton, Maurice : *S. François d'Assise*, Paris, 1923.

Bonaventura, Saint : *Selecta Scripta*, Quaracchi, 1923.

Brewer and Howlett : *Monumenta Franciscana*, London, 1858 and 1882.

Chérancé, Léopold de : *S. Francis of Assisi*, English tr. by R. F. O'Connor, London, 1879.

Coulton, G. G. : *Five Centuries of Religion* ; Vol. II, *The Friars and the deadweight of tradition*, Cambridge, 1927.

Christ, S. Francis and Today, Cambridge, 1919.

Cowley, Patrick : *Franciscan Rise and Fall*, London, 1933.

Cuthbert, Father : *S. Francis of Assisi*, London, 1912.

The Romanticism of S. Francis, New Ed., London, 1924.

Douie, Decima : *The Nature and Effect of the Heresy of the Fraticelli*, Manchester, 1932.

Felder, Hilarin : *The Idealism of S. Francis*, tr. Berchmans Bittle, London, 1925.

Firmamentum Trium Ordinum, Paris, 1512.

Freer, Arthur S. B. : *The Early Franciscans and Jesuits*, London, 1922.

Gebhart, Émile : *L'Italie Mystique*, Paris, n.d.

Gemelli, Agostino : *The Franciscan Message to the World*, tr. by H. L. Hughes, London, 1924.

Gilliat Smith, Ernest : *S. Clare of Assisi*, London, 1914.

S. Anthony of Padua according to his contemporaries, London, 1926.

Gilson, Etienne : *The Philosophy of S. Bonaventura*, tr. by Trethowan and Sheed, London, 1938.

Goad, Harold E. : *Franciscan Italy*, London, 1926.

The Dilemma of S. Francis in *Essays in Commemoration*, 1926.

The first Walter Seton Memorial Lecture, London, 1929.

Brother Elias in *Franciscan Essays*, II, *B.S.F.S.*, 1932.

Golubovich, Girolamo : *Biblioteca Bio-bibliografica*, I, 1906.

Gratien, Père : *Histoire de la Fondation et de l'Évolution de l'Ordre des Frères Mineurs au XIIIᵉ Siècle*, Paris, 1928.

Saint François d'Assise, Paris, 1928.

Jörgensen, J. : *Saint Francis of Assisi*, English tr. by T. O'Conor Sloan, London, 1912.

Kerval, Léon de : *S. Antonii de Padua Vitae Duae* in *Collection d'Études*, V, Paris, 1904.

Knox-Little, W. J. : *Saint Francis of Assisi*, London, 1897.

Lempp, Édouard : *Frère Élie de Cortone* in *Collection d'Études*, III, Paris, 1901.

Little, A. G. : *Studies in English Franciscan History*, Manchester, 1917.

The Grey Friars at Oxford, Oxford, 1891.

The Franciscans in the University of Cambridge in *Méianges Mandonnet*, II, Paris, 1930.

Macdonnel, Anne : *Sons of Francis*, London, 1902.

Monnier, L. le : *History of Saint Francis of Assisi*, English tr., London, 1894.

Oliger, Livarius : *De Origine Regularum Ordinis S. Clarae* in *A.F.H.*, V, 1912.

Rashdall, Hastings : *Universities of Europe in the Middle Ages*, New Ed., London, 1936.

Sabatier, Paul : *Vie de S. François d'Assise*, Paris, 1894.

Regula Antiqua Fratrum et Sororum de Poenitentia in *Opuscules*, fasc. i, 1901.

Salvatorelli, Luigi : *Vita di San Francesco d'Assisi*, Bari, 1926.

Sbaralea, Hyacinthus : *Bullarium Franciscanum*, Rome, 1759, etc.

Scott-Davison, Ellen : *Forerunners of Saint Francis*, London, 1928.

Scudder, Vida : *Franciscan Adventure*, London, 1931.

Seton, Walter : *Blessed Giles of Assisi* (*B.S.F.S.*), VII, 1918.

The Last Two Years of the Life of S. Francis in *Essays in Commemoration*, London, 1926.

Speculum Minorum, Rouen, 1509.

Strong, Mrs. Eugenie : *S. Francis in Rome* in *Essays in Commemoration*, London, 1926.

Wadding, Luke : *Annales Minorum*, Rome, 1731–45.

LIST OF ABBREVIATIONS

THE following abbreviations have been used:

TEXTS

1 Cel.	. .	Celano's *Vita Prima S. Francisci.*
2 Cel.	. .	Celano's *Vita Secunda S. Francisci.*
Leg. 3 Soc.	.	Legenda Trium Sociorum.
Sp. S.	. .	Speculum Perfectionis (ed. Sabatier).
Sp. L.	. .	Speculum Perfectionis (ed. Lemmens).
Per.	.	Legenda Antiqua de Perugia.
Bon.	.	Bonaventura's *Legenda Maior S. Francisci.*
Little	.	Dr. Little's Franciscan MS.
V.C.	.	Verba Conradi.

MODERN WORKS

An. Bolland.	.	Analecta Bollandiana.
An. F.	.	Analecta Franciscana.
A.L.K.G.	.	Archiv für Litteratur und Kirchengeschichte.
A.F.H.	.	Archivum Franciscanum Historicum.
B.S.F.S.	.	Publications of the British Society of Franciscan Studies.
Bull. Franc.	.	Bullarium Franciscanum.
E.H.R.	.	English Historical Review.
Misc. Franc.	.	Miscellanea Francescana.
Opuscules	.	Opuscules de Critique Historique.

CORRIGENDA

p. 8	Line 11:	For 1852 read 1849.
	Line 12:	For 1855 read 1885.
	Note 1, line 2:	For *Son* read *Sun.*
	Note 2, line 2:	For (1855) read (1885).
p.19	Line 15:	For *in the Sacristy of* read *in a chapel in* .
p.23	Note 2, line 2:	For 1210 read 1223.
p.26	Line 21:	Omit the word *Umiliati* .
p.29	Line 22:	For *hath* read *has* .
p.46	Line 5 from bottom:	Read *begging, and some of it is certainly* .
p.51	Line 10:	For *abnegat* read *abneget* .
p.54	Line 6 from bottom:	For *he* read *He* .
p.57	Line 24:	For *Minister General* read *Vicar General* .
p.67	Line 3:	For *May* read *July* .
p.71	Line 27:	For *pecasse* read *peccasse* .
p.71	Line 35:	For § 42 read § 32.
p.72	Bottom line:	Leave space between *se* and *praeparat.*
p.75	Line 14:	For *May* read *July* .
p.75	Note 3:	For *3 Soc.13* read *3 Soc. 14.*
p.83	Line 27:	For *Assisi* read *Perugia* .
p.89	Line 6:	For *Iesi* read *Jesi* .
p.97	Line 22:	For *1320* read *1322* .
p.99	Line 4 from bottom of text:	After 93 insert 103a before words *and 106* .
p.107	Line 14:	Add in last column the number 216.
p.109	Line 9 from bottom:	For *Jacqueline da* read *Jacoba dei* .
p.128	Line 2:	for *de* read *dei.*
p.130	Bottom line:	For *de Casale* read *da Casale* .
p.132	3 last lines of text should read as follows:	
		No. 83 is from *I Cel.* 106.
		No. 84 is a poem about the Portiuncula which may possibly come from a document which was preserved there.
p.138	Line 14:	For *Iesi* read *Jesi* .
p.139	Line 11 from bottom of text:	For *1255* read *1257* .
p.147	Line 8 from bottom of text:	For *Jacoba de'* read *Jacoba dei* .
p.166	Line 15:	For *Iesi* read *Jesi* .

AUTHOR'S NOTE - 1966

This book was written more than 25 years ago and was published in the middle of the Second World War. This meant that many of the channels for the dissemination of knowledge were closed, and the book could therefore reach only a limited public. Without exception, the theories which I propounded about the relationship between the various sources for the Life of S. Francis were approved by the leading scholars of the day,[i] and the book, of which only a small edition could be printed, was quickly sold out.

It was not until after the War that English books were able to reach other parts of Europe, and by that time copies of this book were practically unobtainable. A copy did, however, reach the Franciscans at Quaracchi (from Ireland) where it came under the fire of that great scholar, Fr. Michael Bihl, O.F.M. Fr. Bihl not only reviewed it but also wrote an article on it, which he called "Contra duas novas Hypotheses prolatas a Ioh. R. H. Moorman", which occupied 35 pages of the *Archivum Franciscanum Historicum.* [ii] This article was a severe and lengthy attack by a man who was rightly regarded as the most learned Franciscan scholar of his generation.

To answer Fr. Bihl's criticisms would need a great deal of time and space, neither of which is available at this moment. Fr. Bihl was a German scholar who had devoted the whole of his life to the study of medieval history, with special reference to the history of his own Order.[iii] Yet I am quite sure that, in his discussion of the theses which I had propounded, especially about the relationship between the *Vita Prima* of Celano and the *Legenda Trium Sociorum*, he completely misunderstood my intention. My theory, as set out in detail in Chapter IV of this book, is that a comparison of the texts in these two documents leads one to the conclusion that the stories of the early life of S. Francis, as told in *Leg. 3 Soc.*,

(i)   See, for example, F.M. Powicke in *Journal of Theological Studies* (Jan. - April, 1942); Walter Gumbley, O.P. in *English Historical Review* (July, 1942); Decima Douie in *History* (June, 1941); Paulinus Lavery, O.F.M. in *The Tablet* (10 May, 1941); Thomas Plassmann, O.F.M. in *Speculum* (Jan. 1942); A.H. Sweet in *American Historical Review* (April, 1942); Kevin Smyth, O.F.M. Cap. in *Franciscan Studies* (March, 1942).
(ii)   *A.F.H.* XXXIX (1946), pp. 3 - 37 and cf. pp. 279 - 87.
(iii)   See "Occasione Iubilaei religiosi R.P. Michaelis Bihl (1896 - 1946) Notae quaedam biographicae" in *A.F.H.* XXXVII (1944), pp. 355 - 402. He died in 1950.

are clearly a more primitive version than that contained in *I Celano*, and may possibly have been written up, by some unknown scribe, from the rough notes which Thomas of Celano made in the years 1228 - 29 when he had been invited to write the official Life of the saint.

In reaching this conclusion I was using the fairly simple rules which I had learned in my New Testament studies at Cambridge some years before, which enable one to determine, generally without great difficulty, which of two texts appears to be the original and which the copy. In order to demonstrate this I printed, in parallel columns (see pp. 72 - 74) the two accounts of the dream which S. Francis had when on his way to Apulia, and I endeavoured to show that the narrative in *Leg. 3 Soc.* was clearly a more primitive version than that in *I Celano*. That Fr. Bihl was unfamiliar with the critical methods, which had long been in use in Biblical scholarship, is clear from what he says about this passage (pp. 17 - 19). Here he makes much of the fact that the story is concerned with a dream, in which all sorts of strange things can happen, and suggests that the matter should be referred to Sigismund Freud, or some other psychologist, for a solution.

A good deal has been written on the early Franciscan literature during the last 25 years,[i] and some of what is said in parts of this book would have to be revised if an entirely new edition (rather than a reprint) was being prepared for the press. But I still hope that the main arguments of the book will stand up to reasonable criticism, and that scholars will find them useful in trying to solve the complex and fascinating problem of how and when the early Lives of S. Francis came to be written.

JOHN MOORMAN

Bishop of Ripon.

(i) See especially: K. Esser, *Das Testament des Heiligen Franziskus von Assisi: eine Untersuchung über seine Echtheit und seine Bedeutung* (Münster-i-W. 1949); Jacques Cambell, "Les écrits de Saint Francois d'Assise devant la critique" in *Franz. Studien,* XXXVI (1954), pp. 82 - 109, 205 - 64; S. Cavallin, "La Question Franciscaine comme problème philologique" in Eranos, LII (Upsala, 1954), pp. 239 - 70; S. Clasen, "S. Bonaventura, S. Francisci legendae maioris compilator" in *A.F.H.* LIV (1961), pp. 241 - 72; LV (1962), pp. 3 - 58, 289 - 319.

I

THE FAME OF SAINT FRANCIS

In the year 1926 Christendom celebrated the seventh centenary of the death of Saint Francis of Assisi. Centenaries are apt to be transient affairs, but this one made a deeper impression than most, since of all the figures of the past who have captivated the religious imagination of later ages Francis has good claim to stand supreme. Ernest Renan's description of him as "the one perfect Christian" [1] would seem to most of us to be an exaggeration; yet we should find it hard to point to anyone who has come closer to the Christian ideal as it is outlined for us in the Gospels. Nor is it surprising that he, above all others, should have won the honour and respect of our generation, for in an age which has worshipped materialism and security, comfort and convenience, S. Francis has been loved as one who held all these things in contempt, and who set out to perform the daring experiment of taking Christ's words literally. Every sensitive Christian is bound to be worried by the hard sayings of Christ. When we read such statements as "He that renounceth not everything that he·hath, he cannot be my disciple," or the commands "Go and sell all that thou hast and give to the poor," or "Give to every man that asketh of thee, and of him that taketh away thy goods ask them not again," we feel that such demands are excessive and even fantastic; and in order to avoid the difficulty of having to fit them into our lives, we argue that Christ did not mean quite what He is reported to have said, or that His words are not of general application. So in the life of each Christian disciple there is always a compromise, an interpretation limited by the measure of his courage and of his zeal, the drawing of a line beyond which he is not prepared to go. But when we are introduced to the life of S. Francis we find ourselves face to face with a man who would allow no such compromise in his life. Here was one who gaily cut the knot wherewith we try to fasten together our Christianity and our desire for security, and who, by becoming quite indifferent to the future, separated himself for ever from all that this world holds dear. Few there are in any day

---

[1] *Nouvelles Études d'Histoire Religieuse*, p. 334: "On peut dire que, depuis Jésus François d'Assise a été le seul parfait chrétien."

who would be prepared to go as far as he went, but many must be attracted by the boldness of his enterprise.

The centenary of S. Francis in 1926 was marked not only by a number of significant events such as a Papal Encyclical, the printing of a special issue of postage stamps and, in our own country, by an exhibition of Franciscan manuscripts in the British Museum, but also by a prodigious output of books and articles dealing with the life of S. Francis and his Order. Camille Pitollet in an article in the *Revue d'Histoire Franciscaine*,[1] gives a list of no less than two hundred and fifty-four books and essays on this subject published between 1920 and 1926 by the presses of Western Europe and the United States of America. Publishers, like all others whose livelihood depends upon their power to dispose of their wares, must consult public taste and public needs ; and an output of Franciscan literature as great as this presupposes an abnormally high demand. No one could doubt that the " Fame of S. Francis " was already well established.

If we ask what is the cause of this remarkable popularity, we should, I think, be right in attributing it to three things—the character of S. Francis himself, the wealth of evidence about his life, and the fact that he has had in recent years so sympathetic and so brilliant an interpreter as Paul Sabatier. Dr. Seton in his essay on " The Rediscovery of S. Francis " dates the re-awakening of interest in S. Francis from the publication of Karl Hase's " Life " in 1856,[2] but the bibliographical evidence points rather to Sabatier's *Vie de S. François* in 1894 as the book which really introduced the Poverello to the modern world. Sabatier's work was immediately successful. Within a few years it had run into more than thirty editions and had been translated into English, German, Italian, Dutch, Swedish, Polish and Russian, the last under the direction of Tolstoi.[3] For a time it was " the book of the day ". All over Europe men and women, many of whom were not accustomed to reading the lives of medieval saints, were enjoying this delightful biography, combining as it does the fruits of sound and painstaking scholarship with a style inspired by a fervent admiration for its subject.

The *Vie de S. François* is an inspired interpretation of an unusually inspired life ; but, like every other study of the past, it depends ultimately upon the raw material which is supplied by the testimony of contemporaries. It is a truism to say that all history is based on evidence and that all evidence is derived from experience ; yet it is a fact which can easily be forgotten or ignored. That is why it is so important for every historian and biographer to examine with the utmost care the sources upon which he bases his judgments. Nor is it

---

[1] Tome III, 1926, Nos. 3-4, pp. 579-91.   [2] *Essays in Commemoration*, p. 249.
[3] See A. G. Little in *E.H.R.*, 1902, p. 647.

enough that he should confine himself to sources which are derived from the actual experiences of eye-witnesses, for he must also know something of the writers themselves in order to satisfy himself that their evidence is reliable. In dealing with the sources for the life of S. Francis we shall see that the history of the Order compels us to walk very warily, and it will be the purpose of this study to determine which of our various documents have most claim to be authentic and trustworthy.

S. Francis was himself a writer, and we shall therefore have to begin our study of the sources with an examination of his own works. These were collected within a few years of his death,[1] and some of them were printed in such works as the *Speculum Minorum* in 1509 and the *Firmamentum Trium Ordinum* in 1512 ; but the edition which has been mostly used by historians has been that produced by the Irishman, Luke Wadding, who printed the works of S. Francis in the volume called *Beati Patris Francisci Assisiatis Opuscula* in 1623.[2] This remained for 250 years the standard edition, though it was re-edited at various times by such editors as de la Haye (1641) and J. von der Burg (1849). It was only in comparatively recent years that the canon of S. Francis's Writings was subjected to historical criticism, the pioneer in this field being Karl Müller, who published his *Anfänge des Minoritenordens* in 1885.

Next in importance to the Writings of S. Francis are the two " Lives " by Thomas of Celano. The first of these (*1 Celano*) was known to Wadding and other early Franciscan scholars, but was not actually printed until the Bollandist Fathers included it in the second October volume of the *Acta Sanctorum* in 1768. Celano's *Vita Secunda S. Francisci* (*2 Celano*) was curiously neglected by eighteenth-century writers and was not published until 1806, when Rinaldi brought out his *Seraphici viri S. Francisci Assisiatis Vitae Duae auctore B. Thoma de Celano*. Rinaldi's edition was limited to a very small issue which was soon exhausted. So in 1880 Leopoldo Amoni, who had already published an Italian version of *1 Celano*, brought out a new edition of the two Lives. This remained the standard text until Edouard d'Alençon produced a new edition with *apparatus criticus* in 1906.[3] This volume included the *Tractatus de Miraculis*, a kind of supplement to the *Vita Secunda*.[4]

---

[1] Perhaps as early as 1250. Cf. Burkitt's study of MS. *Assisi* 338 in *Revue Bénédictine*, July, 1922, p. 203.

[2] For biographical notes on Wadding, see Gemelli, *The Franciscan Message to the World*, pp. 152–8.

[3] *S. Francisci Assisiensis Vita et Miracula auctore Fr. Thoma de Celano*, Rome, 1906.

[4] This had been already edited by van Ortroy in *An. Bolland.*, XVIII, 1899. The latest edition of *1 Cel.*, *2 Cel.* and the *Tract. Mir.* is to be found in Tome X of the *Analecta Franciscana*.

The charming account of the early years of S. Francis and his disciples known as the *Legend of the Three Companions* (*Leg. 3 Soc.*) was known to Wadding, but, like *1 Celano*, was not printed until 1768, when it appeared in the *Acta Sanctorum*. The indefatigable Amoni published a somewhat unreliable text of it in 1880, but the first really scholarly edition was that of Faloci-Pulignani published at Foligno in 1898. He also printed a similar text in the seventh volume of his *Miscellanea Francescana* in the following year.[1]

From 1266 onwards the " official " Life of S. Francis has been the *Legenda Maior* of S. Bonaventura. This exists in a very large number of manuscripts and has been constantly reprinted since the fifteenth century. The latest and most authentic edition is that of the Quaracchi Fathers in Vol. VIII of the *Opera Omnia S. Bonaventurae*.[2]

The unsatisfactory nature of Bonaventura's official portrait of S. Francis becomes abundantly clear when we compare it with what is by far the best known and most loved of all the Franciscan sources, the *Fioretti* or " Little Flowers of S. Francis ". How far this can be regarded as authentic evidence, and how far it must be considered as later tradition, will be discussed in a subsequent chapter. Suyskens, the learned editor of the *Acta Sanctorum*, held it of so little importance that he confesses that he had not even troubled to read it—a strange confession from one who set himself to study the Franciscan sources.[3] However much it may have been mistrusted by the more scholarly of Franciscan students, this delightful series of tales has always captivated the imagination of readers and there have been many editions of it since printing first began. Amoni and Passerini are two modern editors who have both given us convenient editions.[4]

These five were the main sources for the Life of S. Francis before Sabatier began his work towards the end of the nineteenth century. But they were not all. Sabatier was convinced that the *Legenda Trium Sociorum* was only a fragment of the writings of the Three Companions and that it had, in fact, been deliberately mutilated by the relaxing party in the Order. He was, moreover, determined to institute a search for the missing chapters, an enterprise which was rewarded by the discovery of a number of manuscripts called *Speculum Perfectionis*,

---

[1] The *Leg. 3 Soc.* shows every sign of being an incomplete or mutilated work, and various attempts have been made from time to time to supplement it from other Franciscan material. Cf. Melchiorri, *Leggenda di S. Francesco scritta dalli suoi compagni*, Recanati, 1856, and Marcellino da Civezza and Teofilo Domenichelli, *Leggenda di S. Francesco*, Rome, 1899.

[2] Quaracchi, 1882. A handy edition of the *Legenda Maior* and *Legenda Minor* was reprinted from this.

[3] *Acta Sanctorum*, Oct. ii, p. 865 : " Floretum non legi, nec curandum putavi."

[4] L. Amoni, *Fioretti di S. Francesco*, Rome, 1889 : G. L. Passerini, *I Fioretti del glorioso santo Francesco*, Florence, 1903.

which he believed to be the original writings of Brother Leo. In 1898 he triumphantly published this collection with the bold sub-title: *S. Francisci Assisiensis Legenda Antiquissima auctore Fratre Leone*. Further research revealed the fact that Sabatier was mistaken in the date to which he had attributed this work, and we shall have occasion later to discuss this question, together with the whole intricate problem of what were the original writings of Brother Leo and his two collaborators, Angelo and Rufino. Previous to his discovery of the *Speculum Perfectionis*, however, Sabatier had studied an early sixteenth-century collection of Franciscan material known as the *Speculum Vitae*,[1] from which he had extracted a number of chapters which seemed to him to have the appearance of coming from primitive sources. With these chapters, in addition to the works already known, Sabatier was in possession of practically all the earliest sources for a "Life of S. Francis". It was his triumph that he made of his material a book which everyone recognised as a work of genius.

There had been, of course, many Lives of S. Francis before Sabatier. The first work which could be described as an "interpretation", after the original sources had been composed, was the great collection of Franciscan material which Bartholomew of Pisa presented to the Chapter General of the Order in 1399 under the title: *Liber de Conformitate Vitae b. Patris Francisci ad Vitam Domini Nostri Iesu Christi*, which now occupies two large volumes of the *Analecta Franciscana*.[2] This strange work shows that the writer was familiar with most of the early sources. He quotes from some of the Writings of S. Francis, from *2 Celano* (though not from the *Vita Prima*[3]), from the Three Companions, from the *Speculum Perfectionis*, and of course extensively from *Bonaventura*. He refers also to a *Legenda Antiqua*, which seems to be the collection known as *Fac secundum exemplar*.[4] The purpose of Bartholomew's thesis was, as the title suggests, to show how closely the life of S. Francis approached to the life of Christ; his method was to take some aspect of the character or work of Christ from the Gospels, and then quote passages from the Life of S. Francis which refer to similar virtues or activities. Many of his stories are legendary.

The early years of the sixteenth century saw the production of three works, all of which deal fairly extensively with the life of S. Francis: the *Chronica Ordinis Minorum* of Nicholas Glassberger,[5] the *Fasciculus*

---

[1] *Speculum Vitae Beati Francisci et Sociorum Eius*, Venice, 1504. Sabatier has given a description of this in the 6th fascicule of his *Opuscules*.

[2] *An. F.*, IV and V.

[3] See *An. F.*, IV, p. xiii.

[4] See p. 165.

[5] First published in 1508 and reprinted in *An. F.*, II. See also *Nicholas Glassberger and his Works* by W. Seton (*B.S.F.S.*), 1923.

Chronicarum of Mariano of Florence [1] and the *Chronicae* of Mark of Lisbon.[2]   Although these writers refer to some of the primitive sources, it is clear that most of their information comes either from Bonaventura or from Bartholomew of Pisa, and it is doubtful whether any of them had access to any early material.[3]   Even the learned Wadding, head of the Irish Franciscan College of S. Isidore at Rome, who began the publication of his massive history of the Order, *Annales Minorum*, in 1625,[4] was almost entirely dependent upon Mariano of Florence and Mark of Lisbon for his information about S. Francis.

About a century later, in 1725, Père Chalippe wrote a Life of S. Francis which achieved a very considerable popularity.   It was early translated into Italian [5] and even found an English translator in F. W. Faber, the writer of a number of well-known hymns.[6]   Chalippe's book is frankly propagandist, written without any attempt to criticise his sources ; yet it probably served a useful purpose until more scholarly biographers took up the tale.

The chief event in Franciscan bibliography in the eighteenth century was certainly the publication of the October volumes of the *Acta Sanctorum* in 1768.   Here are printed in full Celano's *Vita Prima*, the *Legenda Trium Sociorum*, and Bonaventura's *Legenda Maior*, with a commentary by the learned Bollandist, Constantius Suyskens.   This commentary is brilliantly written, but is strangely limited.   We have already referred to Suyskens' refusal even to look at the *Fioretti*, and he seems to have taken little interest in a manuscript of *2 Celano* to which his attention was drawn.[7]   At the same time, the publication of this volume must be regarded as an event of first-rate importance, for it marked the first attempt to study the sources with a critical mind and to print them in full for the use of scholars.

At this point we might pause a moment to see what effect the growing interest in S. Francis was having in Protestant countries.   During the fourteenth and fifteenth centuries the Friars had gradually deteriorated in public esteem ; and it was perhaps no wonder that, after the Reformation, men looked back to them as representative of the worst evils from which they felt that they had been delivered.   We get a good

---

[1] Written sometime before 1527, in which year he died ; cf. Sabatier, *Tractatus de Indulgentia*, pp. 140 ff.

[2] Published at Venice in three folio volumes between 1556 and 1568.

[3] See le Monnier, *History of S. Francis* (Eng. tr.), p. 17.

[4] It took twenty-nine years to complete the work, which in the first edition filled eight volumes.   A second and enlarged edition was published at Rome, 1731–45, in nineteen volumes.

[5] I am not certain in which year this translation was made.   My own copy was published at Milan in 1760.

[6] His translation appeared in 1847.

[7] Le Monnier, *History of S. Francis* (Eng. tr.), pp. 19–20.

example of this in the apologetic tone with which an English Franciscan, Anthony Parkinson, introduces his history of the Minorites in England, which he published in 1726 with the title *Collectanea Anglo-Minoritica*. He begins his Preface with these words:

COURTEOUS Reader,

If the writer of these Sheets had presented the World with an Account of the ancient Heathens, and their Manners, Rites and Customs, studious Men wou'd have been ready enough to turn over the Work, and the Subject wou'd not have been Scrupled at, if the Performance had proved to be Ingenious. Shou'd he have Writ of the *Flamins* or the *Druids*, from whom sprang the superstitious Worship of the *Britans*, he wou'd not have wanted Subscribers to the Tract: Nay, the old Rhyming *Bards* (Pagans as they were) wou'd have found a kind Reception. This gives me Hopes, that he may be permitted to pick up a few Gleanings of *Christian History*, and may not be blamed for rescuing the Characters of many renowned *English Franciscans* from Moths and Worms. They were a Society of wel-meaning Christians, and our Country-Men; and on these Considerations, I presume, they cannot be disagreeable to all. . . . It's true they were *Friers*; but they are dead and gone many a fair Year ago, and it is Pity, methinks, that all the Memory of their Merits shou'd die too.

Such was the apologetic tone of an English writer of the early eighteenth century in offering his history to Protestant readers. He clearly hopes that his work will be received with a tolerance which he could certainly not have expected on the Continent. Great indignation had there been aroused among Protestants by the publication, in 1510, of the *Liber de Conformitate*, with its analogies between the life of Christ and that of S. Francis. A reply to it was written by Erasmus Alber under the title *Alcoranum nudipedum*, which was later printed in French and Latin as *L'Alcoran des Cordeliers : recueil des plus notables bourdes et blasphèmes de ceux qui ont osé comparer Sainct François à Iésu Christ*. This work, which achieved considerable popularity, opened the gate to a stream of anti-Franciscan literature, such as the scurrilous *Les Avantures de la Madona et de François d'Assise*, with the sub-title: *Recueillies de plusieurs ouvrages des Docteurs Romains ; Écrites d'un stile récréatif ; en même tems capable de faire voir le ridicule du Papisme sans aucune controverse*.

This spirit of mockery died away before the opening of the nineteenth century, the century which brought, first, the Romantic Movement in literature and art, and then the growth of scientific historical research. To both of these activities of the human mind the story of S. Francis had much to offer. There was something undeniably "romantic" about this Christian Troubadour, with his love of nature and poetry, who sang the *Chansons de Geste*, preached sermons to the birds, and picked up the worms out of the road lest they should be trodden on. Furthermore, the nineteenth-century intellectuals, tired of the limitations of classical study, turned with a new interest to the Middle Ages; and no one can study the Middle Ages without, sooner or later, coming up against S. Francis. In literature it was he who wrote the oldest surviving poem in any modern language [1] : in art it was his life which inspired Berlinghieri and Giotto [2] : in Church History it was he who led the last and greatest of the revivals of religious life. Meanwhile, for those who enjoyed the critical study of medieval documents there was a rich field to be worked. The old antagonisms were forgotten. Catholics and Protestants could now meet on common ground.

The " romanticism " of S. Francis was first studied by the German writer Goerres, who in 1826 published a book with what seemed then to be an original and significant title, *Der Heilige Franziscus von Assisi, Ein Troubadour*.[3] It was followed by Frederick Ozanam's famous book on the Franciscan Poets in 1852 and Thode's *Franz von Assisi und die Anfänge der Kunst der Renaissance* in 1855. English men of letters like Ruskin also began to do homage to the " little poor man ", though it is doubtful, as Mr. Goad says, whether they ever really understood him.[4] Meanwhile many historical and critical studies were being produced, such as Papini's Essay on S. Francis in 1822, followed by the *Life* in 1825, and Karl Hase's *Franz von Assisi* in 1856. Then in 1885 the Franciscan Fathers at Quaracchi, near Florence, began the publication of sources in the *Analecta Franciscana*, and in the following year Faloci-Pulignani founded his bi-monthly review of Franciscan research, the *Miscellanea Francescana*. Meanwhile in this country, in addition to Faber's translation of Chalippe, we find Mrs. Jameson writing most appreciatively of S. Francis in her *Legends of the Monastic Orders* in 1850, Mrs. Oliphant's charming *Life of S. Francis* in 1870, while Messrs. Burns and Oates were publishing English versions of the *Works of S. Francis, Bonaventura* and the *Fioretti*, as well as a translation of the French Life of S. Francis by Léopold de Chérancé.

But perhaps the event which had most significance was the publication of Ernest Renan's delightful and enthusiastic essay on S. Francis in his *Nouvelles Études d'Histoire Religieuse* in 1884. It came rather unexpectedly in a volume which has been described as " a delightful

---

[1] I take this phrase from a leaflet containing a new translation of *The Song of Brother Son*, by F. C. Burkitt.

[2] The chief works on S. Francis and Italian art are Thode's *Franz von Assisi und die Anfänge der Kunst der Renaissance* (1855), Bughetti's *Vita e miracoli di S. Francesco nelle tavole istoriate dei secoli XIII e XIV* in *Arch. Franc. Hist.*, 1926, Arnold Goffin's *S. François d'Assise et l'Art primitif Italien* (1909), Koltonski's *S. Francis and Giotto*, Corrado Ricci's *Umbria Santa* (1926) and Miss Gurney Salter's *Franciscan Legends in Italian Art* (1905).

[3] In the same way there is something rather significant in the title of an American work : *Francis of Assisi : Saint, Mystic, Poet, Democrat*, by Richard Whitwell, 1923.

[4] *The First Walter Seton Memorial Lecture, 1929*, p. 29. Contrast with Ruskin's attitude that of Goethe, who visited Assisi towards the end of the eighteenth century. He went only to see the little Temple of Minerva in the piazza, and refused even to look at the " medieval barbarities " in the Church of S. Francesco. See Mary Cameron, *A Pilgrim's Guide to Assisi*, p. 6.

theosophical pot-pourri ",[1] dealing as it does with Paganism, Buddhism, the mystics of Persia, Galileo and Spinoza. Renan writes with undisguised admiration not, as others had written, for what Francis inaugurated, but for what he himself was. Although Renan himself was far from being a loyal son of the Church he comes little short of the attitude of Bartholomew of Pisa,[2] whose thesis was so indignantly repudiated by the Protestant writers of the sixteenth century. But not only is Renan's essay remarkable in itself, it has a further significance in that it was Renan who entrusted to Paul Sabatier the task of writing the Life of S. Francis which he himself had planned but had never been able to perform. The story is as follows : " Towards the end of 1884 Renan, after his lecture, talking to some of his students said : ' When I began to work I dreamt of devoting my life to the study of three periods. Blessed be the illusions of youth ! Three periods ! The origins of Christianity in connection with the history of Israel, the French Revolution, and the marvellous renewal of religion realized by S. Francis of Assisi. I have only been able to carry out the first third of my programme. You, M. Leblond, must write the religious history of the Revolution, and you (he said, putting his hand on Sabatier's shoulder), you will be the historian of the Seraphic Father.' "[3]

Sabatier worked for eight years on his Vie de S. François which appeared in 1894 and quickly took the intellectual world by storm. Immediately the printing presses of Europe began to hum with Franciscan literature of all kinds and of widely different value. Works appeared with such " bewildering rapidity "[4] that it would be almost impossible to draw up a complete bibliography of Franciscan literature even for the last fifty years. But it may be of interest to give some indication of what has been done in this country alone. Since 1894 there has been offered to the public a new (and, incidentally, very inaccurate) translation of S. Francis' Writings by Constance, Countess de la Warr, an excellent version of Celano's two Lives of S. Francis by A. G. Ferrers Howell, no less than three separate translations of the Speculum Perfectionis by Sebastian Evans, Robert Steele and Lady de la Warr, a new translation of Bonaventura's Legenda Maior, an English version of the Legenda Trium Sociorum by Miss Gurney Salter, three different translations of the Fioretti, the best by Thomas Arnold, and

---

[1] H. E. Goad, The First Walter Seton Memorial Lecture, p. 31.

[2] Cf. Nouvelles Études, p. 325 : " C'est, après Jésus, l'homme qui a eu la conscience la plus limpide, la naïveté la plus absolue, le sentiment le plus vif de sa relation filiale avec le Père céleste. Dieu a été vraiment son commencement et sa fin. En lui, Adam semblait n'avoir pas péché." Again on p. 326 : " François d'Assise a toujours été une des raisons les plus fortes qui m'ont fait croire que Jésus fut à peu près tel que les évangelistes synoptiques nous le dépeignent."

[3] See A. G. Little's Memoir of Sabatier (B.S.F.S.), 1924, p. 4.

[4] Cf. A. G. Little in E.H.R., 1902, p. 643.

the others by Professor Okey and W. Heywood, together with a transla-
tion into English verse by James Rhoades, and two versions of the
Sacrum Commercium, one by Canon Rawnsley and one by Montgomery
Carmichael. There have also been works on S. Francis by A. G. Little,
Father Cuthbert, Canon Knox-Little, G. K. Chesterton, two by James
Adderley, J. O. Dobson, John Hoyland, Hermitage Day, Amy Stoddart,
H. F. B. Mackay, T. S. R. Boase, Dr. Coulton, W. H. Leatham,
E. M. Wilmot Buxton, Seymour van Santvoord, Elizabeth Grierson,
Anne Macdonnell, E. Salusbury, Alice Heins, Mrs. Harper, Laurence
Housman, Horatio Grimley, Father Oswald, W. G. Pearse, Caroline
Duncan Jones, Elizabeth Lukens, Anne Pritchard, Archibald Campbell,
D. H. S. Nicholson, Pascal Robinson, N. H. Westlake, and a remarkable
volume by Brigadier Eileen Douglas of the Salvation Army called
" Brother Francis, or Less than the Least ", chosen to be the first
volume of a series known as the " Red Hot Library ". In addition to
these English works there have been translations published of Sabatier's
Vie de S. François, Jörgensen's *Life of S. Francis*, Lives by Salvatorelli
and Abel Bonnard, Nino Tamassia's *S. Francesco e la sua Leggenda*,
Hilarin Felder's *Die Ideale des hl. Franziscus von Assisi*, Gemelli's *Il
Francescanesimo* and Auguste Bailly's hopelessly inaccurate narrative,
The Divine Minstrels.

Besides these works dealing with the Life of S. Francis there have
been at least two Anthologies of Franciscan literature,[1] plays by
Laurence Housman, Henri Ghéon,[2] Harry Lee, Father Cuthbert and
J. A. Peladan.[3] Books on Franciscan Italy have been written, often
with a wealth of detail, by H. E. Goad, Peter Anson, Beryl de Selincourt,
Ernest Raymond, Mrs. Goff, Lina Duff Gordon, Mary Cameron, Francis
Newton and Sir William Richmond, with translations of Jörgensen,
Gabriel Fauré and Corrado Ricci. To these we should add various
collections of Franciscan Essays—notably the volume called *S. Francis :
Essays in Commemoration, 1926*—the twenty-two volumes published by
the British Society of Franciscan Studies, and many books and articles
on Franciscan history and art.[4]

Such is the effect which the " rediscovery of S. Francis " has had on
this country alone. But the revived interest in the saint led not only
to the production of a large number of books about him ; it also drove
scholars to ransack the libraries of Europe in the hope of finding further
Franciscan material. Nor were their labours in vain, for four important
" finds " were made—the various copies of the *Speculum Perfectionis*

---

[1] *Franciscan Days*, ed. by A. G. Ferrers Howell ; and *The Little Brown Company*,
ed. by Louis Vincent.

[2] Translated by C. C. Martindale.   [3] Translated by H. J. Massingham.

[4] I make no claim that this list is complete, but even as it stands it gives some indication of what the " Fame of S. Francis " means to this country to-day.

discovered by Sabatier, the works of Brother Leo in the manuscript known as *S. Isidore 1/73* edited by Leonardus Lemmens, the *Legenda Antiqua* discovered by Ferdinand Delorme at Perugia and the manuscript discovered and bought by Dr. A. G. Little in 1910. All these have now been published, and the Franciscan scholar is in the happy position of having before him, in a convenient form, all the material which is now available for a Life of S. Francis.[1]

But even when we have all our sources before us, and have established the text beyond all reasonable doubt, there is still much to be done. Biblical scholars used to draw a distinction between " lower " and " higher " criticism, the " lower " being concerned with the text and the " higher " with the history of the sources and their relations one with another. For many years the " higher criticism " of the Gospels has attracted students of all degrees of learning; perhaps now the " higher criticism " of the Franciscan sources may provide an equally interesting subject, for the two problems have much in common.[2] But the study of the Franciscan documents depends even more than that of the early Christian literature on the history of the times in which they were written. For the history of S. Francis and of the early years of the Order which he founded is the story of a conflict between the uncompromising idealism of the Saint himself and the determination of others, both within the Order and without, to turn the power which he had generated to practical use, even though it meant some departure from the declared intentions of the Founder. This conflict has left its mark on all the documents upon which our knowledge of S. Francis rests. It will therefore be our task in these pages to study these documents against the background of the circumstances in which they were written and to try to assess their reliability.

[1] Lemmens's edition of *S. Isidore 1/73* in *Documenta Antiqua Franciscana* is unfortunately now a rare book, of which there are only a few copies in this country. I should like to put on record here my thanks to Mrs. Burkitt for allowing me to have Professor Burkitt's copy of this book after his death in 1935.

[2] See Coulton's essay, *The Story of S. Francis of Assisi* in *The Beginnings of Christianity* (ed. Foakes Jackson and Kirsopp Lake), Vol. II, pp. 438–63, and especially p. 439, on which he gives, in parallel columns, a comparison of the dates of the early Christian and early Franciscan sources.

THE WRITINGS OF SAINT FRANCIS

ALTHOUGH S. Francis distrusted learning and would not allow his followers to become scholars, he was himself a writer; and we must therefore begin our study of the sources for his life with an examination of his own works. But before we embark upon this we shall do well to make up our minds as to what we can accept as authentic. Wadding, the seventeenth-century Franciscan historian, prints in the volume called *Beati Patris Francisci Assisiatis Opuscula* the works which were at that time regarded as the Writings of the saint. This list consisted of the following: seventeen letters, twelve prayers, the Testament of S. Francis, the two Rules of the Order, the Rule of S. Clare and the Rule of the Third Order, the collection of short exhortations known as the Admonitions, the brief Salutation of the Virtues and the Salutation of the Virgin, the chapter from the *Actus* on Perfect Joy, a Paraphrase of the Lord's Prayer, the little act of Praise called *Laudes Domini*, twenty-eight " Monastic Collations ", an Office of the Passion, the Canticle of the Sun, a group of Poems, and finally a large collection of apophthegms, sayings, parables, and prophecies. We know now that this list is far too long, that some of the letters and many of the poems were not written by S. Francis at all, and that most of the last group of Sayings are from the works of S. Bonaventura. We know also that the Rules for S. Clare and the Third Order which Wadding prints, though based on S. Francis's intentions, are not actually from his hand. In order, therefore, to arrive at a satisfactory canon of the Saint's Writings we shall have to shorten this list very considerably.

By way of comparison with the collection made by Wadding we turn to a much earlier and shorter compilation. In a manuscript in the Sacro Convento at Assisi, known as MS. *Assisi 338*, we find one section devoted to the Writings of S. Francis. Professor Burkitt considers this manuscript to be not later than the middle of the thirteenth century,[1] and therefore written within twenty-five years of the death of S. Francis. In contrast to Wadding's substantial catalogue, this early document gives us only the following works : the Second Rule written in 1223, the Testament of S. Francis, the Admonitions, only two letters,

---

[1] Cf. above, p. 3, n. 1.

two short documents known as *De Reverentia Corporis Domini* and *De Religiosa Habitatione in Eremis* (which Wadding included among the Monastic Collations), the Canticle of the Sun, the Paraphrase of the Lord's Prayer and the Office of the Passion. It has been suggested [1] that this collection represents the views of the " Conventual " party in the Order, those of the friars, that is to say, who were in favour of a relaxation of the strict standards set by S. Francis ; but the presence of the Testament contradicts this. Of all the writings of the Saint this was the one which led to most controversy, and was at the same time most warmly defended by the " Spirituals " and deliberately ignored or explained away by the " Conventuals ". The nature of the documents here collected does not, in fact, suggest any particular bias on the part of the collector, and the contents were probably determined by the facilities which the compiler had for his work. But his collection is far from complete, for there are several well-authenticated Writings of S. Francis which we do not find here.

There is, fortunately, almost complete unanimity among modern critics as to what may be regarded as the authentic Writings of S. Francis.[2] They are as follows :

The *Regula Prima* of 1221.
The *Regula Secunda* (or *Regula Bullata*) of 1223.
The Testament.
28 Admonitions.
De Reverentia Corporis Domini.
De Religiosa Habitatione in Eremis.
The Canticle of the Sun.
Seven Letters (addressed " to all the faithful ", " to all the brethren ", " to a certain minister ", " to the rulers of the people ", " to Brother Leo ", " to Brother Anthony ", and " to all the *custodes* ".
The Paraphrase of the Lord's Prayer, or *Laudes Domini.*
The Blessing of Brother Leo with the Praises written on the reverse.
The Salutation of the Virtues.
The Salutation of the Virgin.
The Office of the Passion.
The prayer " *Absorbeat* ".

But there is no reason to suppose that this is all that S. Francis wrote. Indeed, we know from our other sources of various writings of S. Francis

---

[1] E.g. by Father Cuthbert, *Life of S. Francis*, p. 494.
[2] See Boehmer, *Analekten zur Geschichte des Franciscus von Assisi* (1904) ; Goetz, *Die Quellen zur Geschichte des hl. Franz von Assisi* (1904) ; Fr. Lemmens, *Opuscula Sancti Patris Francisci* (1904) ; Fr. Cuthbert, *Life of S. Francis* ; Sabatier, *Vie de S. François* and *Quelques Travaûx récents sur les Opuscules de S. François* in *Opuscules*, fasc. x (1904). Fr. Lemmens' edition is the most convenient, though he rejects the Letter to Brother Anthony and unfortunately omits the Canticle of the Sun on the grounds that it was written in Italian and not in Latin.

which are now lost. We know, for example, from Celano's *Vita Secunda* (§ 163) of a letter which Francis wrote to S. Anthony of Padua in which he addressed him as " Brother Anthony, my Bishop " ; we know of Letters to Cardinal Ugolino (*1 Celano*, 5 and 100) ; we know of written messages to S. Clare, one of which Francis sent from his death-bed (*Spec. Perf.* 90 and 106) ; we know of a letter to the people of Bologna mentioned by Eccleston (*De Adventu*, cap. 6) ; and another to the brothers in France (*ibid.*) ; and we know of a short Testament which S. Francis wrote previous to the Will which has been published (*Spec. Perf.* 87). But by far the most important of all the lost documents is the original Rule which S. Francis wrote in 1210 to present to Innocent III for his approbation. It is surprising that Boehmer, in giving a list of all the " lost writings " of S. Francis, makes no mention of this.

There are, besides this, two other documents of great importance which we shall, unfortunately, have to include among the " lost writings " of S. Francis. These are the Rules for what came to be called the Second and Third Orders, the Poor Clares and the Penitents. The origins of the Rule of the Poor Clares have been closely studied by Fr. Oliger, who published his conclusions in the *Archivum Franciscanum Historicum* in 1912.[1] Of the six states of the Rule between 1212 and 1263 we are only concerned with the first, the *forma vivendi* which Francis gave to Clare when she made her escape from Assisi and was professed by Francis himself at the Portiuncula. Within a few hours of this event Clare herself was safely interned in a convent of Benedictine nuns at Bastia, a few miles from Assisi, where she remained for a short time. Later she moved to S. Angelo di Panzo on the slopes of Subasio, where she was joined by her sister Agnes before finally settling at S. Damiano, which now became the home of an enclosed Order. It is probable that Francis did not write out a Rule for these new disciples of his, whose devotion and importunity he may have found rather embarrassing, until it had become quite clear that their foundation was going to be a permanent one. When he actually set himself to the task of composing a Rule for them he was faced by considerable difficulties. So far as his own brethren were concerned he was quite satisfied that they were to live as homeless beggars, dependent upon the alms of the faithful even for the bare necessities of life. But he could not expose a group of women to the dangers which he and his men friends could willingly face, nor could he impose upon them the same rules as he had drawn up for the friars. In his perplexity he seems to have turned to the Benedictine Rule which gave

[1] *De Origine Regularum Ordinis S. Clarae* in *Arch. Franc. Hist.*, v, pp. 181–209 and 413–47. Cf. E. Gilliat Smith, *S. Clare of Assisi : her Life and Legislation*. Part ii, esp. pp. 133–48.

him most of what he wanted, and only needed the addition of a clause to forbid the Clares from holding corporate property.

When we turn to such evidence as we have, we find that it does not help us very much. Celano, in the *Vita Prima S. Francisci* (§ 37) tells us that Francis gave " to either sex " a " manner of living and way of salvation " (*norma vitae ac salutis via*) ; Ugolino, after he had become Pope as Gregory IX, wrote a letter to Agnes of Bohemia in 1238 in which he speaks of the " form of life " (*formula vitae*) which Francis gave to Clare. Clare herself, in the Rule which she wrote in 1253,[1] refers to this formula which Francis drew up for her, but tells us very little about its details. We are therefore left with the assumption that Francis, perhaps in conjunction with the Bishop of Assisi and Cardinal Ugolino,[2] wrote out a form of life for the Poor Clares more or less in the terms of the existing Benedictine Rule for women, though with certain important qualifications with regard to the holding of corporate property. There must have been something about this Rule which made it not altogether acceptable to Ugolino, for we find him, a few years later, trying to bring the Clares more and more into line with the established Orders by the imposition of what were called the " Ugoline Constitutions " in 1219, while Clare, to the end of her life, fought for the liberty of living in that absolute poverty, corporate as well as private, which she regarded as the distinguishing mark of the Order of S. Francis. We must conclude, then, that the original Rule which Francis wrote for the Poor Clares has perished and is unlikely now to be retrieved. All that we can content ourselves with is the short message which he sent to S. Clare in which he implored her to stand fast by Lady Poverty.[3]

The origin of the Third Order presents problems which are full of difficulty, and which have led to considerable controversy. Père Mandonnet was of the opinion that large numbers of people, inspired by the preaching and example of S. Francis, attached themselves to him, being afterwards divided into three groups—those who gave up everything to follow him (the Friars Minor), the women who were content to live a cloistered life under his direction (the Poor Clares), and those who wished to live a life of simplicity under his inspiration (the Order of Penitents).[4] The more generally accepted theory is that

[1] *Seraphicae Legislationis Textus Originales* (Quaracchi), 1897, pp. 62–3 ; cf. Wadding, *Annales, ad an.* 1253, n. 5.

[2] The Poor Clares were under the authority of both Francis and the Bishop of Assisi. Cf. *Legenda S. Clarae*, n. 18.

[3] " *Rogo vos dominas meas et consilium do vobis, ut in ista sanctissima vita et paupertate semper vivatis. Et custodite vos multum ne doctrinâ vel consilio alicuius ab ipsa in perpetuum ullatenus recedatis.*" This is printed on p. 76 of the *Opuscula S. P. Francisci*. Cf. Oliger in *A.F.H.*, v, p. 193.

[4] *Les Origines de l'Ordo de Poenitentia* in *Comptes-rendus du Quatrième Congrès Scientifique International des Catholiques.*

the Friars Minor formed the first group, to which later the Poor Clares were added as an organisation for women existing side by side with that for men, and that the Third Order was a society of persons loosely attached to S. Francis and living under a rule of life for which he was responsible. The evidence which we possess is not enough to enable us to say with certainty exactly what happened.

But what of the Rule which Francis gave to the Penitents? The problem has been studied by Sabatier and Mandonnet in the first and fourth fascicules of the *Opuscules de Critique Historique* and by Lemmens in the *Archivum Franciscanum Historicum*.[1] Sabatier prints the text of the Rule from the manuscript at Capistrano which dates from between 1228 and 1234 and which he regards as a second edition of the original Rule, much as the *Regula Bullata* of the Friars represents a later stage of their Rule. The original Rule seems to have been drawn up in 1221, but it is impossible to say how far the text of the Capistrano MS. reflects the original wording.[2] On the whole, then, we must class the original Rule of the Third Order among the " lost works " of S. Francis.

The works which have survived are of varying importance and deal with a wide range of subjects. Boehmer divides them into three groups [3] : those in which Francis writes as the head of a great fraternity, those in which he writes as an individual and a father in God, and those in which he gives free rein to his own personal convictions. Into the first of these groups Boehmer puts the two Rules, the Testament, the Admonitions and most of the Letters. To the second group he assigns the Letter to the Minister General, the Letter to Leo and the Blessing of Leo ; and in the third group he collects together the liturgical works such as the Office of the Passion, the Canticle of the Sun, the *Laudes* and Salutations. In spite of the fact that Sabatier thinks so highly of this passage of Boehmer as to print a translation of it in full,[4] I am bound to admit that it does not seem to me to be a very satisfactory method of classifying the works of S. Francis. For example, can one possibly say that in the Testament Francis is speaking as the head of a great fraternity ? On the contrary, we shall see reasons later on for believing that in this document Francis is speaking directly against the wishes of the great fraternity, of which, though he was still the leading figure, he was no longer the official head.

---

[1] *Regula Antiqua Ordinis de Poenitentia* in *A.F.H.*, vi, pp. 242–50. See also Fr. Cuthbert, *Life of S. Francis*, Appendix III, pp. 486–91.

[2] Mandonnet regards the Capistrano MS. as a faithful rescript, Boehmer classes it among the " spurious works of S. Francis ", Goetz considers it a mere *pastiche* of other documents.

[3] *Analekten zur Geschichte*, pp. xlv–liii.   [4] *Opuscules*, fasc. x, pp. 144–50.

Rather, I should prefer to group the writings of S. Francis into these three classes : those in which he expresses himself quite freely and unhampered by a sense of responsibility as head of a great Order ; those in which he is writing to urge some particular cause or in which he is anxious to convey some particular message ; and those in which it is not he alone who is speaking but the voice of those who shared among themselves the control of the Order, sometimes inducing Francis to write things with which he did not altogether agree. For we must remember that Francis as a writer was not wholly free. Normally when we compare the actual writings of a man with what others have said about him we are at liberty to regard the man's own works as giving a more accurate impression of his thought than any external evidence. So far as some of the writings of S. Francis are concerned this is true ; but it is not true of them all. Sabatier says, speaking of the writings of S. Francis as a whole, that they " shew us his real spirit ; each phrase has been not only thought out but lived out, and brings us, still quivering, the emotions of the Poverello ".[1] This is certainly true of the Testament and the Canticle of the Sun and some of the Letters, but it could not possibly be regarded as an accurate description of the *Regula Bullata*. We must, therefore, make a distinction between those works in which Francis felt himself free to express his innermost feelings and those in which he is the mouthpiece of the Order as a whole, and sometimes even writing against his own convictions.

Among the writings in which Francis is speaking quite freely and irresponsibly I should include the Canticle of the Sun, the Prayers, the Salutations, the Blessing of Brother Leo with the *Laudes* which accompany it, the Letter to Leo and all the liturgical works. Into the second group—works which express the deepest emotions of S. Francis but are yet written with a sense of responsibility and to plead a particular cause—I should put the Admonitions, the first five Letters, the *de Reverentia Corporis Domini*, the *de Religiosa Habitatione in Eremis*, the lost Rule of 1210, and, what is the most intimate and revealing of all his writings, the Testament. The third category consists of those official documents in which Francis is deeply under the influence of the Order as a whole, the Rule of 1221 and the *Regula Bullata* of 1223.

Among the writings which may be said to represent the true spirit of S. Francis pride of place must be given to the *Canticum Solis*, the Song of Brother Sun, which is believed to be the oldest extant poem in any modern language.[2] There has been some discussion as to

---

[1] *Vie de S. François* (1896 ed.), p. xxxvi : " ses œuvres nous montrent son ame même ; chaque phrase a été non seulement pensée, mais vécue, et nous apporte encore palpitantes les émotions du Poverello."

[2] See Bracaloni, *Il Cantico di Frate Sole* ; Goad, *Franciscan Italy*, pp. 115–19 ; Sabatier, *Spec. Perf.*, *Étude speciale du chapitre 120*, etc. There are many translations and versions, notably that by Matthew Arnold in *Essays in Criticism*.

whether Francis is here exhorting the heavenly bodies and the four elements to praise God, after the manner of the *Benedicite*, or whether he is inviting man to praise God for these gifts. God is to be praised " *per* " sun, moon and stars, earth, air, fire and water ; but there is some doubt as to the meaning of *per* in this connection. This Italian preposition has to do all the work which, in French, is shared by the two words *par* and *pour*. Celano says that it is the creatures who are to praise God,[1] but the language of the *Speculum* suggests that the poem was written to encourage men to give thanks to God for His good gifts.[2] Whichever way we take it, the poem gives us an insight into those tender feelings which Francis certainly had for the creatures of God, though they were feelings which were obviously not altogether shared by all of his disciples.[3]

The circumstances in which the poem was written are of great interest. Brother Leo tells [4] us how Francis lay for seven weeks in a little hut in the garden at S. Damiano in great pain and discomfort. He was blind and suffering a great deal internally, and was besides so weak that he was unable to prevent the mice from running all over him where he lay. Thus he spent many sleepless nights ; but never did he lose his courage and gaiety. " Brothers," he said to his companions, " I ought to be very happy and rejoice in my sufferings and discomforts and be comforted in the Lord and be ever giving thanks to God the Father and to His only Son Jesus Christ our Lord and to the Holy Spirit." Then he sat and meditated awhile and afterwards said : " O Almighty, Omnipotent, good Lord God . . . etc." Then, when he had written his poem, which must originally have consisted of the first five stanzas only, he taught the brethren to sing it whenever they went out preaching. Shortly afterwards he wrote another verse, the occasion of which was a dispute between the Bishop and the Podestà of Assisi. The Bishop had excommunicated the Podestà, and the Podestà had retaliated by placing an embargo on the tradespeople to prevent their selling anything to the Bishop, so that a very uncomfortable situation had arisen. It was then that Francis intervened, telling some of the brothers to go up to the piazza and sing the *Canticum Solis* with an extra stanza in which God is to be praised for those who forgive one another : " Praised be my Lord for all those who pardon one another for His love's sake ; and who endure weakness and tribulation. Blessed are they who peaceably shall endure, for thou, Most Highest, shalt give

---

[1] " *Invitabat omnes creaturas ad laudem Domini* ", 2 Cel. 217.

[2] " *Volo . . . facere novam laudem de creaturis Domini quibus quotidie utimur et sine quibus vivere non possumus* ", Spec. Perf. 100.

[3] In the well-known story of Brother Juniper cutting off a pig's trotter while it was yet alive, no suggestion of cruelty is ever made.

[4] *Per.* 78 = *Spec.* (*Sab.*) 100.

them a crown." Two years later, when he had been carried down from the Bishop's palace to a little hut close to the Portiuncula and he knew that he was going to die, he called for Brothers Angelo and Leo to sing to him the Canticle of the Sun. At the end he added these words : " Praised be my Lord for our Sister the Death of the body, from whom no man escapeth. Woe to him who dieth in mortal sin ! Blessed are they who are found walking by thy most holy will, for the second death shall have no power to do them harm." It was not long after this that he died ; and we are told that his last words were " Welcome, Sister Death ! " [1]

Another of the works of S. Francis which deserves particular mention is the famous parchment which he gave to Brother Leo in memory of the holy days which they had shared on the inhospitable summit of La Verna in the autumn of 1224.[2] The little scrap of parchment is now exhibited in a silver reliquary in the Sacristy of the Lower Church at Assisi, its folds and creases showing how for many years it lay in the bosom of Brother Leo, a dearly loved memento of his master. There is not much doubt that we have here a genuine holograph of S. Francis himself. On the reverse is an act of praise, *Laudes Dei*, which was almost certainly written by S. Francis at the same time.

With this precious *chartula* we should also consider the very short letter of S. Francis to Brother Leo in which he refers to some previous conversation " on the road " (*in via*) and invites Leo to come to him at any time if he should need any advice or comfort. Both Faloci-Pulignani and Goetz accept the Vatican MS. of this letter as a genuine holograph of S. Francis.[3]

Among the other writings which may be regarded as expressive of the innermost feelings of S. Francis we should include, first, the Prayer : " *Absorbeat, quaeso, Domine, mentem meam . . .*" which was quoted by Ubertino da Casale in his *Arbor Vitae Crucifixae* in 1305. Then there is also that paraphrase on the Lord's Prayer known as the *Laudes*, which Francis told the brothers at the Portiuncula that they must say regularly to keep them from idle words,[4] and which has been preserved among his writings. Again, Celano mentions certain *Laudes de Virtu-tibus*,[5] apparently a reference to the *Salutatio* of the six Virtues of Wisdom, Simplicity, Poverty, Humility, Charity and Obedience which is one of the accepted works of the saint. The short and rather banal *Salutatio Beatae Virginis* should also be included here. Lastly comes

---

[1] " *Bene veniat soror mea mors !* ", *Per.* 97.
[2] See Mrs. Reginald Balfour, *The Seraphic Keepsake*, and an interesting article by M. Faloci-Pulignani in *Misc. Franc.*, vi, pp. 33–9, called *Gli autografi di S. Francesco*.
[3] *Gli autografi*, etc., *Misc. Franc.*, vi, p. 39 : Goetz, *Die Quellen*, p. 16.
[4] *Spec. Perf.* 82 : *Pater Noster dicat pro anima sua cum Laudibus Domini ut dictum est.*
[5] *2 Cel.* 189 *ad fin.*

the *Officium Passionis Domini,* which may probably be identified with the *Officium Crucis* mentioned by Celano in his life of S. Clare.

'This brings us to the second group, containing those documents in which Francis is writing to fulfil some particular purpose or to plead some special cause. By far the most important of these is the Testament of S. Francis ; but it will be more convenient to discuss this after we have dealt with the writing of the Rules.

Next in importance to the Testament stand the *Admonitions,* a collection of twenty-eight short exhortations, beatitudes and sermons on a number of texts and subjects upon which Francis wished to make his ideas known to the brethren. Although their authenticity is nowadays generally accepted, there has been considerable discussion about the circumstances in which they were written. Sabatier believes them to be the basis of the *Regula Prima* of 1221 and to have been the result of the conversations which we know took place between Francis and Ugolino in 1218 and again in 1221.[1] They have certainly much in common with the Rule [2] ; but this is only natural as they deal with the subjects which were uppermost in S. Francis's mind and which constantly recur in all his writing and teaching. The Admonitions are concerned with such things as Poverty (Nos. 14 and 19), Humility (Nos. 4, 5, 17, 20 and 24), Obedience (Nos. 2 and 3), Respect for the Clergy (No. 26), and the Dangers of Learning (No. 7). On all these subjects Francis had much to say, while many of them were the cause of controversy and litigation for many years to come. Hints of these controversies sometimes occur in the Admonitions. For example, Francis always insisted that if the brothers wanted to follow the Rule strictly they should be allowed to do so even though their vow of obedience might be in jeopardy. In trying to enforce this principle on the Order he was defeated by the Pope,[3] but his wishes are made clear in the third Admonition : " If a superior give any order to one who is under him which is against that man's conscience, although he do not obey it yet he shall not be dismissed."

As to the question of the occasions when the Admonitions were written, Goetz suggests that they were originally words of counsel addressed separately to the various Chapter Meetings and collected together either during the saint's lifetime or shortly after his death.[4] There is some support for this theory in the *Vita Secunda* of Celano, where we read that Francis " at a certain Chapter had these words written down ".[5] The difficulty here is that the quotation which

---

[1] *Vie de S. François,* pp. 297 f.

[2] Cf., for example, *Admon.* 4 and *Reg. I,* cap. 6.

[3] See the chapters known as *Legenda Vetus* in *Opuscules,* fasc. iii.

[4] *Die Quellen,* p. 45.   [5] *2 Cel.* 128.

follows is taken not from the Admonitions at all but from the *Regula Prima*. Jörgensen suggests that they were set forth by S. Francis at the Pentecost Chapters and were meant to be regarded as more or less official additions to the Rule.[1] Since there is nothing to enable us to settle with certainty their provenance, we can only suppose that from time to time Francis addressed to the Chapter Meetings short expositions of scripture and words of counsel both before 1221 and afterwards. Whether they are actually " writings " of S. Francis which he read to the Chapter, or whether they are really spoken words which his hearers afterwards wrote down, it is impossible to say. But one thing is certain, and that is that they clearly represent the thought and the spirit of S. Francis.

The little exhortation known as *De Religiosa Habitatione in Eremis* may be one of the Admonitions which has become separated from its fellows, or possibly an unofficial addition to the Rule to meet the needs of those who, as years went on, were tending to withdraw into the remoter hermitages of the Apennines. If the Admonitions were addressed to the Chapter Meetings this exhortation can hardly be included among them, as it is clearly addressed to those who were more or less cut off from the official life of the Order. The problem of choosing between the life of an evangelist and the life of a hermit was one which Francis himself found difficult.[2] No doubt some of the brothers were faced with the same problem ; and though Francis himself decided, on the advice of Sylvester and Clare, that his future was as a wandering preacher, yet he must have had some sympathy with those who chose the other course. But the hermit life was one which was open to peculiar temptations of which Francis himself was fully aware.[3] His message to those who choose this way of life is, therefore, full of such advice as will help them to combat their peculiar difficulties.

The *De Reverentia Corporis Domini* treats of a theme which was very dear to the heart of S. Francis. One of the first acts of his new life was to present church ornaments to poor priests in order that the elements might be more worthily housed,[4] while later in life we find him sweeping out dirty churches[5] and picking up fragments of parchment for fear that the Name of God might be written on them.[6] This reverence for the Church and its ministers, and for everything sacred, appears constantly in S. Francis's writing and teaching. Besides this little tract the first Admonition and the Letter " to all the faithful " are concerned with the same subject. In full accord, then, with what we know to have been S. Francis's practice, he writes here to exhort

---

[1] *S. Francis of Assisi* (Eng. tr.), p. 324.
[2] See *Actus* (or *Fioretti*) 16. Bonaventura, *Leg. Maior*, xii, 1.
[3] *2 Cel.* 179.   [4] *2 Cel.* 8.   [5] *Per.* 54.   [6] *1 Cel.* 82.

priests and others to see that holy things are properly cared for, the elements kept in a decent place, the altars kept clean, and sacred things treated with respect. The tenor of this exhortation makes it probable that it was a circular letter sent round to different provinces.

We are now left with five Letters addressed respectively " to all the faithful ", " to the Chapter General ", " to a certain Minister ", " to the rulers of the people " and " to all the *custodes* ". There is also a short letter to S. Anthony of Padua, accepted as genuine by Wadding, Goetz and others, but rejected by Lemmens and so not included in the Quaracchi edition. It is perhaps the most interesting of all the Letters because it deals with a development in the Order of some importance. Anthony began his life in the Order as a hermit at Monte Paolo near Bologna, but before long he was invited to take charge of the Province of Romagna.[1] Realising that this would mean a break in his life as a contemplative, and the assumption of duties as a teacher and preacher, he may well have written to S. Francis for advice. We know something of Francis's fear of the sterility of intellectual work, and the reply to Anthony bears this out :

> Brother Francis to my dearest Brother Anthony,
> Greetings in Christ.
> I am willing that you should expound the words of theology to the friars provided that neither in you nor in the others (and this I most particularly desire) should be extinguished the spirit of holy Prayer according to the Rule which we profess.
> > Farewell.

The Letter " to all the faithful " was written towards the close of S. Francis's life when his infirmities prevented him from further travelling. Like the *De Reverentia Corporis Domini*, this must have been a circular letter sent round and read by the friars in the course of their evangelistic work. It is concerned with reverence for the sacred mysteries, repentance, almsgiving and humility, honour to the priesthood, abstinence and discipline, simplicity and renunciation.

The Letter " to the Chapter General " was written shortly before Francis died, and when he was too weak to attend the meeting. It implores the priest-brothers to be reverent and conscientious in the performance of their office, to have Mass said once a day in]each convent (though if there be more than one priest the others must be content to listen), and he begs all the brothers to observe the Rule strictly. As the letter proceeds the tone of the writer becomes more and more urgent, thereby revealing something of the anguish of mind which Francis felt through the carelessness and disloyalty of some of the brothers. " Whosoever of the brothers ", he writes, " will not observe the Rule I cannot regard as Catholics nor as my brothers, nor do I even wish to see them or speak to them until they have done penance."

[1] L. de Kerval, *S. Antonius de Padua*, p. 35.

The Minister to whom the third Letter is written is believed to be Elias, who was Minister General from 1221 until after the death of S. Francis. The letter is an appeal to him not to waver in his love for the brethren, especially those who cause him the greatest distress and sorrow.

The fourth Letter is addressed " to the rulers of the people " begging them not to let earthly cares hinder their love of God and admonishing them to receive the Sacrament regularly and devoutly. The *Custodes* to whom the fifth Letter is addressed were the heads of the friaries or *loci* as they are called in the legends. The appeal which Francis makes to them is to honour the Sacraments and to provide suitable vessels for them, to show reverence to the Scriptures, and to exhort the people to do the same.

The third group of S. Francis's Writings consists of two documents only, the *Regula Prima* of 1221 and the *Regula Bullata* of 1223. We shall, however, consider with them the Testament of S. Francis. These three works owe both their origin and their form to certain events in the life of S. Francis and of the Order. We can only, therefore, discuss them in the light of these events and so endeavour to find out how far they may be said to represent the true wishes and emotions of S. Francis and how far they reflect ideas which were imposed upon him from without.

Whether it were part of his intentions or not, Francis was the instigator of a great movement which spread rapidly throughout Europe and drew within its orbit very large numbers of people.[1] It soon became essential that some organisation should be set up and some regulations promulgated to control the progress of so energetic a movement. In other words, the Fraternity of which Francis, though the Founder, was for a time little more than *primus inter pares*, gradually developed into a popular Religious Order; and a Religious Order cannot exist without a Rule. It was over the writing of the Rule that the controversies arose, Francis reluctant to accept the changing conditions or to surrender any of his intransigeance; Ugolino, Elias and Honorius III desperately anxious to direct the spiritual forces which Francis had generated into a channel which would be not only *ad maiorem Dei gloriam* but also to the advantage of the Catholic Church. Our records tell us that Francis wrote at least four Rules.[2] The first was in 1210 when he had a small band of eleven disciples whom he

---

[1] The *Spec. Perf.* tells us that at the Chapter of 1221 there were 5,000 brethren present. It is sometimes thought that this number included members of what came to be called the Third Order.

[2] There may have been more, for, according to the *Leg. 3 Soc.* 35, Francis tried out various Rules before the one which was finally adopted in 1210.

took with him to Rome to seek the official approbation of Innocent III ;
the second was in 1221, soon after his return from the East on that
tragic journey which let loose the troubled waters of disaffection and
disloyalty ; the third was in 1223, when Francis was at Fonte Colombo,
but this was either lost or destroyed ; the fourth was the second edition
of this same Rule and was the only one to receive official papal sanction
with the authority of a Bull.

Referring to the original Rule, or *Regula Primitiva* as I shall call it,
Celano tells [1] us that when Francis had raised the number of his
followers to eleven, and when they had had some experience of the
evangelistic work to which their lives were dedicated, he wrote for them
a Rule, " simply and in a few words, mainly using the precepts of the
Holy Gospel to whose perfection he earnestly aspired. A few other
things he included which were obviously necessary for the living of
a holy life." Writing of these early days in his Testament, Francis
himself bears witness to the simplicity and brevity of the original Rule.[2]

It is quite clear that this description cannot possibly refer to what
is generally known as the *Regula Prima*, which is a long, rambling
document of twenty-three chapters, containing a number of repetitions
and even contradictions,[3] while many of the regulations presuppose
conditions and developments in the Order which were considerably
later than 1210. It is, however, generally agreed that the Rule of 1221
is only an amplified and extended version of the *Regula Primitiva*, and
that if everything that can be proved to be of a later date be removed
from the *Regula Prima*, we shall be left with something like the actual
words which S. Francis wrote for himself and his friends in 1210. In
the next chapter an attempt will be made to do this on the lines already
explored by Karl Müller in 1885 in his *Die Anfänge des Minoritenordens*,
by Father Cuthbert in 1912 in the first appendix to his *Life of S. Francis*,
and by Dr. Dominicus Mandić in 1924.[4]

Almost from the beginning events in the Fraternity took a turn for
which Francis was quite unprepared, and it seems probable that had
things gone as he expected there would never have been any need for
a Rule apart from the words of Christ in the Gospels. For it cannot
be too often stressed that the " conversion " of S. Francis was at first

---

[1] *1 Cel.* 32.

[2] *Testamentum* : " *ego paucis verbis et simpliciter feci scribi.*" Cf. *1 Cel.* 32 : " *simpliciter et paucis verbis . . . sancti evangelii praecipue sermonibus utens*".

[3] Cf. cap. 17 : " *Nullus fratrum praedicet contra formam et institutionem sanctae romanae
ecclesiae et nisi concessum fuerit sibi a ministro suo*" with cap. 21 : " *Hanc exhortationem
. . . omnes fratres mei, quandocumque placuerit eis, annuntiare possunt inter quoscumque
homines.*"

[4] Cf. *De Legislatione Antiqua Ordinis Fratrum Minorum*, p. 122. A French translation of the Primitive Rule as reconstructed by Dr. Mandić is given in *Revue d'Histoire
Franciscaine*, II, pp. 265–6. It consists of three chapters only.

an entirely personal and individual affair. This is amply borne out both by the *legendae* and by his own Testament. From the vision at Spoleto which put an end to his career as a soldier, from the solitary communings with God in the forests and caves of Subasio and the Tescio valley, and from the experience in S. Damiano which gave him a specific piece of work to do for God and His Church, he was driven to do the only thing which would satisfy his conscience and give him peace of mind. From these experiences he was led to adopt a particular manner of living, his choice being ratified by hearing the Gospel read at the Portiuncula on S. Matthias's day. This process of change seems to have taken two or three years to complete, during which there was, so far as we know, no suggestion of others being associated with him. For a longer time than is often realised by his biographers he was *vox clamantis in deserto*, a solitary and strange figure in the streets of Assisi, misunderstood, mocked and insulted. But he seems to have been content to plough this hard and lonely furrow, and hardly to have realised that others might want to make him their leader, since he was obviously most reluctant to accept the offer of Bernard of Quintavalle to join him in this rough life, and was only finally convinced by the threefold opening of the Bible in the Church of S. Nicholas.

Bernard was only the first of several who gathered round the Poverello and turned what had begun as a friendship into a Fraternity. How were they to live ? Francis had found the answer to this question so far as it concerned himself by years of prayer and experiment and by a succession of spiritual experiences ; but was it to be supposed that what was right for him was right for all ? As far as the first few disciples were concerned, each had had his own problem to face and his own reluctance to overcome, and there seemed no doubt of the genuineness of their vocation. It was enough, then, at first that the newcomers should accept without demur the standards and ideals which Francis put before them both by word and example. But this could not go on for ever. Francis had had a vision in which he had seen " a great multitude of men coming to us and desiring to live with us in the habit of holy life and under the rule of blessed religion ".[1] But what was he going to do with them all ? He could hardly test the vocation of each one as he had tested that of Bernard of Quintavalle. Therefore some Rule was necessary, some *forma vivendi* which should make clear what they were trying to do. But Francis was most anxious that his Fraternity should not become just another monastic Order with a Rule like that under which the Benedictines lived, with its seventy-three chapters regulating every detail of the monk's daily life. Francis was an artist and a poet who could never understand or appreciate the legal mind, while he had seen enough of the failure of monasticism, and even of

[1] *1 Cel. 27.*

the attempts at reform which had been made in the twelfth century, to convince him that what was needed was something different from any other existing Order, something much more simple, more directly based on the teaching of Christ and more susceptible to the directing influence of the Spirit of God. It is probable that at first he had in his mind the idea that, if a Rule were demanded by his followers, he would point to the Gospels and say : " There is your Rule ; what more do you want ? " or, as he said at the end of his life : " I have done my duty ; may Christ teach you yours." [1] So also he wrote about the same time in his Testament : " After the Lord had given me brothers no one shewed me what I ought to do ; but the Almighty Himself revealed to me that I was to live according to the manner of the Holy Gospel." There was, to his mind, no need for anything more specific than that.

But the problem was not quite so simple. The latter part of the twelfth century had been a time of considerable anxiety for the Church. Many social and political changes had combined with a general dissatisfaction with the methods and privileges of the clergy to bring into being a number of Fraternities practising poverty, proclaiming the right of the layman to preach, staunchly pacifist and bitterly critical of the Church. These movements, bearing such titles as Umiliati, Cathari, and Poor Men of Lyons, flourished most luxuriantly in the Lombard plain and in the south of France, but their influence was constantly spreading southwards. Now the position of Assisi in the Tiber valley, and the fact that it was one of those cities where communal liberty was growing at the expense of feudal autocracy, made it the sort of place where such ideas would be sure of a welcome; and, as Miss Scott Davison has pointed out,[2] it is impossible to ignore the fact that young Francis Bernardone must have had some knowledge of them. Moreover, the commercial expeditions of his father into the south of France (on some of which the young Francis may have been taken) would further bring him into touch with this great movement of liberal and anti-clerical thought.[3]

When Francis found himself the leader of a movement which was obviously growing rapidly, it is clear that he did not want it to become just another of the many communities which were causing so much anxiety to the ecclesiastical authorities. But as he and his companions, most of them laymen, went about preaching and living in voluntary poverty, how was the world to distinguish them from the other roaming bands, or to know that they were there to help the Church, not to find fault with it ? The only solution was to have some Rule which would

<hr />

[1] *2 Cel.* 214.   [2] *Forerunners of S. Francis,* pp. 282–3.

[3] We know that Francis often spoke quite naturally in French, though the *3 Socii* tell us that he was not very fluent.

be acceptable to the Pope and which would thereby give them authority to speak in the Church's name.

It was fortunate for Francis that he had to approach so wise a man as Innocent III. This far-seeing Pope realised that there were good grounds for this great urge for Church reform, and that no good would come to the cause of Christianity by alienating those who were demanding a return to apostolic simplicity. Had he been less sympathetic, it is unlikely that the Franciscan movement would ever have made any progress, for he must have regarded the little band of penitents from Assisi who presented themselves to him in 1210 as just another of these semi-heretical movements which were causing him so much trouble. But fortunately Innocent was a man who was prepared to take infinite pains to sort out the bad from the good ; and so when Francis appeared before him he was at least ready to give him a hearing.

Knowing the character of the Pope and the kind of questions which he would be likely to ask, Francis realised that he must have with him some written document which would explain what it was that he and his companions were trying to do. To go to Rome and say " We wish to live according to the Gospel, but we do not feel that we can bind ourselves by any Rule " would have been to court disaster. But here lay the problem. On the one hand the Rule must state definitely what were to be the guiding principles of the movement, while, on the other hand, it must leave ample scope for the direction of the Holy Spirit. The result was something quite simple (*simpliciter*), and quite short (*paucis verbis*), using as its main precepts the words of Christ which Francis had already made the guiding principles of his life.

This *Regula Primitiva* was either written out by S. Francis himself or dictated by him to one of the brothers in 1210,[1] and taken to Innocent III who confirmed it, though without a Bull. It was one of the last Rules to be approved by the Church, for the Lateran Council of 1215 passed a decree that any new foundations must adopt one of the existing Rules—Benedictine, Augustinian, Cistercian, etc. Although the primitive Rule of the Friars Minor was not officially approved in 1210, it seems to have been treated as an " existing Rule " in 1215 and was allowed to stand. But there was certainly a party among the brothers after the time of the Lateran Council who thought, quite conscientiously, that the original Rule of S. Francis was not in the technical sense one of the " existing Rules " in 1215 and were anxious to abandon it in favour of some other.

In 1217 a most important step was taken in the development of the Order by the appointment of provinces and ministers to supervise them. This was agreed upon at the Pentecost Chapter. At the same time it

---

[1] Celano says " *scripsit* " (*I Cel.* 32), but Francis himself says " *feci scribi* " (*Testamentum*).

was decided to make new efforts in evangelism, with the result that Francis himself immediately set off for France. But on reaching Florence he came into contact with Cardinal Ugolino, the man who was to exert so great an influence on the history of the Order. We do not know whether they had actually met before, although Ugolino was already Protector of the Order, a position to which he had succeeded on the death of Giovanni di San Paolo in the previous year. Moreover, we know from Eccleston that Francis was at Perugia when Innocent III died there in 1216, and it is probable that Ugolino would be there too.[1] Celano's account of the meeting at Florence does not say definitely that they had met before. What he says is : " Not yet were they joined together in any special intimacy, though the fame of each one's holy life had brought them together in affection and charity." [2] What is clear is, that by the time of their meeting in 1217 Ugolino was already in a position to exercise some authority over Francis, as he succeeded in persuading him to abandon his proposed evangelistic journey over the Alps, and to remain in Italy for the time being. Ugolino was a states-man who saw already the potential value to the Church of this brother-hood of men so completely surrendered to the will of God, so humble and so obedient. To him it seemed a mistake for the brothers to be scattered over the world, dying of cold and hunger, when they might be used nearer home in building up the prestige of the Church. " Why," he asked Francis, " have you sent your brethren so far away to die of hunger ? " [3] So a damper was put on the missionary zeal of the brothers, and Francis, abandoning his proposed journey, stayed in Italy.

This meeting between Francis and Ugolino in Florence in July 1217 was therefore one of great importance for the future development of the Order. Giovanni di San Paolo, the first Protector of the Order, does not appear to have had much influence over the ebullient enthusiasm of S. Francis ; but in Ugolino the Poverello found a man of strong purpose and great force of character who was able, from the very first, to bend the will of the saint to his own.

Early in 1218 Francis went to Rome.[4] There he found Ugolino, who was in the city from December 1217 to April 1218.[5] Another visitor to Rome that spring was S. Dominic, who arrived there in January.[6] The future of the friars and the decree of the Lateran Council must have been discussed between these three men, and pressure was probably put upon Francis then to give up his own Rule and adopt one of the great monastic Rules which were already in

---

[1] Eccleston, *De Adventu* (ed. Little), p. 119.   [2] *1 Cel.* 74.   [3] *Spec. Perf.* 65.
[4] Sabatier, *Vie de S. François*, p. 243, n. 1.   Cf. *1 Cel.* 73, which seems to refer to this visit, as Francis is more or less unknown to Honorius III.
[5] Potthast, *Regesta*, I, 5269–747.
[6] Bede Jarrett, *Life of S. Dominic*, p. 77.

existence. This step had already been taken by Dominic whose Order is described in a Bull of December 22nd, 1216, as " *ordo canonicus secundum beati Augustini regulam* ".[1] But Francis was much less amenable. " The Almighty has revealed to me that I must live according to the manner of the Holy Gospel," [2] he said, and he would not submit to anything else. Ugolino tried everything : he sketched for the benefit of the Poverello, his idea of what the Church might become if the friars would only work with him. He pointed out that in the early Church it was poor men who were chosen as leaders, and admitted that his ambition was to see poor men taking the lead again. " Why," he asked, " should we not make of your brethren Bishops and Prelates ? " Francis had his reply ready. " My lord," he said, " my brothers are called ' lesser ' just so that they may not aspire to become ' greater '." [3] Ugolino had to give in ; but the following June he presided in person over the Chapter Meeting at the Portiuncula and saw to it that Dominic was there also.

It was at this Chapter that certain of the brothers went to Ugolino and asked him to try to persuade Francis to give up his own Rule and adopt one of the existing Rules of the monastic Orders. When Francis had listened to the advice of Ugolino on this point he led him by the hand into the Chapter and said to the brothers there assembled : " Brothers, brothers ; the Lord hath called me by the way of humility, and He has shown me the way of simplicity ; and I do not want you to mention to me any other Rule, neither that of S. Augustine, nor of S. Benedict, nor of S. Bernard. And the Lord told me that He wished me to be a new fool in the world and that He did not want to lead us by any other way than by that wisdom ; for by your learning and your wisdom God will confound you." [4] Ugolino had failed again ; but if he was not able to induce Francis to give up his Rule at least he was able to arrange that certain additions were made to it to make it a little more comprehensive. The framework of texts upon which Francis had hung a few exhortations in 1210 could hardly bear the strain which was put upon it now that the numbers had increased so vastly.

At the Chapter Meeting in the following year (1219) the main subject of discussion was the missionary work of the Order, and a new attempt was made to organise evangelistic work on a big scale. As usual, Francis was determined to set a good example to the others, and on

June 24th he left Ancona on his expedition to Damietta and the Holy Land. He had the encouragement of the Pope behind him, for on June 11th Honorius had issued a Bull in support of the missionary work of the Friars Minor.[1] Francis was away until July or August 1220. During his absence various significant changes took place in the life of the Community. In the first place Ugolino forced upon the Poor Clares a set of regulations which, as Father Cuthbert says,[2] " were altogether lacking in that sweet reasonableness which breathes in the legislation of the great monastic founders . . . They exhibit all the rigidity and harsh externalism of a Rule meant to correct and guard against abuses, with none of the inspiring idealism which is the very life of a religious Order ". An examination of these " Ugoline Constitutions " [3] shows that they are definitely based upon the Benedictine Rule, while the first visitor of the nunneries appointed by Ugolino was a Cistercian, a member of the strictest Order then in existence.[4] Meanwhile the Poor Clares of Monticello, Siena, Perugia and Lucca had been forced to accept the Benedictine Rule in its entirety.[5] Then at the Chapter in May 1220 new regulations about fasting were imposed upon the brothers which were so contrary to the spirit and intention of S. Francis that a certain Brother Stephen rushed straight off to Acre to implore the saint to come home and deal with the trouble that had arisen.

Francis hurried home, arriving at Venice about the end of July. He proceeded to Bologna, where, in great indignation, he rushed into the house which he found the brothers had built and turned them all out, including some who were sick.[6] A Chapter Meeting was summoned for Michaelmas Day (September 29th); but if Francis was preparing to make a last bid for the liberty which he had always claimed and fought for, the wind was taken out of his sails at the last moment by the Pope, who, on September 22nd, issued the Bull, *Cum secundum*,[7] in which a year's novitiate for all postulants to the Order was enjoined. Thus a further step was taken in bringing the Rule of the Friars Minor into conformity with the existing monastic Rules. When the Chapter met a week later Francis abdicated.

With the resignation of S. Francis the position of Minister General

[1] Sbaralea, *Bullarium Franciscanum*, I, p. 2. Potthast, *Regesta*, 6081. In the previous year Honorius had announced his intention of making a big missionary effort. Potthast, *Regesta*, 5891.

[2] *Life of S. Francis*, p. 292. For a full discussion, see Oliger, *De Origine Regularum Ordinis S. Clarae* in *A.F.H.*, v (1912).

[3] They are dated July 25th, 1219. Cf. the Bull, *Sacrosancta* in Sbaralea, *Bull. Franc.*, I, p. 3.

[4] Sbaralea, *Bull. Franc.*, I, p. 46.

[5] Oliger in *A.F.H.*, v, p. 195. The decrees are dated July 27th, 29th and 30th, 1219.

[6] *2 Cel. 58 = Spec. Perf.* (Sabatier) 6.   [7] Sbaralea, *Bull. Franc.*, I, p. 6.

was given to his friend Peter Catanii. Francis retired to the Portiuncula for that winter and set himself to revise the Rule and to offer it to the Chapter in 1221. Here with the aid of some of those whom he could trust—Peter Catanii, Caesarius of Speyer and others—Francis worked away at the Rule. Then, early in 1221, he went again to Rome, where he met Ugolino and Dominic again for further consultation.[1] Gradually the Rule was hammered out in readiness for the Pentecost Chapter which was held on May 30th. Ugolino, strangely enough, was not present, his place being taken by Cardinal Rainerio.[2] Probably Ugolino was dissatisfied with the final draft of the Rule and thought it wise to stop away, for it was the only Chapter Meeting which he missed in those early years. It was to this Chapter, then, that Francis offered the so-called *Regula Prima*. Father Cuthbert says of this Rule [3] : " It was not a treaty of peace : it was a challenge thrown down to those who would change the vocation of the fraternity ; and as such it was taken by the dissident ministers." Yet we cannot accept the Rule of 1221 as a true expression of the will of S. Francis, for there is much in it which runs counter to what we know to have been his intentions. For example, in chapter ii we read that the postulant " shall sell all his goods if he wishes to do so and can do so in a spiritual way and without let or hindrance " [4] ; and again, " if a man comes who cannot give his goods away without hindrance and yet has a spiritual desire to do so, let him leave them and that shall suffice ". Concessions such as these are not in keeping with the uncompromising words of the *Regula Primitiva* and of the Testament. Or again, on the subject of clothes : " let them have one tunic with a hood and another without a hood ", though in the early days only one tunic was allowed. Again, in chapter iii we read : " they may have such books as are necessary for saying the offices ", which is quite contrary to the declared wishes of S. Francis in the *Intentio Regulae* and elsewhere. Again, on the subject of preaching, the Rule says : " no friar shall preach unless permission has been given to him by his minister, and let the minister be careful not to give that permission without discretion ", which contrasts with the more liberal decree of the *Regula Primitiva* giving the friars leave to exhort the people whenever it pleases them to do so.[5]

On the other hand, there are undoubtedly some moments in the Rule where Francis is expressing his own ideas, even though they may run contrary to the capitular decrees of the Ministers. For example, in chapter ix permission is given to the brothers, if necessity arise, to eat

[1] Sabatier, *Vie de S. François*, pp. 301 ff.   [2] Jordano, *Chronica*, cap. 16.

[3] *Life of S. Francis*, p. 314.

[4] " *Si vult et potest spiritualiter et sine impedimento, vendat omnia sua* " (*Reg.* I, cap. ii).

[5] " *Hanc vel talem exhortationem et laudem omnes fratres mei quandocumque placuerit eis annuntiare possunt inter quoscumque homines* " (*Reg.* I, cap. xxi).

all kinds of food—a direct challenge to the decrees of 1220 which forbade the brothers to eat meat.[1]   Again, in chapter viii the brothers are forbidden, under any circumstances, to receive or solicit money for the building of houses ; and we are reminded of the occasion upon which Francis had found the brothers at the Portiuncula building themselves a house, and had climbed on to the roof and begun throwing the tiles to the ground.[2]   Or again, in chapter xvi he overrides the authority of the Ministers by ordering them to give a licence to any brother who wants to go abroad so long as he is fit for such work.

So the true S. Francis keeps appearing in the Rule ; and this was what made it unacceptable to those who were determined to bend the Order to their own will.   Without the restraining hand of Ugolino the Rule may have passed the Chapter : it did not pass the Pope, for it was never officially approved, and so remained for ever ineffectual. What happened to it we do not know.   The *Speculum* says [3] that many things were taken out of it by the Ministers, but there is no real authority for this statement as it is not in the *Verba S. Francisci* from which this chapter is taken.   Rather it seems to have been one of those compromises that fail, being acceptable neither to Francis himself nor to the dissentient ministers.

Sabatier says [4] that after the Chapter of 1221 almost everything that was done in the Order was done either without Francis's knowledge or against his will.   Francis certainly withdrew more and more from taking any active part in the affairs of the community.[5]   Peter Catanii had died in March 1221 and Elias was now at the head of the Order, put there possibly by Ugolino without the brethren being consulted at all.[6]   Francis meanwhile was rapidly becoming a sick man and, as such, was losing something of the old fighting spirit which had previously spurred him on.   His thoughts turned more and more towards the life of a mystic and contemplative, while he travelled about among the smaller hermitages, avoiding the controversies and the dust of the conflict which was being waged among his brethren.

In the meanwhile Elias and Ugolino were busy.   On March 22nd, 1222, they persuaded Honorius to issue a Bull giving to the Friars Minor the privilege of saying Mass in their churches in time of interdict.[7] " We accord to you," he wrote, " permission to celebrate the Sacraments in time of interdict in your churches, *if you come to have any*." [8]

---

[1] Jordano, *Chronica*, cap. 11.   [2] *Per.* 48d.   [3] *Speculum* (Sabatier), cap. 1.
[4] *Vie de S. François*, p. 316.   [5] Cf. *2 Cel.* 157 : " *subtrahebat se a consortio fratrum.*"
[6] Lempp, *Frère Élie de Cortone*, p. 46.   But the *Chronica XXIV Generalium* says that Elias was appointed by S. Francis : " *B. Franciscus posuit ad regendum fr. Heliam.*" *An. F.*, III, p. 31.
[7] Sbaralea, *Bull. Franc.*, I, p. 9.
[8] A similar privilege had been granted to the Dominicans a few days before (March 7th).   Ripolli, *Bull. Praed.*, I, p. 15.

These last words are significant. As yet the friars had no churches, and it was against their Rule to have them; but Honorius clearly expected that this Rule would soon be superseded. A week later, on March 29th, he gave to the Dominicans and Franciscans of Lisbon special permission to proceed against the Bishop and clergy of that city,[1] in spite of Francis's declared intention that the friars should not seek any such privileges from the Holy See.

Sometime in 1222 or early in 1223 Francis sought out Ugolino again. Things were becoming chaotic and the whole future of the Order was at stake. The Rule of 1221, even with the concessions which it contained, was being openly ignored by the dissentient Ministers, and something had to be done to restore order. Ugolino tells us himself of the conversations which he had with Francis at this time, as they talked over the question of a new Rule.[2] At the Whitsuntide Chapter which followed these talks a definite demand for a new Rule was made, and Francis retired to Fonte Colombo to write it. While he was there a rumour was started that the new Rule was going to be too severe, and Elias and some of the other Ministers came to say that they were not prepared to accept the Rule which Francis was now writing.[3] According to Brother Leo, however, the voice of Christ intervened and declared that everything in the Rule was written at His dictation and was to be observed *ad litteram, sine glossa*.[4] Francis went on with the work, and in due course presented the new Rule to the Ministers. But the next thing we hear is that it was lost! Bonaventura says charitably that it was lost " through carelessness ",[5] but there can be little doubt that it was destroyed deliberately. So Francis retired again to Fonte Colombo to dictate a new copy. But this time, before it was made public, he took it to Rome to consult Ugolino and Honorius. Perhaps he hoped to get their approval before it was put into the hands of the Ministers, but what actually happened was that his distinguished consultants prevailed upon him to modify what he had written.

An account of these conversations is given in chapter 2 of the *Legenda Vetus* which Sabatier published in 1902 in the *Opuscules de Critique Historique*.[6] According to this account Francis had given the brothers liberty to observe the Rule *ad litteram*, even if the Ministers ordained otherwise. This would have been a valuable concession to the strict party, but, at the same time, a blow to the authority of the

---

[1] Potthast, *Regesta*, 6809.

[2] In the Bull, *Quo elongati* of 1230.

[3] *Verba S. Francisci*, 4. Cf. *Spec. Perf.* (Sabatier) 1.

[4] Cf. Burkitt's essay on " Fonte Colombo and its Traditions " in *Franciscan Essays*, Vol. II (*B.S.F.S.*).

[5] " *per incuriam* ", *Leg. Maior*, iv, 11.

[6] *S. Francisci Legendae Veteris Fragmenta Quaedam* in *Opuscules*, fasc. iii.

D

Ministers.   So Honorius prevailed upon Francis to omit this passage.[1]
Even more significant is the omission of chapter xiv of the *Regula
Prima* : " When the brothers are going about the world, let them carry
nothing with them," which comes down from the original Rule of 1210
and is an essential part of the Franciscan ideal.   We cannot believe
that Francis would ever have willingly submitted to the omission of
this phrase.

Pious pilgrims in Franciscan Italy point to Fonte Colombo as
the " Sinai " of the Order.   But the document which proceeded from
that wooded gorge expresses but a poor shadow of the real wishes of
S. Francis.   Over and over again in the Rule of 1223 we see points
which were all in all to S. Francis being either given up or reduced
to a feeble image of their original ideal.   At first everyone who wished
to join the Fraternity was ordered to sell all that he had and give to
the poor, for the brothers were committed to the service of Lady
Poverty.   By 1221 this had been toned down a little.   If the distribution
to the poor could not be made *sine impedimento*, then it would suffice
that they should just renounce everything that they had.   But in 1223
a much greater concession is made, a concession which destroys the
whole force of the original injunction.   After repeating the phrase
about selling all and giving to the poor Francis now writes :   " and if
they cannot do this, their good will shall be enough ".[2]   Again, the
brother's outfit, which began with *tunica unica* and was increased in
1221 by the addition of *alia cum caputio*, is now further enlarged by
a *caparone*, or large cape reaching to the waist, and a pair of sandals, in
spite of Francis's wish that the brothers should go barefoot like the
apostles.   Further restrictions are now put upon preaching, for the
brother must now obtain permission not from his Provincial Minister
but from the Minister General.   Clerks in the Order are now given
leave to possess breviaries, and the ministers are ordered to see that the
sick brethren are well cared for and the brothers everywhere properly
clad.

Of course there is much, even in this Rule, which represents the real
wishes of S. Francis.   But there is a note of pleading running through
it all which shows that the writer is not happy in his own mind.
" *Consulo, moneo et exhortor*," he writes three times over in chapters ii,
iii and x.   In chapter vi he suddenly breaks into the second person,

---

[1] Unfortunately, the authority of the *Legenda Vetus* is not very great.   Sabatier
accepted it without demur :   " je n'hésite pas . . . à voir dans ce morceau une des
plus précieuses données historiques que nous ayons sur la vie de S. François ", *op. cit.*,
p. 90.   But it comes from a fourteenth-century manuscript which cannot claim first-
rate authority.   Sabatier's theory that these chapters are part of the missing portion of
Leg. 3 Soc. is no longer tenable.   For further notes on the *Legenda Vetus*, see below,
p. 166.

[2] " *Quod si facere non potuerint sufficit eis bona voluntas* " (*Reg. II*, cap. ii).

imploring the brothers to stand fast in their profession of Poverty, while in chapter iv he begins with the phrase : " I firmly order all the brothers that on no account must they receive coins or any money either themselves or through a third party." [1] But even allowing for these things the Rule of 1223 cannot be regarded as representative of the real wishes of S. Francis. It was taken to the Pope, who, on November 25th, 1223, confirmed it and sealed it with a Bull.[2] Three weeks later another Bull was issued excommunicating those who left the Order.[3]

Sick at heart as well as in body, disillusioned, unhappy, anxious for the future and with a feeling of having failed in his mission, Francis retired to Greccio, where he spent the winter and stayed on over the following Easter.[4] There he spent much time in solitary prayer ; " he came not down from his cell except at meal times and immediately returned thither ".

During these long hours of meditation and prayer he must have brooded over the course which events in the Order had taken. His own dear Rule of 1210 was long since dead and buried under the weight of capitular legislation ; the Rule of 1221 had been superseded and was out of date ; it was the *Regula Bullata* which was now the official Rule of the Order, and Elias would not even accept *that*, although it had papal sanction behind it.[5] Francis must have longed to go back to the beginning, to start again with a new Rule and new ideals. But he had no authority apart from his personality. He could only exhort the brethren, and plead with them, and try to get them to see what his real wishes were.

It was in this mood that he put together his Testament. It is the most moving of all his writings. Calm and unimpassioned, it makes, by its very simplicity, an appeal more touching than all the Rules and Admonitions. But it is not only an appeal ; it is also an autobiography. The sanction which lies behind his will for the brethren is the example which he himself has set. He begins with a passage from his own life : " Thus did the Lord give to me, Brother Francis, to begin to do penance, for when I was in sin it seemed to me very bitter indeed to see lepers ; but the Lord Himself led me among them and I showed pity upon them . . . And then after a little while I came out from the world." Then he goes on to state his own faith in the Church

---

[1] " *Praecipio firmiter fratribus universis ut nullo modo denarios vel pecuniam recipiant per se vel per interpositam personam* (*Reg. II*, cap. iv).

[2] Sbaralea, *Bull. Franc.*, I, pp. 15–19.   [3] *Ibid.*, p. 19.

[4] See *Per.* 66–7, where *dies nativitatis* has been written in mistake for *dies resurrectionis.* This is clear from the fact that a few lines previously the writer says *erat quadragesima.* It is further borne out by *2 Cel.* 61, where the same incident is dated *quodam die Paschae.*

[5] Eccleston, *De Adventu*, p. 85.

and her priests, which was so great that " if they should persecute me I would yet wish to have recourse to them ", while he would on no account preach in their parishes without their consent.[1] After this he declares his reverence for the Sacraments and his desire that the elements should be worthily kept. This was a common theme in his writings and a practice of his from early days when, as a young man, he used to send vessels for the adornment of Churches.[2] Then he writes of his veneration for the Scriptures and of his desire that they also should be honourably preserved, which again reminds us of the statement in *1 Celano* that whenever he found any writing, sacred or profane, he would pick it up and place it most reverently in some safe place in case the name of the Lord should be written upon it.[3] After this he writes again in a reminiscent tone of the first brothers which the Lord gave him, and of how God revealed to him that they were to live according to the precepts of the Gospel,[4] and of how he wrote the original Rule which Innocent III confirmed for him. Then he tells how in those early days they gave everything which they had to the poor and were satisfied with one habit, patched within and without, if they so wished, and the cord and breeches : " and we did not want anything else ".[5] Having recalled their personal renunciation, he next writes of their life together. He tells how they said their prayers with the greatest simplicity, considering themselves *idiotae et subditi omnibus*. He refers to the manual labour which he and the others performed, and to their begging for alms if they received no reward for their work. Then he records how God revealed to him the salutation which they were to use on their journeyings : " The Lord give you peace."

So far Francis has been in reminiscent mood ; there are few injunctions and little pleading ; simply the story of the early days is told and the reader is left to draw his own conclusions. But from this point onwards Francis states his own wishes for the future of the Order. First he warns them against accepting buildings for their convenience ; then he orders them (*praecipio firmiter*) not to seek privileges from Rome under any pretext whatsoever. After this he enjoins them all to obey the Ministers and guardians appointed over them and to adhere to the Rule, in the meanwhile laying down most careful instructions how to treat the recalcitrant brother, who is to be guarded day and night like a prisoner in chains until he be brought

---

[1] The friars' claim to be allowed to preach in the parishes without the consent of the incumbents was a constant source of friction.

[2] *3 Soc.* 8.

[3] *1 Cel.* 82, and cf. Admonitions, Letters and *De Reverentia Corporis Domini*.

[4] Cf. *3 Soc.* 29 and *1 Cel.* 32.

[5] Cf. *1 Cel.* 39 : " *sola tunica erant contenti, repetiata quandoque intus et foris . . . fune succincti femoralia vilia gestabant . . . nihilque habere amplius propositum pium habebant.*"

to Cardinal Ugolino, the Protector of the Order, lest he should escape and so put himself under the sentence of excommunication which Honorius had declared to be the fate of those who left the Order.[1]

The last part of the Testament is an appeal. " Let not the brothers say," he writes, " ' This is a new Rule ' ; for this is a memorial, an admonition, an exhortation, and my Testament which I, little Brother Francis, make for you, my blessed brothers, on this account, that we may observe in a more orthodox way the Rule which we have promised before God." Then he asks them not to interfere with what he has here written, but to keep it together with the Rule, and to read it at every Chapter Meeting. And they are not, on any account, to put glosses and interpretations upon it or upon the Rule.

So he ends his last appeal to the brothers, imploring them, " as the Lord has granted to me simply and plainly to speak and to write these words ", to observe what he has written for them loyally, faithfully, for ever. It is his last will and testament.

On September 28th, 1230, just four years after the death of S. Francis, Ugolino, now raised to the Papacy as Gregory IX, declared authoritatively [2] that the brothers were not bound to observe the injunctions laid down in the Testament because Francis had no right, without the consent of a Chapter General, to lay any commands upon them, nor had he the power to commit his successors in any way. A few years later copies of the Testament were being deliberately burned by command of the Ministers.[3]

---

[1] Bull of Dec. 18th, 1223. Sbaralea, *Bull. Franc.*, I, p. 19.
[2] In the Bull, *Quo elongati* in Sbaralea, *Bull. Franc.*, I, p. 68.
[3] Ubertino da Casale quoted in Sabatier, *Vie de S. François*, p. xxxvii, n. 2.

III

THE *REGULA PRIMITIVA* OF 1210

THE precious document which Francis carried in his bosom on that journey to Rome in 1210 has long since disappeared, and our only hope of reconstructing it is to see whether it is embedded in the Rule of 1221. In order to guide our choice, we have four things to consider. First, there are the descriptions of the primitive Rule in Celano's *Vita Prima* and in the Testament of S. Francis. Celano says that it was written " simply and in a few words, using mainly the precepts of the Holy Gospel, to whose perfection he earnestly aspired ",[1] and S. Francis himself, in the Testament, says that, having learnt from God that he was to live according to the manner of the Holy Gospel, he had it written down " in a few words and simply ". Secondly, we know from Jordano's *Chronicle* that when S. Francis was preparing the Rule in 1221 to present to the Chapter he called in the help of Caesarius of Speyer, who was a well-educated man, to adorn it with some suitable texts from the Bible.[2] Thirdly, many of the regulations in the Rule of 1221 obviously belong to a later stage in the development of the Order. For example, anything to do with Provincial Ministers must have been added after 1217 when these officers were first appointed. Fourthly, we must bear in mind all that we know of the life of the friars in the early days when as yet there were few of them. For this we must rely mainly upon the *Legenda Trium Sociorum* and *1 Celano*.

The Rule begins with a Prologue announcing the fact that this is the way of life to which Innocent III gave his approbation. These words may have been inserted by the Pope himself immediately after giving his licence, or they may have been added by S. Francis as he came out from the audience. They cannot, of course, have been part of the original document as the verbs are all in the perfect tense : *petiit, concessit, confirmavit*. The second paragraph of the Prologue, which declares that " Brother Francis and whosoever shall be the head of this Religion ", shall promise obedience and reverence to Innocent and his successors, may well be original. The word " *religio* " gave place in later years to the word " *ordo* ". Moreover, it would be both wise and natural for Francis to state at once that this *religio* was to be in

[1] *1 Cel.* 32. [2] Jordano, *Chronica*, cap. 15.

38

the Church and in complete loyalty to the Pope. Such a statement standing at the head of the Rule would be calculated to make a good impression, and dispose the Pope to give a hearing to what this strange little man had to say. On the other hand, the last sentence of the Prologue which states that all the brothers shall obey Francis and his successors is certainly later, as at the moment when the primitive Rule was written it was Bernard and not Francis who was in command, as he had been appointed the leader on the journey to Rome.[1]

Chapter i declares that the brothers are to live in obedience and in chastity and without property, and to follow the teaching and the footsteps of Christ. These simple words are followed by four texts : " If thou wilt be perfect go and sell that thou hast and give to the poor, and come, follow me " ; " If any man will come after me let him deny himself and take up his cross and follow me " ; " If any man come to me and hate not his father and mother and wife and children and brethren and sisters, yea, and his own life also, he cannot be my disciple " ; and " Everyone that hath forsaken father or mother or brothers or sisters or wife or children or houses or lands for my sake shall receive a hundredfold and shall inherit eternal life." This chapter corresponds with our descriptions of the original Rule and is in perfect harmony with the declared wishes of S. Francis. It was, moreover, quoted by Jacques de Vitry in a letter written in 1220.[2] We need have no hesitation, therefore, in regarding it as a genuine part of the Regula Primitiva.

Chapter ii, which deals with the reception of the brothers and their dress, is perhaps the most important part of the whole Rule. It has been modified and extended a good deal from the original words which Francis wrote, and, in its present form, shows several departures from his early intentions. There appear to be five distinct stages in the development of this chapter.

(a) The original words of S. Francis seem to be represented by these two sentences : " If anyone by divine inspiration and willing to accept this life (i.e. the life of obedience, chastity and poverty mentioned in chapter i) shall come to our brothers, let him be kindly received by them . . . And he must sell all his goods and be careful to give everything to the poor " (vendat omnia sua et ea omnia pauperibus studeat erogare). We should note here the repetition of the word omnia. The renunciation was to be complete ; everything was to be given to the poor, and not either appropriated by the brotherhood nor distributed among the man's relations. The second passage which appears to be primitive runs as follows : " And let all the brothers be dressed in shabby clothes (vilibus vestibus), and let them patch them with sackcloth and other rags with the blessing of God ; for the Lord

<hr />

[1] 3 Soc. 46. 　　　　[2] Golubovich, Biblioteca, I, p. 9.

says in the Gospel: *They which are gorgeously apparelled and live delicately are in kings' courts."* These two injunctions—complete renunciation and rough clothing—are in full accord with our accounts of the early days, with the words of S. Francis himself in the Testament, and with the description of the Rule in *Celano*.

(b) The original intention of the saint was that postulants should sell everything and give the money to the poor. This was based upon the words of Christ to the rich young man: "*Go and sell that thou hast and give to the poor, and come, follow me."* But from quite early days there appear to have been two dangers attendant upon this renunciation. One was that the existing members of the Order should try to get some of the money to form a reserve fund to be used in emergency. That this was always a danger is shown by a passage in *2 Celano* (§ 67) where Peter Catanii, the Minister General, anxious about providing enough sustenance for the large numbers of brothers who attended the Chapter Meeting at Michaelmas, 1220, appealed to the saint to allow some of the property of novices entering the Order to be set aside for contingencies such as this. Francis, of course, was horrified by this suggestion and ordered Peter to " strip the altar " if he were really in need ; but the whole incident shows how great the danger was. The second danger was much more difficult to combat. When a man of property came to the brothers and asked to be accepted by them, declaring at the same time his willingness to give away everything that he had to the poor, we can readily imagine that a certain amount of " lobbying " went on among some of the brothers. No doubt many of them had poor relations in the world who might as well have a share in what was going as anyone else. Suggested names of suitable recipients would therefore be given to the man who was distributing his wealth. Such action would be abhorrent to S. Francis. So the second stage in the development of this chapter gives us a clause which is intended to deal with these two dangers. The injunction is as follows : " Let the brothers be most careful not to meddle in any way with his affairs (i.e. those of the man who is distributing his goods) and not to accept any money either themselves or through a third party " (*Caveant autem sibi fratres . . . quod de negotiis suis nullo modo se intermittant neque accipiant aliquam pecuniam, neque per se neque per interpositam personam*).

(c) The third stage is reached by the appointment of Provincial Ministers in 1217. Various additions to the Rule are now necessary, the Ministers being given the task of instructing the novices and eventually receiving them into the Order. We get, therefore, the following clause added : " If he (the postulant) shall be determined to accept our life, let the brothers be very careful not to meddle with his affairs, but let them take him as soon as possible to their Minister.

And let the Minister receive him kindly and comfort him and explain to him carefully the main object of our life."

(d) A fourth stage is reached three years later by the issue of the Bull, *Cum secundum*, on September 22nd, 1220.[1] This Bull made two provisions for the Order; one was that all newcomers should serve a year's novitiate before being finally professed; the other that anyone who left the Order to join another would be excommunicated. Further additions to the Rule are therefore necessary to make allowance for these new regulations. The Minister is ordered to " hand over to him (the new member) the uniform of a probationer (*panni probationis*) for a year; that is to say, two tunics without a hood and the cord and breeches and a cloak (*caparone*) down to the waist. And when the year of probation is over, let him receive him ' into obedience '. After that he shall not be allowed to go over to any other Order, nor to wander away from obedience (*extra obedientiam evagari*) according to the command of the Lord Pope." It is possible also that at this same time, when the dress of the probationer was under discussion, a further concession to the brothers themselves was made. We know from Celano and the Testament of S. Francis that the early brothers were content with one tunic, and that Francis frequently admonished those who wanted to have more than one; and yet in this so-called *Regula Prima* we read: " The other brothers, who have promised obedience, may have one tunic with a hood and another without a hood, if it should be necessary, and the cord and breeches."

(e) Finally, there are certain things in this chapter which ill accord with what we know to have been the wishes of S. Francis. When they were added we do not know, but they can certainly be no part of the original Rule. One of these almost entirely destroys the force of the clause bidding the man who joins the Order to sell all that he has and give to the poor, for these words have been added: " If he is willing and is able to do so spiritually and without hindrance (*si vult et potest spiritualiter et sine impedimento*)." Again, a little later: " If anyone comes who cannot give his property away without hindrance, and yet has a spiritual intention (*spiritualem voluntatem*), let him leave everything and that will do (*relinquat illa et sufficit ei*)." Probably about the same time was added this other concession which again cuts across what Francis intended. When a postulant is distributing his goods, the friars, " if they are in need, may accept things necessary for the body, so long as the need is great, like other poor men; but not money (*si tamen indigerent, alia necessaria corporis praeter pecuniam recipere possint fratres causa necessitatis, sicut alii pauperes*)." This cannot have been done with Francis's consent, as is clear from his words to Peter Catanii to which allusion has already been made.

[1] Sbaralea, *Bull. Franc.*, I, p. 6.

Chapter iii is entitled " Of the Divine Office and Fasting ". With regard to the first part, the saying of the canonical hours, Celano tells us expressly that in the early days the brothers did not know the Church services (*ecclesiasticum officium ignorabant*) and that Francis could only teach them to say the *Paternoster* and this short prayer : " We adore thee, O Christ, here and in all thy churches which are in the whole world, and we bless thee in that thou hast redeemed the world by thy holy cross." [1] Yet in this chapter, as it now stands, specific instructions for all the brothers, whether clerks or laymen, are given, in spite of the fact that in the early days this distinction hardly existed. We must conclude, then, that the whole of this chapter is later. This is borne out by the permission given to the priest brothers to have such books as were necessary for the saying of their offices (*libros tantum necessarios ad implendum eorum officium possint habere*), and that even laymen were to be given breviaries provided that they could read them. All this, of course, directly contradicts the regulations laid down in the first two chapters of this Rule and the declared intentions of S. Francis, expressed in such a work as the *Intentio Regulae*, that books were not allowed.[2]

With regard to the second part of this chapter, which is concerned with the question of fasting, Jordano tells us that " according to the first Rule " the brothers fasted on Wednesdays and Fridays and, by permission of S. Francis, on Mondays and Saturdays as well ; but that on other days they were free to eat what they liked.[3] On the authority of this statement Müller says that regulations about fasting were " without doubt " part of the original Rule.[4] But what did Jordano mean by the " First Rule " ? He surely cannot have meant the *Regula Primitiva* which had become swamped by a mass of later developments long before Jordano joined the Order. But if he is referring to what is generally known as the " First Rule " (1221), then he is making a mistake, for there are no such specific statements as he alleges. What this chapter says is that the friars are to fast from All Saints' Day to Christmas, and from the Epiphany to Easter, and on all Fridays. Father Cuthbert regards this as part of the original Rule, but my own feeling is that the conditions in which the brothers lived in 1210 were so severe, and the chances of getting enough to eat at any time so remote, that prescribed fasts can hardly have been necessary. The more we try to enter into the thoughts and intentions of

---

[1] Cf. *1 Cel.* 45 and the *Testamentum*.

[2] That Francis was not opposed to the study of Scripture is shown by a story told by Bonaventura that when the friars one day received a New Testament Francis divided it up into single leaves so that each might have a portion to read. *Epistola ad magistrum innominatum* in *Opera Omnia*, VIII, p. 334.

[3] Jordano, *Chronica*, cap. 11.   [4] *Anfänge des Minoritenordens*, p. 20.

S. Francis in those early days, the less likely does it seem that he would have included any such regulations as are here given. It seems much more probable that these injunctions were added later, and that the last sentence of this chapter, which after all largely contradicts all that has gone before, is the only part which belongs to the *Regula Primitiva*. If that is so, this chapter would read: "And they may eat anything that is set before them according to the Gospel," with the probable addition of the words from S. Luke x. 8: "*Eat what is set before you.*" When the Order became more ecclesiastical, and regular fasts were instituted, these words from the Gospel were tactfully dropped.

It is also quite possible that these words in the original Rule did not form a chapter by themselves but were really part of chapter ii, which would then deal with clothes and food together. In that case the last part of that chapter would read: "And let all the brothers be dressed in shabby clothes . . . since the Lord says in the Gospel: '*They which are gorgeously apparelled, etc.*'; and let them eat whatever is set before them, according to the words of the Gospel: '*Eat what is set before you.*'" This would bring the whole thing into line with Celano's description of the Rule as "using mainly the words of the Holy Gospel".

Chapter iv, which deals entirely with Ministers and Provinces, must be later than 1217 when Provincial Ministers were first appointed.

Chapter v is concerned with the correction of those who do wrong. The first part is later than 1217, for it consists of instructions to the Ministers how to deal with recalcitrant brothers. The middle section is more doubtful. It says: "None of the brethren shall have any power or domination, especially over other brothers. As our Lord says in the Gospel: *The princes of the Gentiles exercise dominion over them and they that are great exercise authority over them but it shall not be so* among the friars; but *he that is greatest* among them shall be *as their minister* or servant, and *he that is greatest* among them *let him be as the younger.*" In form this agrees entirely with our descriptions of the Primitive Rule, but it does not altogether agree with the account of the early days in the *Legenda Trium Sociorum*, which tells us [1] that, on the journey to Rome, Bernard of Quintavalle was elected as "*vicarius Iesu Christi*" and "*dux*" of the whole party. In spite of this, however, Francis may have been anxious to include in the Rule some safeguards against the ambitious friar, and this section may therefore be primitive. The third section, forbidding the brothers to speak or act maliciously against one another, would hardly seem necessary in the days when the group was so small. Indeed, the whole of this paragraph, with its reference not only to unkind words and deeds but

[1] *3 Soc.* 46.

also to rank disloyalty and disobedience, is probably later than the troubles of 1220 which brought Francis back from the East. The independence of some of the brothers, such as the one mentioned by Celano [1] who " severed himself from the religion of the brethren and wandered through the world like a stranger and a pilgrim ", would provoke Francis to include in the Rule something about those who " fall away from the commandments of God and wander away from authority " (declinant a mandatis Domini et extra obedientiam evagant).

Chapter vi is very short but of considerable interest. It says, first of all, that if a brother finds that he can no longer live the life of a Minorite, he must go as quickly as possible to his Minister and lay the matter before him. This sentence, then, is clearly later than 1217. The chapter then, rather inconsequentially, says : " And no one is to be called prior, but all alike shall be called Friars Minor. And let each wash one another's feet " (Et nullus vocetur prior, sed generaliter omnes vocentur fratres minores. Et alter alterius lavet pedes). It looks as if this short chapter consisted of two regulations which are quite independent of each other. The first one is, as we have seen, comparatively late. What of the second ? Celano informs us that the name " Fratres Minores " was given by S. Francis to the Order after he had written in the Rule the phrase " sint minores ".[2] " He himself ", he writes, " first planted the Order of Friars Minor and on that very occasion gave it that name ; since, as is well known, it was written in the Rule : et sint minores. And in that hour when those words were uttered, he said : ' I will that this brotherhood be called the Order of Friars Minor (Fratres Minores).' " It looks, from this account, as if, having written in the Rule the phrase containing the two words sint minores, Francis was struck by the appropriateness of the word minores and made it the title of the Order. Having done this, he may have inserted into the Rule which he had already written the words " all alike shall be called Friars Minor ". That this is what occurred is borne out by Brother Leo in the Intentio Regulae, where he writes that it was revealed to S. Francis that they ought to call themselves " the Order of Friars Minor " and that he had this fact written in the Rule which he carried to the Lord Pope Innocent.[3] On both internal and external evidence, then, this phrase must be accepted as part of the original Rule.[4]

---

[1] 2 Cel. 32–3.   [2] 1 Cel. 38.

[3] Intentio Regulae, cap. 6 = Spec. Perf. 26.

[4] Dr. Little draws my attention to the fact that Honorius III in 1220 calls the prelates of the Friars Minor priores, and asks whether he would have done this if the Rule approved by his predecessor had said that they were not to be so called. The title prior was certainly common enough by 1220, as Jacques de Vitry writes in that year : " Habent autem unum summum Priorem, cuius mandatis et regularibus institutis reverentes

Müller suggests that chapters iv, v and vi were originally a separate document drawn up at a Chapter Meeting to discuss and define the position of the Ministers. He points out in support of this that chapter iv begins with the words : *in nomine Domini*. If this is so, it probably dates from 1217 when the Chapter first appointed Ministers. On the other hand, we must remember that in it is incorporated a certain amount which we have shown reason for regarding as primitive.

Chapter vii deals with service and labour. It begins in this way : " All the brothers, in whatever place they may be staying with other people to serve them and work for them, shall not be chamberlains (*camerarii*) nor chancellors (*cancellarii*) nor have any rule over the households of those whom they serve ; nor shall they take any office which might cause scandal or harm to the soul ; but let them be underlings (*minores*) and in subjection to all who are in that house." We have already seen reasons for supposing that the phrase *sint minores* formed part of the original Rule, and the tone of this sentence as a whole certainly seems to belong to the early days, for the friars are spoken of not as a religious Order living in communities, but as labourers and servants in other people's houses. On the whole, then, this section must be regarded as primitive.

The second section says : " And those brothers who know how to work shall work, and pursue whatever trade they have learnt, so long as it is not contrary to the good of the soul and can be honestly carried on." There follow three quotations from the Bible, and then : " For their labour they may accept what is necessary, but not money. And when necessity shall arise let them go begging like the other brothers." These words are obviously in keeping with Celano's description of the brothers. " Day by day," he writes,[1] " those who were able, worked with their hands, and they stayed in lepers' houses, or in other suitable places, serving all with humility and devotion. They would exercise no calling whence scandal might arise." S. Francis, in his Testament, also expresses the same convictions : " I laboured with my hands and I wish so to labour ; and I most sincerely hope that all the other brothers will work at any task that is honest. Those who know not how to do so, must learn, not because they have any desire to receive the reward of their labours, but to set a good example and to expel idleness." All this in the Rule about labour is probably, therefore, primitive. The permission for the brothers to have the tools necessary for the work will be later, for at first they were to work as

---

obediunt minores priores ceterique eiusdem ordinis fratres " (Golubovich, *Biblioteca*, I, p. 8). Yet the words " *et nullus vocetur prior* " must have been written in the Rule at some time. If they are not part of the Primitive Rule, how could they have been added in later years when the title had become so well established ?

[1] *1 Cel.* 39–40.

hired labourers, using only such tools as were provided by their employers.

The third section of this chapter which merely repeats what has gone before, with the addition of two apt quotations, one from S. Jerome and one from S. Anselm, is probably an example of the work of Caesarius of Speyer in embellishing the Rule in 1221. Francis himself is unlikely to have been familiar with either of these writers.

The fourth section refers to friars in hermitages or friaries (*loci*) [1] and must therefore be later. The last part, about the friars not appearing depressed (*nubilosus*), is quoted by Celano in the *Vita Secunda*.[2] " Now Francis so much loved a man full of spiritual joy that at a certain Chapter he had these words written down for general advice, ' Let the brothers be careful not to shew themselves outwardly miserable or gloomy hypocrites ; but rather let them appear rejoicing in the Lord, and gay and joyful and duly thankful.' " It appears, then, that these words belong to the same category as the Admonitions and were inserted into the Rule at a later date.

Chapter viii, " That the friars must not accept money ", is a sermon on the text : " *Take heed and beware of covetousness.*" It is much in the style of the Admonitions and contains several phrases reminiscent of S. Francis's teaching about money. It was obviously Francis's intention that the brothers should not handle money at all, and Celano tells us of occasions when brothers who touched it were severely rebuked.[3] The earlier chapters of the Rule are explicit on the point that no money is to be received.[4] However, in this eighth chapter an exception is made " when there is obvious necessity for the sick brothers " (*propter manifestam necessitatem infirmorum fratrum*). This decisively proves that this chapter is later, as there would be no use in making a concession on behalf of the sick until the time had come when the brothers had houses in which the sick could be cared for. This chapter also suggests various malpractices which had crept in among the friars and which needed to be suppressed. For example : " In no circumstances must the brothers ask for money for houses or friaries, nor go round with another person to do the asking for money for such places (*neque cum persona pro talibus locis pecunias vel denarios quaerente vadant*)."

Chapter ix deals with the subject of begging, some of it being certainly primitive. It begins thus : " All the brothers must seek to follow the humility and poverty of our Lord Jesus Christ, and must remember that we ought not to possess anything in this world except what the Apostle says : ' *having food and raiment let us be therewith content.*

---

[1] The early name for a house belonging to or inhabited by the brothers was just the word *locus*. It cannot be literally translated, but " friary " is what it means.
[2] *2 Cel.* 128.   [3] *2 Cel.* 65, 66 and 68.   [4] See *supra*, chapters ii and vii.

And they ought to rejoice when they are living among common and despised people, among the poor and the weak, the sick and the lepers, and those who beg by the wayside. And when it is necessary, let them go for alms and not be ashamed." This is so entirely in accordance with what we know to have been the wishes of S. Francis from the beginning of the Order that we need have no hesitation in accepting it as primitive. The rest of the chapter is in the nature of an encomium on the joy of living on charity. It may be a fragment of S. Francis's own writings, or it may have come from the hand of Caesarius of Speyer. It is unlikely that it was part of the *Regula Primitiva*. The last part, which grants permission to the friars to eat any kind of food, reminds us of what has already been enjoined in chapter iii of the Rule, and Father Cuthbert suggests [1] that it may have been added in reply to the decrees of the Vicars General, who, at the Pentecost Chapter of 1220, when Francis was away in the Levant, had issued a number of decrees about fasting.

Chapter x, which is concerned with the treatment of sick brothers, presupposes an organisation more advanced than was possible in the early days. It is quoted by Celano in the *Vita Secunda*, § 175.

Chapter xi ordains that the brothers must not blaspheme nor quarrel among themselves, but must love one another. " And all the brothers must be careful not to speak evil of one another nor to wrangle ; but rather they should make a point of being silent whensoever God shall confer His grace upon them. Nor must they quarrel among themselves nor with others, but they must take care to answer humbly, saying : ' *We are unprofitable servants.*' " All this is borne out by Celano, who says : " No envy, malice, rancour, evil-speaking, suspicion or bitterness had place in them, but great concord, continual quietness, thanksgiving and the voice of praise were in them." [2] We can therefore safely accept this as part of the original Rule, though the rest of the chapter, consisting mainly of quotations from the Epistles, was probably added later, perhaps in 1221.

Chapter xii, on avoiding familiarity with women, deals with a subject upon which Francis had a good deal to say. Celano devotes a whole section of his *Vita Secunda* to this subject, telling us with pride that Francis knew only two women by sight,[3] and there is not much doubt that Francis, from the first, would not allow himself to have much to do with women. But this chapter shows signs of being later, for it speaks of priest-brothers hearing the confessions of women, a practice which can hardly have been contemplated in 1210.

Chapter xiii, which declares that a friar who commits fornication

---

[1] *Life of S. Francis*, p. 474. Cf. Jordano, *Chronica*, cap. 11.
[2] *1 Cel.* 41. Cf. *2 Cel.* 54 and 182.
[3] *2 Cel.* 112–14.

must be expelled from the Order, is also later. It is unlikely that Francis would have made any such provision in the early days.

Chapter xiv, " How the brothers are to go about the world ", is almost certainly primitive. It simply says (*simpliciter et paucis verbis*, as Francis described it) : " When the brothers are going about the world they must carry nothing with them, *neither scrip, nor purse, nor bread, nor money, nor staff. And into whatsoever house* they *shall enter* they shall *first say, ' Peace be to this house.' And in the same house* they shall *remain eating and drinking such as they give.* They shall not *resist evil,* but *unto him that smiteth* them *upon the one cheek* let them *offer also the other ;* and *him that taketh away their cloak* let them not *forbid to take away their coat also.* Let them *give to every man that asketh* of them, and *of him that taketh away their goods* let them not *ask them again.*"

Chapter xv says that the brothers, as they go about the world, must not ride on horseback or on any other animal. This chapter is later than 1210, for it bears no resemblance to our descriptions of the early Rule. It should be noted that Francis himself was obliged to ride an ass towards the end of his life.[1]

Chapter xvi treats of missionary journeys to the Saracens and other heathen. As it stands it is clearly later than 1210, when such expeditions can hardly have been contemplated ; but parts of it may well represent primitive regulations about evangelistic work in general. Both Celano and the Three Companions tell of journeys undertaken by the brothers before the expedition to Rome in 1210, and it may well be that Francis wanted to make some stipulations as to how such journeys were to be conducted. According to the *Legenda Trium Sociorum* the brothers were often very roughly treated.[2] Hearing of this, and having himself experienced similar things, Francis would naturally recall the words of Christ : " *Behold, I send you forth as sheep among wolves,*" or " *Blessed are they that are persecuted for righteousness' sake.*" It is possible, therefore, to regard the latter part of this chapter as primitive, though it has probably been extended by Caesarius. The early version would read : " Let all the brothers, wherever they may be, remember that they have given themselves and surrendered their bodies to our Lord Jesus Christ, for love of whom they ought to expose themselves to their enemies both visible and invisible. As our Lord says : ' *Whosoever shall lose his life shall find it, etc.*' " On the other hand, the earlier part of the chapter, with its direct reference to expeditions to the Saracens and its mention of Ministers, must be later.

Chapter xvii is devoted to the subject of preaching. From the very first, preaching had been one of the chief activities of the brothers,[3]

---

[1] Cf. *1 Cel.* 98, *2 Cel.* 46, 98 and 142.   [2] *3 Soc.* 37–40.
[3] See *1 Cel.* 29.

and it would be necessary to make some provision for this in the Rule. But this chapter of the Rule cannot represent the original regulations. For one thing, it is actually contradicted by a passage in chapter xxi, which we shall be considering in a moment. For another, it pre-supposes the existence of Ministers and an organisation of the friars such as had not been envisaged in the early days. Like certain other chapters, it is more of an admonition or sermon than a Rule.

Chapter xviii makes provision for the annual Chapter General at the Portiuncula at Pentecost and for Provincial Chapters at Michaelmas. The mention of Ministers *ultramarini* and *ultramontani* shows that this chapter must have been composed after the Order had spread overseas.

Chapter xix, " that the brothers are to live as catholics ", is probably original for the same reasons as were adduced in support of the words of the Prologue. Francis, being anxious to show that his brotherhood was to be essentially within the Church, would naturally stress this fact in the Rule. " All the brothers shall be catholics and live and speak as catholics (*catholice*). If, however, any shall err from the catholic faith and life, either by word or deed, and shall not mend his ways, let him be expelled from our brotherhood." What could be more calculated to win the approval of the Pope ? The word *fraternitas* represents a very early tradition, giving place later to *religio* and finally to *ordo*. The second part of this chapter, which declares Francis's submission to the priesthood, is in full accord with his own sentiments expressed in many of his works, and not least in the Testament.

Chapter xx, on Confession and Communion, is later. The phrase " clerks and laymen alike " (*tam clerici quam laici*), which occurs more than once in this Rule,[1] is always a sign of a later tradition. Although there was one priest in the party which went to Rome, Sylvester, the distinction between the priest-brothers and the rest, which became so important later on, was not drawn in the early days. There is no reason to suppose that Sylvester was treated any differently from the others on account of his orders, though Francis always had the greatest respect for a priest. It is interesting, therefore, to notice the permission given in this chapter to the brothers to confess to a layman if a priest cannot be had, though of course the layman cannot give absolution.[2]

Chapter xxi, which is headed " Of the Praise and Exhortation which the friars can give ", belongs to the primitive Rule. In chapter xvii, which belongs to the later tradition, permission to preach could only be given by a Minister : in this chapter the brothers are given leave to proclaim their message " whenever they like ". Of these two

---

[1] E.g. capp. iii, xv and xx.

[2] " Si vero tunc sacerdotem habere not poterunt, confiteantur fratri suo." Cf. *Epistola ad quendam ministrum : " Si non fuerit ibi sacerdos confiteatur (frater) fratri suo." Opuscula S. Francisci*, p. 110.

statements the latter is obviously the more primitive. Most of the chapter is in the form of an outline sermon for the friars to deliver, based on a few texts from the Gospels.

Chapter xxii, entitled " Of the Admonishing of the Brothers ", is very long and contains the whole of the explanation of the parable of the Sower from S. Mark iv. 15–20. Müller accepts it as a genuine part of the original Rule, but Father Cuthbert rejects it, pointing to the parallels between it and the Letter " to all the faithful ". I am inclined to feel that it cannot have been part of the Rule of 1210, for the simple reason that it does not make any specific demands. We know that that Rule was very concise, but here is an Admonition or Meditation rather than a Rule. It begins : " Let all of us, brothers, listen to what our Lord says : ' *Love your enemies* ' and ' *Do good to those who hate you*,' " and then goes on to explain a number of texts, but always in the first person plural—*caveamus, custodiamus, faciamus*, etc. It then ends with a long quotation from S. John xvii. If we are to accept Müller's theory that it is a part of the original Rule, we shall have to reckon with the fact that it is exactly the same length as all the rest of that Rule put together. And could a Rule which contained this chapter be described as written *simpliciter et paucis verbis* ?

Chapter xxiii is again very long. It is called : " Prayer, Praise and Thanksgiving ", and is mostly of a later date for the same reasons as in the previous chapter. The last part of it, however, shows signs of being a fragment of the original Rule. After a long act of Praise, Francis turns to the brothers with these words : " In the name of the Lord, I beseech all the brothers to learn the purpose and meaning of those things which are written in this way of life, to the salvation of our souls ; and to commit them frequently to memory. And I pray God, the Almighty, Three in One, that He may bless all those who teach or learn or hold or memorise or do these things, whensoever they call to mind and carry out the things which are here written for our salvation. And I implore them all, kissing their feet, to respect, keep and lay up all these things." These words are probably part of the *Regula Primitiva* which would almost certainly end with some such admonition. On the other hand, the concluding sentence, which refers to those who would take away from or alter what was written in the Rule, probably belongs to the time when trouble had broken out.

If we bring together the results of this examination we shall get the following as a suggested reconstruction of the *Regula Primitiva* of 1210.

REGULA PRIMITIVA SANCTI FRANCISCI (1210)

In nomine Patris et Filii et Spiritus Sancti.
Amen.

Frater Franciscus promittat obedientiam et reverentiam Domino Papae Innocentio et eius successoribus.

1. *Regula et vita fratrum haec est, scilicet vivere in obedientia, in castitate et sine*
[cap. i] *proprio, et Domini nostri Iesu Christi doctrinam et vestigia sequi, qui dicit:* Si vis perfectus esse, vade et vende omnia quae habes, et da pauperibus, et habetis thesaurum in caelo; et veni, sequere me; *et:* Si quis vult post me venire, abnegat semetipsum et tollat crucem suam et sequatur me; *item:* Si quis vult venire ad me, et non odit patrem et matrem et uxorem et filios et fratres et sorores, adhuc autem et animam suam, non potest esse meus discipulus. *Et*, omnis qui reliquerit patrem aut matrem, fratres aut sorores, uxorem aut filios, domos aut agros propter me, centuplum accipiet et vitam aeternam possidebit.

2. *Si quis divina inspiratione volens accipere hanc vitam venerit ad fratres nostros,*
[cap. ii] *benigne recipiatur ab eis: et vendat omnia sua et ea omnia pauperibus studeat erogare. Et omnes fratres vilibus vestibus induantur, et possint eas repeciare de saccis et aliis peciis cum benedictione Dei; quia dicit Dominus in Evangelio:* Qui in veste pretiosa sunt et in deliciis et qui mollibus vestiuntur, in domibus regum sunt. *Et liceat eis manducare de omnibus cibis qui apponuntur eis,*
[cap. iii] *secundum Evangelium:* Manducate quae apponuntur vobis.

3. *Omnes fratres non habeant aliquam potestatem vel dominationem maxime inter*
[cap. v] *se. Sicut enim Dominus dicit in Evangelio:* Principes gentium dominantur eorum, et qui maiores sunt potestatem exercent in eos, non sic erit *inter fratres; sed* quicumque voluerit inter eos maior fieri sit eorum minister et servus; et qui maior est inter eos fiat sicut minor. *Et nullus vocetur prior,*
[cap. vi] *sed generaliter omnes vocentur fratres minores. Et alter alterius lavet pedes.*

4. *Omnes fratres in quibuscumque locis steterint apud alios ad serviendum vel*
[cap. vii] *laborandum, non sint camerarii nec cancellarii, nec praesint in domibus eorum quibus serviunt; nec recipiant aliquod officium, quod scandalum generet vel animae suae faciat detrimentum; sed sint minores et subditi omnibus qui in eadem domo sunt. Et fratres qui sciunt laborare laborent et eandem artem exerceant quam noverint, si non fuerit contra salutem animae suae et honeste poterint operari. Et possint pro labore accipere omnia necessaria praeter pecuniam. Et, cum necesse fuerit, vadant pro eleemosynis sicut alii fratres.*

5. *Omnes fratres studeant sequi humilitatem et paupertatem Domini nostri Iesu*
[cap. ix] *Christi et recordentur quod nihil aliud oportet nos habere de toto mundo, nisi, sicut dicit Apostolus:* Habentes alimenta et quibus tegamur, his contenti simus. *Et debent gaudere quando conversantur inter viles et despectas personas, inter pauperes et debiles, infirmos et leprosos et iuxta viam mendicantes. Et cum necesse fuerit vadant pro eleemosynis, et non verecundentur.*

6. *Et omnes fratres caveant sibi ut non calumnientur aliquem, neque contendant*
[cap. xi] *verbis, immo studeant retinere silentium, quandocumque eis Deus gratiam largietur. Neque litigent inter se, neque cum aliis, sed procurent humiliter respondere dicentes:* Servi inutiles sumus. *Et diligant se ad invicem, sicut Dominus dicit:* Hoc est praeceptum meum, ut diligatis invicem, sicut dilexi vos.

7. *Quando fratres vadunt per mundam, nihil portent per viam, neque sacculum,*
[cap. xiv] *neque peram, neque panem, neque pecuniam, neque virgam ; et in quam-*
cumque domum intraverint, dicant primum : Pax huic domui. Et in eadem
domo manentes edant et bibant quae apud illos sunt. Non resistant malo ;
sed, si quis eos in maxillam percusserit, praebeant ei et alteram ; et qui
aufert eis vestimentum, etiam tunicam non prohibeant. Omni petenti se
tribuant ; et si quis aufert ea quae sua sunt, non repetant.

8. *Et omnes fratres, ubicumque sunt, recordentur quod dederunt se et reliquerunt*
[cap. xvi] *corpora sua Domino nostro Iesu Christo, et pro eius amore debent se exponere*
inimicis tam visibilibus quam invisibilibus ; quia dicit Dominus : Qui perdiderit
animam suam propter me salvam faciet eam in vitam aeternam.

9. *Omnes fratres sint catholici, vivant et loquantur catholice. Si quis vero*
[cap. xix] *erraverit a fide et vita catholica in dicto vel in facto, et non se emendaverit, a*
nostra fraternitate penitus expellatur. Et omnes clericos et omnes religiosos
habeamus pro dominis in his quae spectant ad salutem animae et a nostra religione
non deviant, et ordinem et officium eorum et administrationem in Domino
veneremur.

10. *Et hanc vel talem exhortationem et laudem omnes fratres mei, quandocumque*
[cap. xxi] *placuerit eis, annuntiare possunt inter quoscumque homines cum benedictione*
Dei : Timete et honorate, laudate et benedicite, gratias agite et adorate Dominum
Deum Omnipotentem in Trinitate et Unitate, Patrem et Filium et Spiritum
Sanctum, Creatorem omnium. Agite poenitentiam, facite dignos fructus
poenitentiae, *quia scitote quod cito moriemini.* Date et dabitur vobis.
Dimitte et dimittetur vobis. Et si non dimiseritis hominibus peccata
eorum, Dominus non dimittet vobis peccata vestra. Confitemini *omnia*
peccata vestra. *Beati qui moriuntur in poenitentia quia erunt in regno caelorum.*
Vae illis qui non moriuntur in poenitentia, quia erunt filii diaboli, cuius opera
faciunt, et ibunt in ignem aeternum. Cavete et abstinete ab omni malo et
perseverate usque ad finem in bono.

[cap. xxiii] *In nomine Domini rogo omnes fratres ut addiscant tenorem et sensum eorum*
quae in ista vita ad salvationem animae nostrae scripta sunt, et ista frequenter
ad memoriam reducant. Et exoro Deum, ut ipse, qui est omnipotens, trinus et
unus, benedicat omnes docentes, discentes, habentes, recordantes et operantes ista,
quoties repetunt et faciunt quae ibi ad salvationem nostram scripta sunt. Et
deprecor omnes, cum osculo pedum, ut multum diligant, custodiant et reponant
haec.

Gloria Patri et Filio et Spiritui Sancto.
Sicut erat in principio et nunc et semper,
et in saecula saeculorum. Amen.

(Translation)

In the name of the Father and of the Son and of the Holy Ghost. Amen.

Brother Francis shall promise obedience and reverence to the Lord Pope Innocent and
his successors.

1. The Rule and Life of the Brothers is this ; to live in obedience, in chastity and
without property, and to follow the teaching and the footsteps of Christ, who says :
If thou wilt be perfect go and sell that thou hast and give to the poor and thou shalt

have treasure in heaven, and come follow me; and : *If any man will come after me let him deny himself and take up his cross and follow me;* and again : *If any man come to me and hate not his father and mother and wife and children and brothers and sisters, yea, and his own life also, he cannot be my disciple;* and : *Everyone that hath forsaken father or mother or brothers or sisters or wife or children or houses or lands for my sake shall receive a hundredfold, and shall inherit eternal life.*

2. If any man, by divine inspiration and willing to accept this life, shall come to the brothers, let him be kindly received by them ; and he must sell all his goods and be careful to give everything to the poor. And let all the brothers be dressed in shabby clothes and let them patch them with sackcloth or other rags with the blessing of God ; for our Lord says : *They which are gorgeously apparelled and live delicately are in kings' houses.* And they may eat anything that is set before them according to the Gospel : *Eat what is set before you.*

3. None of the brethren shall have any power or domination especially among themselves. As our Lord says in the Gospel : *The princes of the Gentiles exercise dominion over them, and they that are great exercise authority over them, but it shall not be so among* the friars ; but *whosoever would be the greatest* among them *let him be their minister* and servant ; and, *he that is greatest among them let him be as the younger.* And no one is to be called prior, but all alike shall be called Friars Minor. And let each wash one another's feet.

4. All the brothers, in whatever place they may be staying with other people to serve them and work for them, shall not be chamberlains or chancellors nor have any rule over the households of those whom they serve ; nor shall they take any office which might cause scandal or harm to the soul ; but let them be underlings and in subjection to all who are in that house. And those brothers who know how to work shall work and pursue whatever trade they have learnt, so long as it is not contrary to the good of the soul and can be honestly carried on. And for their labour they may receive all things necessary, but no money. And when necessary let them go begging like the other brethren.

5. All the brothers must seek to follow the humility and poverty of our Lord Jesus Christ, and must remember that we ought not to possess anything in this world except what the Apostle says : *Having food and raiment let us be therewith content.* And they ought to rejoice when they are living among common and despised people, among the poor and the weak, the sick and the lepers, and those who beg by the wayside. And when it is necessary let them go for alms and not be ashamed.

6. And all the brothers must be careful not to speak evil of one another nor to wrangle ; but rather they should make a point of being silent whensoever God shall confer His grace upon them. Nor must they quarrel among themselves nor with others, but they must take care to answer humbly, saying : *We are unprofitable servants.* And let them love one another, as our Lord says : *This is my commandment, that ye love one another as I have loved you.*

7. When the brothers are going about the world they must carry nothing with them *neither scrip, nor purse, nor bread, nor money, nor staff.* And *into whatsoever house they shall enter, they shall first say :* " *Peace be to this house.*" *And in the same house* they shall *remain eating and drinking such things as they give.* They shall *not resist evil,* but *unto him that smiteth* them *upon the one cheek let them offer also the other ;* and *him that taketh away their cloak let them not forbid to take their coat also.* Let them *give to every man that asketh* of them, and *of him that taketh away their goods* let them *not ask them again.*

8. Let all the brothers, wherever they may be, remember that they have given themselves and surrendered their bodies to our Lord Jesus Christ for love of whom they ought to expose themselves to their enemies both visible and invisible. As our Lord says : *Whosoever shall lose his life for my sake, the same shall find it unto eternal life.*

9. All the brothers shall be catholics and live and speak as catholics. If, however, any shall err from the catholic faith and life, either by word or deed, and shall not mend his ways, let him be expelled from our Brotherhood. And let us treat all clerks and religious as our superiors in everything that concerns the salvation of the soul and is not contrary to our religion, and let us respect their order and their office and their work in the Lord.

10. And this or some such exhortation and praise shall all my brothers proclaim whenever they like and among whomsoever they may be, with the blessing of God : " Fear and honour, praise and bless, give thanks and adore the Lord God Almighty, Three in One, Father, Son and Holy Spirit, Maker of all things. *Repent ye and bring forth fruits worthy of repentance* knowing that we shall shortly die. *Give and it shall be given unto you. Forgive and ye shall be forgiven.* And *if ye do not forgive men their trespasses neither will the Lord forgive you your trespasses. Confess all your sins.* Blessed are they who die in penitence for they shall be in the Kingdom of God. Woe to those who do not die in penitence for they shall be children of the devil whose works they do, and they shall go into the eternal fire. Beware and keep yourselves from all evil and persevere unto the end in what is good."

In the name of the Lord I beseech all the brothers to learn the purpose and meaning of those things which are written in this way of life, to the salvation of our souls, and to commit them frequently to memory. And I pray God, the Almighty, Three in One, that he may bless all those who teach or learn or hold or memorise or do these things, whensoever they call to mind and carry out the things which are written here for our salvation. And I implore them all, kissing their feet, to respect, keep and lay up all these things.

Glory be to the Father, and to the Son, and to the Holy Ghost. As it was in the beginning, is now, and ever shall be ; world without end. Amen.

THOMAS OF CELANO AND THE *VITA PRIMA S. FRANCISCI*

SAINT FRANCIS died on October 3rd, 1226, in a little hut close to the Portiuncula at Assisi. Nine months later appeared the first of a long series of books which either sought to tell the story of his life or were inspired by his teaching. The first bud of the Franciscan flower was a little allegorical work known as the *Sacrum Commercium*, or *The Holy Converse of the Blessed Francis with Lady Poverty*.[1] The late fourteenth-century Chronicle known as the *Chronica XXIV Generalium* ascribed this work to John of Parma, who was Minister General of the Order from 1247 to 1257 [2]; but all the other evidence which we have points to a much earlier date, and there is really no reason to doubt that the date mentioned in the explicit of each of the manuscripts which we possess, namely July 1227, is correct. Who the author was we have no means of telling. Ubertino da Casale says that it was written by " a certain holy doctor " who was an enthusiastic adherent of Holy Poverty,[3] but this does not carry us very far. Attempts which have been made to attribute it to John Parenti, who succeeded Elias as Minister General in 1227, lack both evidence and conviction.

The little book itself is a work of remarkable charm, telling how Francis sought out the poor, despised and hated Lady Poverty and made her his bride. The theme is perhaps suggested by a story which Celano afterwards told of how Francis as a young man said to his friends : " I will marry a nobler and fairer bride than ever you saw, who shall surpass all others in beauty and excel them in wisdom." [4] It almost certainly inspired the famous fresco by Giotto in the Lower

---

[1] The standard edition was brought out by E. d'Alençon in 1900. There are two English translations, one by Montgomery Carmichael : *The Lady Poverty, a 13th Century Allegory* (1901), and one by Canon Rawnsley, who prints also the Latin text from the Codex Casanatensis.

[2] *An. F.*, III, p. 283.

[3] " *Quidam sanctus doctor huius sanctae paupertatis professor et zelator strenuus.*" Quoted by M. Carmichael from the *Arbor Vitae Crucifixae* in *The Lady Poverty*, p. xxxvii.

[4] *1 Cel.* 7, though the Bride is there represented not as Holy Poverty but as the Order to which Francis was wedded. Cf. *3 Soc.* 7.

Church at Assisi. But the fact that it is pure allegory makes it impossible for us to consider it as one of the sources for the life of S. Francis.

More interesting, if less beautiful, are the contemporary references to S. Francis in works by men who had nothing to do with the Order. In 1219 Francis went to Egypt on an attempt to convert the Soldan to the Christian faith and so put an end to the Crusades. He was seen there by Jacques de Vitry, who, in his *Historia Orientalis*, writes as follows :

We saw the founder and head of this Order whom all the others obey as their Prior, a simple and ignorant man, but loved of God and of men, by name Brother Francis. To such a degree of intoxication (*ad tantum ebrietatis excessum*) and fervour of spirit was he seized that when he had come to the Christian army outside Damietta in Egypt he reached the camp of the Soldan of Egypt himself, so bold was he and so fortified with the shield of faith. When the Saracens captured him on the road, he said : " I am a Christian ; lead me to your lord." And when they had dragged him before the Soldan, the cruel beast was turned to gentleness by the expression on the face of the man of God, so that for several days he listened most attentively to his preaching to them the faith of Christ. At length, fearing lest some of his people should be converted to the Lord by the power of his words, and so go over to the Christian army, he ordered him, with all reverence and every safeguard, to return to our camp, saying to him at the last : " Pray for me that God may reveal to me that law and that faith which is to him most pleasing." [1]

Jacques de Vitry was obviously deeply impressed by the courage and fervour of S. Francis ; but although this was probably the first occasion upon which he had been brought into contact with the Saint himself, he had already had various opportunities of appreciating the work of the Friars. In a letter written in 1216, when the Order was still comparatively young, he says : " I believe that, to the disgrace of the prelates, who are like dumb dogs that cannot bark, the Lord will save many souls before the end of the world by simple and poor men of this sort." [2]

Another most interesting witness to the kind of impression which S. Francis made upon his contemporaries is afforded by Thomas of Spalato in his *Historia Salonitanorum*. Writing of the year 1222 he says :

In the same year, on the day of the Assumption of the Mother of God, when I was a student at Bologna, I saw S. Francis preaching in the piazza before the Palazzo Publico where almost the whole town was assembled. The theme of his sermon was : " Angels, Men, Devils." And he spoke so well and so wisely of these three rational spirits that to many learned men who were there the sermon of this ignorant man seemed worthy of no little admiration, in spite of the fact that he did not keep to the method of an expositor

---

[1] Golubovich, *Biblioteca*, tomo I, pp. 8–10. The story told here is confirmed by the narrative in Bonaventura, *Leg. Maior*, ix, 7–9, which is the best account which we have.

[2] Golubovich, *Biblioteca*, I, p. 5.

so much as of a revivalist.[1] Indeed the whole manner of his speech was calculated to
stamp out enmities and to make peace. His tunic was dirty, his person unprepossessing
(*contemptibilis*) and his face far from handsome (*indecora*); yet God gave such power to
his words that many factions of the nobility, among whom the fierce anger of ancient
feuds had been raging with much bloodshed, were brought to reconciliation. Towards
him, indeed, the reverence and devotion of men was so great that men and women rushed
upon him headlong, anxious to touch the hem of his garment and to carry away bits of
his clothing.[2]

Both Thomas of Spalato and Jacques de Vitry were obviously sur-
prised at the power and influence of a man who was not impressive to
look at, and, according to their standards, *illiteratus*. That such was
also the general impression is borne out by the question which Brother
Masseo is said to have put to S. Francis : " Why doth all the world
come after thee, and why is it that all men long to see thee, and to hear
thee and to obey thee ? Thou art not a man comely of form, thou
art not of much wisdom, thou art not noble of birth : whence comes
it then that it is after thee that the whole world doth run ? " [3]

On the night of October 3rd, 1226, the body of this little poor man,
wasted by sickness and wounded by austerity, lay naked on the floor
of a little hut while his ardent spirit returned to God who gave it.[4]
He had been attended during his last sickness by his most intimate
friends, Leo, Angelo, Rufino, Masseo, and probably Bernard of Quintavalle, the first of his disciples.[5] All of them, however, were under
the direction of the Minister General, Elias. In spite of the fact that
Elias did a good deal to wreck the work of S. Francis, there is no doubt
that he and Francis loved each other and that Francis trusted him and
valued his companionship.[6] There is no doubt either that Elias's
ambitions were kept in check by S. Francis during his lifetime. But
now that the Poverello was dead, a crisis was almost inevitable. For
there were, among the brothers, two different points of view which
proved to be irreconcilable. On the one hand Leo and his immediate
friends were representative of those who regretted every departure
from the strictest letter of the Rule, who looked back to the early days
of the Order as to the time of man's innocency, and who were determined, at whatever cost, to keep alive the highest idealism of the saint.
On the other hand, Elias, working in conjunction with Cardinal Ugolino,

[1] " *Non modum praedicantis tenuit sed quasi concionantis.*" Fr. Lemmens explains
this as " not according to the rules and methods of the schools but out of the fulness
of his heart." Cf. *Testimonia Minora Saec. XIII*, p. 10.

[2] *Mon. Germ. Hist. Scriptores*, xxix, p. 580.

[3] *Fioretti*, cap. x (Arnold's translation).   [4] *2 Cel.* 217.

[5] Celano mentions an unnamed disciple prior to Bernard, but he seems to have dropped
out of the Fraternity almost immediately (*1 Cel.* 24). In the *Vita Secunda* Celano once
describes Bernard as the first disciple (*2 Cel.* 109) and once as the second (*2 Cel.* 48).

[6] Cf. *1 Cel.* 98 and 105 and *Per.* 81 (= *Spec. Perf.* 115 a).

had already acquired exalted ideas as to the place which the Order was going to occupy in the affairs of the Church. How far the brothers as a whole were divided into two camps it is hard to say. At either end there were extremists who were determined to press their claims; but it is unwise to assume, as writers like Edouard Lempp have done, that the Order was already hopelessly divided.[1] Miss Scudder is probably nearer the truth when she says: " It is not for a long time accurate to speak of parties, there were so many shades and cross-divisions." [2] But at any rate it is true to say that there were before the brothers two policies, one a policy of strict adherence to the Rule and Testament, and one a policy of relaxation designed to allow the Order to develop in other ways. It was for each of the brothers to decide which way he wanted to go.

At the death of S. Francis, or shortly afterwards, the little circle of his friends seems to have dispersed. Most of them retired into comparative obscurity while the stage was taken by other men. Leo seems to have started to write his reminiscences fairly early,[3] and for this he frequented the smaller hermitages such as the Portiuncula and Greccio. At the latter he was joined by Angelo and Rufino. Meanwhile, both Leo and Angelo kept in fairly close touch with S. Clare at S. Damiano.[4] Bernard lived for a few more years to be a thorn in the flesh to Elias; [5] Giles retired to Fabriano, near Perugia, to divide his time between contemplating the mysteries of God and making caustic remarks on the progress of the Order. Of Masseo we know practically nothing.

On the other hand, Elias was full of activity. Within a few hours of the death of S. Francis he had sent a letter to all the members of the Order, not only to inform them of the loss which they had sustained, but to tell them also of the miracle of the Stigmata which Francis, during his lifetime, had kept so close a secret. The letter has been preserved and may be read in Boehmer's *Analekten* or in Lempp's *Élie de Cortone.*[6] Immediately we read it we feel that it can hardly be the work of Elias himself. Lempp is most suspicious of the whole affair, and sees behind Elias the hand of Ugolino. " This official style ", he writes, " reminds us of the Curia, and one cannot help feeling that one is looking at the first draft of a Bull; the feeling of grief disappears under the flowers of rhetoric in which it is clothed." [7] What we cannot miss in this letter of Elias is the determination of the writer to leave no doubt in the minds of his readers that Francis was

[1] Lempp, *Élie de Cortone* in *Collection d'études et de documents sur l'histoire religieuse et littéraire,* iii, p. 75.

[2] Scudder, *Franciscan Adventure,* p. 81. [3] See below, p. 92.
[4] Sabatier, *Spec. Perf.,* pp. lxxvii f. Angelo and Clare were cousins.
[5] Cf. Wadding, *Annales,* ad an. 1230 (Vol. ii, p. 241).
[6] Boehmer, *Analekten,* pp. 90 ff.; Lempp, *Élie de Cortone,* pp. 70 ff.
[7] Lempp, *op. cit.,* p. 72.

not only a saint, but a saint of most unusual virtue to be considered worthy of so remarkable a manifestation of divine favour. In this letter he says nothing about the manner of Francis's death; he mentions none of his last words; he passes over the story of the blessing of the brothers and the other incidents which took place at his death-bed. The one thing which the brothers must know was that Francis had had worked upon his body this great miracle " hitherto unheard-of ". This was Elias's first objective. Once establish the sanctity of the man beyond all doubt and the way was cleared for the progress which Elias had in mind.

The month of March, 1227, saw an event of signal importance for the Friars Minor in the death of the aged Pope Honorius III and the election of Ugolino, Protector of the Friars Minor and confederate of Elias, to the chair of S. Peter as Gregory IX. A few weeks later, at the Pentecost Chapter, Elias ceased to be Minister General and was succeeded by John Parenti, a Florentine lawyer who had been converted by S. Francis in 1211. John Parenti seems to have been a devout, conscientious and somewhat emotional man [1] who hitherto had made little or no impression upon the Order. His obscurity makes it incredible that he should have been the choice of the brothers over the head of a man like Elias, who would have been so much more eligible a candidate. We can only assume that Elias was unwilling to continue in office, for Lempp's theory that it was his excesses against the " Spirituals " and the appearance of Brother Leo's *Speculum Perfectionis* early in 1227 that made the election go against him, is untenable.[2] Much more reasonable is the suggestion [3] that Elias wanted a free hand to proceed with the building of the Basilica and did not care to be hindered by the necessity of making constant journeys to distant provinces. It is impossible to believe that, with Ugolino in his exalted position to support him, Elias could have lost an election, nor has any record of a dispute or ballot been preserved.

Elias, therefore, with his hands free from the official duties of a Minister General, could devote himself, in co-operation with Ugolino, to the two questions which had to be immediately answered. The first of these was: What was to be the position of the Order in the Church as a whole? and the second: What was to be done to preserve the memory of the Saint?

With regard to the position of the Order we have already observed

---

[1] The *Chron. XXIV Gen.* says of him : " *fuit etiam hic generalis magnarum lacrymarum, qui magnam partem ordinis nudis pedibus visitavit.*" *An. F.*, III, p. 211.

[2] *Élie de Cortone*, p. 77.

⸰ Made, e.g., by Goad in his *Franciscan Italy*, p. 145. He points out that when Francis went on his journey to the East in 1219 he left behind him two Vicars, one to travel round the provinces and one to stay at Assisi.

that Ugolino had a definite plan for the future of the mendicant Orders.[1] Finding the secular clergy often difficult and obstinate, and the regulars independent and exclusive, he recognised, in the friars, a heaven-sent instrument with which to strengthen the authority of the Church. Elected Pope on March 19th, 1227, it was not long before he began a series of enactments designed to help the friars at the expense of the bishops and parochial clergy.[2] On May 13th of this year he issued a Bull allowing the Ministers of the Order to absolve friars who had been excommunicated[3]; on July 26th he issued another giving the friars permission to have their own burial-grounds[4]; on October 20th he issued yet another in which he took under his special protection the friars of Bassano who were getting into difficulties with the local clergy.[5] And yet all of these Bulls were, of course, directly opposed to the intentions of S. Francis, who wished the brothers to seek no privileges or letters of commendation or protection from the Pope. But Ugolino did not propose to grant special privileges to the friars without expecting something from them in return. So in May, 1228, we find him sending two Friars Minor to Frederick II to remonstrate with him about his attitude to the Church,[6] while at about the same time John Parenti was ordered to go to Rome to try to bring the Romans to a more peaceful frame of mind.[7] This mission proving a success, he was later sent on a similar expedition to Florence.

Meanwhile friction between the friars and the secular clergy was increasing. Not only did the parish priest see his authority and position being taken from him by these wandering preachers who came into his parish, shrove his parishioners and gave them spiritual advice which they did not stay to enforce, but he also found his income diminishing by the friars taking to themselves the customary dues. Thus the conscientious parish priest was anxious about his cure of souls, and the mercenary one anxious about his fees, and bitterness and jealousy and friction were the inevitable result. Moreover, a whole series of Bulls, all in favour of the friars' claims against the secular clergy, did not help to mend matters. But Ugolino had his plans well laid. His sympathy was with the friars, for whom he had had, for many years, a great affection, and whose progress he, as Protector of the Order, had so closely followed. A number of Bulls issued between 1229 and 1231 ordered the secular clergy to abstain from trying to hinder the work of the friars, forbade them to excommunicate those who were helping them, and compelled them to give land for the building of churches;

[1] Cf. p. 28.   [2] Cf. Gratien, *Histoire de la Fondation, &c.*, pp. 113–14.
[3] Sbaralea, *Bull. Franc.*, I, p. 28.   [4] *Ibid.*, p. 31.   [5] *Ibid.*, pp. 34 f.
[6] Potthast, *Regesta*, 8189.
[7] *An. F.*, III, p. 211. The Editors give 1230 as the date of this visit, but Lempp is probably right in assigning it to 1228.

while a Bull of August 28th, 1231, gives a list of twenty-one grievances which the friars had brought against the Archbishops of Germany and the diocesan clergy, all of which charges Ugolino finds justified.[1] If anyone thought that the Friars Minor were going to continue as a body of mendicants, without possessions and willing only to work in submission to the parochial clergy, he was very much mistaken.

The other great question was the manner of preserving the memory of the Saint. Elias and Ugolino both saw the necessity for a shrine to serve as a goal for the many pilgrims who wished to pay homage to the Poverello. By March, 1228, therefore, Elias had obtained from a citizen of Assisi named Azzoguidi a site on what was known as the *Collis inferni*. The deed of this conveyance is printed by Lempp from the original copy in the archives of the Sacro Convento.[2] It is interesting to note that Francis is already spoken of as *sanctus*, although he had not yet been officially canonised—a further indication of Elias's determination to have him numbered with the saints. A month later, on April 29th, Ugolino issued a Bull declaring that a church ought to be built in honour of S. Francis [3]; but it will be observed that Elias had already secured the site.

No sooner had the land been acquired than Elias sent out messages to the Provincial Ministers ordering them to start collecting money.[4] Ugolino supported him by granting special privileges to the new church and to those who contributed towards it.[5] The foundation-stone was laid by the Pope on July 17th, 1228, and two years later the basilica was officially declared to be " *caput et mater* " of the whole Order, in spite of the fact that Francis had accorded this same title to the Portiuncula.[6]

But not only was the memory of Francis to be preserved by a great shrine, there must also be an official *Legenda*, so that all who could read should know for themselves something of the man whom the Friars Minor had for their Founder. Thus it came about that, immediately after the ceremonies of the Canonisation, which took place on July 16th, 1228, Ugolino summoned one of the brothers, called Thomas of Celano, and invited him to write the first Life of S. Francis.

The man to whom the Pope entrusted this responsible task appears to have been a well-educated man of good family, possibly in Holy

[1] Sbaralea, *Bull. Franc.*, I, pp. 48, 50, 74 f.   [2] *Élie de Cortone*, pp. 170 f.

[3] Sbaralea, *Bull. Franc.*, I, p. 40.

[4] *An. F.*, III, pp. 33 f. " *Pro fabrica vero eiusdem ecclesiae frater Helias variis modis coepit pecunias extorquere.*" As Elias was no longer Minister General, he had no authority to do this.

[5] Sbaralea, *Bull. Franc.*, I, pp. 46, 48, 50 and 60. The privileges included the right to carry on in times of general interdict, and the right of holding ordinations therein by bishops other than the diocesan.

[6] *Ibid.*, p. 60. Cf. *Spec. Perf.*, c. 55 : " *deberet esse caput et mater pauperum minorum fratrum.*"

Orders,[1] who had joined the Order in 1215 when Francis returned from a visit to Spain.[2] For the next six years we know nothing about him except that he must have been proving himself a man of ability and enterprise. In 1221 he appears again as one of a party chosen to go to Germany on what was regarded at the time as a desperate adventure. In this way he was brought into contact with a number of men who, in one way or another, achieved distinction in the Order.[3] The following year his ability was recognised by his appointment as *Custos* of Mainz, Speyer, Worms and Cologne, the very district of Germany to which the Provincial Minister, Caesarius of Speyer himself belonged, and for which we may expect him to have had a particular affection.[4] Twelve months later, on Caesarius being recalled to Italy, Celano was made his Vicar and therefore acting Provincial Minister of the Friars Minor in Germany.[5]

Caesarius did not return to Germany, his place being taken by Albert of Pisa, who took over the administration of the province in 1223.[6] What happened then to Celano we do not know, though it is probable that he shortly afterwards returned to Italy.[7] One reason for thinking this is that he separates the years 1224 to 1226 in his *Vita Prima S. Francisci* from the previous years, and gives a most careful and detailed account of these years " *prout potuimus recte scire* ".[8] This suggests that he may have been in more direct touch with S. Francis and the inner circle during these last two years of the Saint's life.

It appears, then, from the little information which we possess, that Celano knew nothing at first hand of the years before 1215, nor of the years 1221 to 1223. From 1215 to 1221 and from 1223 to 1228 he was probably in Italy, though he does not seem to have taken a very prominent part in events as he is nowhere mentioned by other chroniclers, except Jordano. Why, then, we may well ask, did the Pope choose him to write the official life of S. Francis when there were so many others whose personal intimacy with the Saint made them so much better qualified for the task? The answer must be, first, that Celano

---

[1] The fact that in *1 Cel.* there are a great many texts from the Bible, no less than twenty-one quotations from liturgical works, and numerous references to the works of the Fathers, suggests that he must have had the sort of education which at that time was generally confined to the clergy.

[2] *1 Cel.* 56.

[3] Jordano, *Chronica*, c. 19. The party included Caesarius of Speyer, a personal friend of S. Francis who helped in the writing of the Rule in 1221, John of Piancarpino who, in 1245, reached the court of the Grand Khan of Tartary in Outer Mongolia, and Jordano himself, whose Chronicle is so valuable a source of information on these early days.

[4] *Ibid.*, c. 30.   [5] *Ibid.*, c. 31.   [6] *Ibid.*

[7] His account of the Presepio at Greccio in 1223 may well be based on his own reminiscences as it is full of detail and is not recorded in any other document which has come down to us.

[8] *1 Cel.* 88.

was known to have considerable gifts as a writer, and, secondly, that at a time when party feeling was beginning to run high he was known to be a man of moderate views who could be relied upon to give an unbiased portrait of the man whom Gregory wished to have presented to the world.

Whether or not Gregory gave any indication of the lines which he wished the book to follow, Celano certainly set out to give the world the life of a Saint.[1] His close acquaintance with the standard works of hagiography not only showed him what was expected of him but also made him well qualified for the task which had been allotted to him. Francis had just been canonised, Celano had been present at the ceremony and had been immediately afterwards summoned into the presence of the Pope and ordered to write an official biography. He was determined that, as a result of his labours, the world should be left in no doubt of the sanctity of his hero.

We see this revealed as we read the book. First we notice that Celano makes little effort to find out about Francis's childhood, though stories must have been abundant in Assisi when he wrote, but is content instead to give a highly-coloured account of the boy's youthful sins with the obvious intention of throwing into greater relief the sanctity of his life after his conversion. After this he adds some general and rather irrelevant observations on the pernicious way in which children were brought up. Again, his account of the " conversion " of S. Francis is written primarily from the mystical point of view, little being said about his growing concern for the poor, while his devotion to the ideal of poverty is not specifically mentioned until § 35, where he is describing the return from Rome after the visit to Innocent III. Now for about twenty chapters Celano dwells upon the devotion of Francis to Poverty, Simplicity, Humility and Obedience.[2] Then comes an account of his missionary journeys (55–57), followed by a collection of stories (58–70), mostly of a miraculous or remarkable nature, to show that the man with whom we are dealing was quite definitely endued with supernatural virtues.[3] Celano ends this section with the remark that miracles " do not make holiness but only shew it ", which recalls a passage in Gregory the Great which Celano must have had in mind.[4] Celano then gives

[1] Nino Tamassia in his book *San Francesco e la sua Leggenda* (Eng. tr. by Lonsdale Ragg) makes this clear, though his arguments are often unconvincing and his style occasionally offensive.

[2] For Poverty, see §§ 35, 39 and 51 ; for Simplicity, see §§ 46, 47 and 50 *ad fin.* ; for Humility, see §§ 40 and 54 ; and for Obedience, see §§ 39 and 45.

[3] Among these stories we should note the following phrases : " truly this man is a saint " (59), " truly he is a saint " (61), " their devotion to God's saint " (62), and " she was kissing his footsteps " (69).

[4] Celano's words are : " *miracula . . . sanctitatem non faciunt sed ostendunt* " ; Gregory writes, in *XL Homiliae in Evangelium* : " *miracula ostendunt aliquando sanctitatem, non faciunt.*" See Migne, *Patr. Lat.*, lxxvi, 1216. The same phrase is used in the Introductory Letter to the *Leg. 3 Soc.*

many beautiful and characteristic stories which, in spite of his rather stilted style, give a very good picture of S. Francis himself, though they purposely tell us little about the development of the Order. The book ends with a number of conventional miracle-stories which appear to have been copied down from a collection made for the purposes of canonisation.

How far we can regard this *Legenda* as an accurate and adequate portrait of the Saint has often been disputed. We are bound, in the first place, to notice that there are some very obvious omissions in the story. We know from our other sources that the latter years of S. Francis's life were clouded by dissension and disaffection in the Order, that the Rule had to be revised and compromised to make it acceptable to the Pope and to the more prominent of the brothers, and that Francis himself was often in great distress because he felt that his disciples were betraying his ideals. We should expect, therefore, in any life of the Saint to read about these things. But Celano passes most of them over in silence, and gives little or no impression of the very unsatisfactory state of the Order by the time Francis died. The only Rule which he mentions was the *Regula Primitiva* of 1210; he says nothing of the Rule of 1221 or of the Rule which he himself had sworn to obey, the *Regula Bullata* of 1223. He says nothing of any Chapter Meetings, although they played a very important part in the history of the Order; nor does he mention Francis's refusal to allow the friars to ask for privileges from the Pope. The reason generally given for these omissions is that Celano was under the domination of Elias, who himself disapproved of Chapter Meetings and held none during his term of office, and who was busy obtaining privileges from the Pope for the new Church of S. Francis at Assisi.[1] At the same time we must remember the conditions under which Celano was writing. His commission had been given to him by the Pope, who, as Cardinal Ugolino, had played a considerable part in the controversies which troubled the Order, and who may well have given some directions as to the lines which he wished Celano to follow. Celano's own sympathies were, on the whole, with the strict party in the Order, as is clear from his *Vita Secunda*; but at the moment he was not a free agent. Whether or not the Pope definitely told him what he was to include in his *Legenda*, and what omit, there is no means of knowing; but if we recollect that Celano's main object was to give the world a picture of a holy man and not to tell the history of the Order, we cannot altogether complain if he felt that such domestic problems as Rules and Chapter Meetings and disputed interpretations of the Franciscan ideal were both irrelevant and misleading. And that he does give some

---

[1] Cf. Sabatier, *Spec. Perf.*, p. cvi, and Little, *Guide to Franciscan Studies*, p. 12.

indication of the anxiety in the mind of S. Francis as to the future of the Order the following passages will show : [1]

For he saw many running after offices of government whose temerity he hated and whom he was striving to recall from such pestilence by his example . . . Especially at that time, when wickedness had grown to such excess, and iniquity abounded, he pronounced that it was dangerous to rule and more profitable to be ruled. He grieved that some had left their first works and had forgotten their old simplicity in new inventions ; and accordingly he lamented that they who were once intent with their whole desire on higher things had descended to things base and worthless, and had left the true joys to range and wander in frivolity and emptiness over the field of a vacuous liberty. Therefore he besought the Divine clemency for the deliverance of his children, and prayed most earnestly that they might be kept in the grace given them (*I Cel.* 104).

And again, in Francis's farewell :

"Fare ye well, all ye my sons, in the fear of God, and remain in Him always, for a great trial is coming upon you and tribulation draweth nigh. Happy are they who shall persevere in the things they have begun, for the scandals that are to be shall separate some from them " (*I Cel.* 108).

A more unfortunate omission in Celano's legend is the names of Francis's intimate friends. It is indeed strange that this Legend should say nothing of Leo, Angelo and Masseo, though no less than forty other people are mentioned by name. The friends of S. Francis are in fact mentioned, though not by name, in § 102,[2] where Celano speaks of them in very warm terms but says that he suppresses their names " to spare their modesty " (*ipsorum verecundiae parcens*). This has been taken as a slight on these men for which Elias was probably responsible ; but it is equally possible to imagine that these men, being out of sympathy with the policy and methods of Elias, and knowing that Celano was working with and for him and Ugolino, may have said, when they gave their evidence : " We would rather that you did not bring our names into it."

Another criticism of Celano's work is that it gives far too much prominence to Elias. Sabatier calls it " un vrai manifeste en sa faveur ",[3] an expression which is repeated by Dr. Little in his article in the *English Historical Review* in 1902. But can this be substantiated ? We find that Elias is mentioned in six chapters in the *Vita Prima :* 69, 95, 98, 105, 108 and 109. Of these, 69, 95, 105 and 109 are insignificant and can therefore be ignored. In § 98 Celano refers to Elias as one whom S. Francis " had chosen to himself in place of a mother and had made the father of the other brethren " (*quem loco matris elegerat sibi et aliorum*

---

[1] The translation is that of A. G. Ferrers Howell in *The Lives of S. Francis by Thomas of Celano* (1908).

[2] Together with Rufino, who is, however, mentioned by name in another connection in § 95.

[3] *Vie de S. François*, p. liv.

fratrum fecerat patrem). But we know that in 1221, on the death of Peter Catanii, Elias had become the official head of the Order, whether he had been expressly chosen by S. Francis or not. The only positive statement which we have is in the *Chronica XXIV Generalium*, which says, " *Beatus Franciscus posuit ad regendum fratrem Heliam* ".[1] Lacking any further evidence we can hardly quarrel with Celano's statement.

Much more important is the famous story of S. Francis's blessing of the brothers shortly before his death, in which Elias is singled out for a particular blessing.[2] It has been said [3] that Celano has here allowed himself to be carried away by his devotion to Elias into giving a description of something which never happened. But before we accept this we must consider the facts. Francis died in October, 1226 ; Celano's book was written in 1229 or 1230.[4] If what he gives us as the death-bed scene of the saint is false, then there were many who could and would have immediately exposed him. Celano tells us that in the course of writing his book he has had occasion to consult " faithful and approved witnesses ",[5] some of whom must have described in detail for him the last few hours of S. Francis's life. Is it conceivable that, with these witnesses still living, Celano could have deliberately falsified the account in order to bring honour on Elias ? After all, it is natural enough that Francis, if he were going to give a special blessing to anyone, should give it to the recognised head of the Order, whatever he may have thought of him personally. The special blessing need not be taken to imply special affection or approval ; but S. Francis, realising the difficulties with which Elias would have to contend—and also perhaps conscious of his essential inability to deal with them—and anxious to do what he could for the future of the Order, would naturally want to give all possible strength to the man who would have the greatest influence and responsibility. We must not regard as a reward what was primarily intended to be a means of grace. Even in 1247, long after Elias had fallen into disgrace, Celano, in writing his *Vita Secunda*, has to concede that Francis did in fact give a special blessing to Elias.[6]

Taking the whole book into consideration, we must admit that it is imperfect ; that there are many things omitted which, though they concern the Order rather than the man, are vital to a proper understanding of S. Francis ; that the relative importance of men like Elias and Leo is not justly appreciated ; and so on.[7] But all the same, the book does give us a remarkable account of a very remarkable life, and was considered good enough to serve as the standard biography for

---

[1] *An. F.*, III, p. 31.   [2] *1 Cel.* 108.   [3] E.g. by Sabatier in *Spec. Perf.*, p. ci.
[4] See below for a discussion on the actual date when the work was finished.
[5] *1 Cel.* Prologue.   [6] *2 Cel.* 216.
[7] Fr. Cuthbert says that Celano was " apt to form his opinion of men by the place which they held in the opinion of the world around him." *Life of S. Francis* p. 501.

seventeen years, becoming immediately popular both among the friars and among those outside the Order.[1]

So then, in May, 1228, immediately after the Canonisation, Gregory IX called Celano to him and invited him to write what was to be regarded as the official biography of the Saint. Celano would naturally feel honoured by such an invitation and would be anxious to produce something really worthy of the occasion. The first thing was to collect his material, then to select what he wanted to use, and finally to work it up into a biography which would take its place among the standard *Legendae* of the saints. This process must have taken some time, and we shall be wise not to tie ourselves down to the very early date of February 25th, 1229, as the occasion upon which the *Vita Prima* was officially approved. The evidence for this date, which has been accepted by most scholars,[2] is a note appended to the Paris MS.[3] of *1 Celano*, which reads : " At Perugia the blessed Lord Pope Gregory IX, in the second year of his glorious pontificate, on the fifth of the kalends of March, received this *legenda*, confirmed it, and considered it worthy of acceptance." But the Paris MS. cannot be placed earlier than the end of the thirteenth century, while the appended note, which is in a different handwriting, is probably nearly a hundred years later.[4] If this note is demonstrably a hundred and fifty years later than the date which it gives, it can hardly be regarded as a primary authority. Another argument for the year 1229 is that Celano says nothing of the Translation of the body of S. Francis to the new Basilica, which took place in May, 1230. But though Celano certainly gives no account of the proceedings, there seems some reason for supposing that the event had already taken place ; for he writes, in § 23, of the church of San Giorgio, that it was here that S. Francis was " honourably buried the first time " (" *in quo loco sepultus est honorifice primum* "). Besides this we know that the behaviour of Elias at the time of the Translation was such as to cause

---

[1] We find references to the *Vita Prima* in Luc de Tuy ; cf. Mariana's *Maxima Biblioteca Veterum Patrum*, Tomus xxv (1677), pp. 188–251, and d'Alençon's edition of *Celano*, Prolegomena, p. xxvii ; the *Annales Monasterii Waverleiensis*, cf. *Recueil des Historiens des Gaules et de la France*, Tome xviii, p. 210, where there is a literal quotation from *1 Cel.* 88 ; the *Chronicon Stadensis*, cf. *Mon. Germ. Hist. Scriptores*, Vol. xvi, p. 360, for a quotation from *1 Cel.* 126 ; the *Chronique Rimée* of Philip Musket, cf. *A.F.H.*, iii (1910), p. 421 ; the *Liber Epilogorum* of Bartholomew of Trent, a Dominican ; the Sermons of Guiard de Laon and of Berthold of Ratisbon, cf. *Testimonia Minora Saec. XIII*, p. 21, and *Études Franciscaines*, Tome xviii, pp. 530 ff. *1 Çel.* also formed the background of a number of legends which will be considered in the next chapter.

[2] E.g. by Sabatier, *Vie de S. François*, p. li, n. 2 ; Little, *Guide to Franciscan Studies*, p. 10 ; d'Alençon's *Celano*, Prolegomena, p. xxvi. Doubt has been cast upon this date by Beaufreton, *S. François d'Assise*, p. 269, n. 3.

[3] *Bibl. Lat.* 3817.

[4] D'Alençon, Prolegomena, p. lvi : " *Illa notula manu diversa scripta fuit, et si legenda indicatur a peritis saeculo xiii exarata, haec additio facta videtur saeculo xiv potius labente.*"

a good deal of scandal which Celano might think better forgotten. It is noticeable that he makes no mention of the Translation in his *Vita Secunda* written in 1247.[1] The evidence, then, in favour of February, 1229, is not very great. On the other hand, there is much to be said against it. The *Vita Prima*, far from showing signs of haste, gives every appearance of having been most carefully written. There is a plan running through the whole of the work, the style is polished, and there are numerous quotations from the Bible and the Fathers for which Celano must have had access to books of reference.

Our next problem is to investigate the sources upon which the *Vita Prima* is based. Celano tells us in the Prologue that some of what he is writing is based upon his own reminiscences (" *ea quae ex ipsius ore audivi* ") ; but this cannot have amounted to very much, as we know that up to 1215 he was outside the Community altogether, and that from 1221 to 1223 he was away from Italy. Most of his material, therefore, must have been collected from the " faithful and approved witnesses " to whom he refers. We must picture him, then, during the summer of 1228 travelling around the towns and villages of Umbria, consulting such people as the townsfolk of Assisi, the intimate friends of S. Francis, and any others who had stories to tell. Some of these would put their testimony into writing, others would have to have their story taken down at their dictation. In this way Celano would collect a dossier of *written* evidence which he would need to sift before sitting down to write his *legenda*. But what became of these sources when he had finished with them ?

To give what can only be a conjectural answer to this question we must turn to that much discussed document known as the *Legenda Trium Sociorum*. This *legenda* consists of an Introductory Letter, stating that it was written in 1246 by Brothers Leo, Angelo and Rufino, and seventy-four chapters. Sabatier, in the Study of the Sources which he appended to his *Vie de S. François*, drew attention to the discrepancies between the letter and the legend which it is meant to introduce, and gave it as his opinion that what we possess of the legend is only a fragment.[2] That was in 1894. In 1900 the Bollandist father, François van Ortroy, published an article in the *Analecta Bollandiana* [3] in which he argued that the *Leg. 3 Soc.* was not a fragment of a larger work but a " pastiche " made up of excerpts from various other *legendae*

---

[1] The other references to the burial are not very helpful. In § 88 Celano says that Francis's body was " taken up and honourably buried where, to the glory of the Almighty, it gleams with many miracles " and repeats this, without any further details, in § 118.

[2] Cf. *Vie de S. François*, p. lxiii : " *Il est évident que la Légende des Trois Compagnons, telle que nous l'avons aujourd'hui, n'est qu'un fragment de l'original.*"

[3] Vol. XIX, pp. 110-97.

such as *1* and *2 Celano, Julian of Speyer, Bernard of Bessa* and others.[1] Sabatier published a spirited reply to van Ortroy in the *Revue Historique* in 1901, and followed it up some years later by a series of articles which were published posthumously in *Studi Medievali* under the heading : " *La Première Partie de la Vie de S. François* ".

The problem presented by the *Leg. 3 Soc.* has led to endless controversy, into the details of which it is not necessary for us now to enter. If the Letter of the Three Companions was really meant to introduce the legend which follows it, then clearly that legend must be mutilated. But it would be equally possible to suppose that the Introductory Letter really belonged not to this legend at all but to a completely different collection of papers sent in by Leo, Angelo and Rufino in 1246. This suggestion, made by van Ortroy, is now generally accepted, and gives us an opportunity of studying the *Leg. 3 Soc.* from an entirely new standpoint.

The 74 chapters may be divided into three sections. The first section (2–60) contains a full and detailed account of the earlier years of S. Francis's life down to the division of his followers into three Orders.[2] The next few chapters (61–67) are written from a somewhat different point of view, which makes one feel that they must have come from another writer altogether. The simple stories of S. Francis and the friars now give place to details about the government of the Order, while the outlook of the writer is definitely more characteristic of one of the " Conventual " party. It is, for example, loud in praise of Ugolino, it suggests that Francis ran to the Pope for protection against the bishops, it tells how Ugolino saved the brothers from persecution, in spite of Francis's declared wish that they should willingly submit to any kind of oppression,[3] and it even says that Francis obtained a papal privilege to allow the brothers to build, although we know that this was entirely contrary to his intentions.[4] When we compare this with the praise of abject poverty and humility, which is so conspicuous in the earlier chapters, we cannot fail to see that the point of view of the writer is now very different. Chapters 68 to 74 are admittedly later,[5] describing the death and canonisation of S. Francis, the appearance of the Stigmata and an account of the Indulgence of the Portiuncula.

It is the first of these sections (§§ 2–60) which is the most important. When we compare it with the writings of Celano we find many passages which are almost identical with the *Vita Prima*, besides some which have a close affinity with the *Vita Secunda*, though here the exact

---

[1] Cf. " *un pastiche* " (p. 128), " *un mythe* " (p. 138), " *une pièce apocryphe* " (p. 138).
[2] The date of this is uncertain and has led to some discussion, but it was certainly in what we may call the " middle period ", say 1212 to 1215.
[3] Cf. *Regula Prima* (1221), capp. xiv and xvi.
[4] Cf. *Testamentum S.F.* in *Opuscula*, p. 80.   [5] Sabatier, *Vie de S. François*, p. lxvi.

parallels are very much fewer. In spite of van Ortroy's theories, no one who takes the trouble to compare the narratives of the Three Companions with those of Celano's *Vita Secunda* can have much doubt that Celano is using the *Legenda* as his source.

But we are mainly concerned in this chapter with the relationship between the *Leg. 3 Soc.* and the *Vita Prima*. Here the parallels are very much more striking, whole sentences being written out in exactly the same words in both documents. Assuming that the *Vita Prima* was written in 1229 and the *Leg. 3 Soc.* in 1246, critics have taken it for granted that what we find common to both must have been copied by the Three Companions from *Celano*. Burkitt, for example, in his essay on the "Sources for the Life of S. Francis" says : "the use of *1 Celano* by the *3 Socii* is impossible to deny " ; and in a paper contributed to the *Miscellanea Francesco Ehrle* he says : "we have here a case of direct literary borrowing. It is not a case of relating the same events or of using a common source."[1] In spite of this judgment I believe that a detailed comparison of the parallel passages in the *Vita Prima* and the *Leg. 3 Soc* will show that, though Celano may not be borrowing direct from the Three Companions, yet that the *Legenda* represents the earlier tradition and *Celano* the copy.

First we will consider the " form " in which Celano plans out his chapters. Each chapter is carefully arranged ; and we know from the *Vita Secunda* that a common practice with Celano was to copy out a source more or less verbatim, and then to add at the end of it some observation of his own, a moral or apophthegm. In the *Vita Prima* we find exactly the same process being carried out. In §§ 5, 7, 9, 11, 12 and 15 Celano's narrative is closely akin to that of the *Leg. 3 Soc.*, with the addition of a few lines at the end in which the moral of the story is pointed.

Again, on the question of style, the *Leg. 3 Soc.* is on the whole more simple than *Celano*. For example, in § 18 the *Legenda* writes : "*tanquam daemonum tentationibus probatus et tentationum documentis instructus*". It is a clumsy sentence which Celano in the parallel passage reduces to : " *tentationum documentis probatus* " (*1 Cel.* 13). Or again, in § 17 the Three Companions speak of the crowd in Assisi staring at Francis " *cernentes enim ipsum sic et pristinis moribus alteratum* ". The " *sic et* " is obviously superfluous ; so Celano leaves it out and says simply : " *cernebant eum a pristinis moribus alteratum* ".

Then again, there are several instances in which Celano has slightly altered the ending of a sentence, or has added an extra phrase, in order to bring it into line with one of the accepted forms of the *cursus*. " If one document ", writes Dr. Little,[2] " uses the rhythms which were

---

[1] *Essays in Commemoration*, p. 27 ; *Misc. Franc. Ehrle*, Tomo iii, p. 3.
[2] *Some recently discovered Franciscan Documents*, p. 11.

generally regarded as marks of good style in the middle ages, and another version of the same story does not use those rhythms, the probability is that the rhythmical version is derived from the un-rhythmical rather than vice versa. No medieval writer would deliberately change what he regarded as good style into bad style." In the parallel passages in *1 Celano* and the *Leg. 3 Soc.* we find the following :

(*a*) *3 Soc.* 12 : *orabat ut Deus dirigeret viam suam.*
    1 Cel. 6 : *orabat devotus ut Deus aeternus et verus dirigeret viam suam et suam illum doceret facere voluntatem.*
(*b*) *3 Soc.* 12 : *sustinebat autem maximam passionem et anxietatem mentis non valens quiescere donec opus compleret quod mente conceperat.*
    1 Cel. 6 : *maximam sustinebat animi passionem et, donec opere compleret quod conceperat corde, quiescere non valebat.*
(*c*) *3 Soc.* 16 : *circuit quaerens quid actum sit de filio suo.*
    1 Cel. 10 : *scire cupiens quid de filio actum sit.*
(*d*) *3 Soc.* 16 : *citissime cucurrit ad locum.*
    1 Cel. 9 : *citissime cucurrit ad locum in quo Dei famulus morabatur.*
(*e*) *3 Soc.* 17 : *et lapides proiiciebant in eum.*
    1 Cel. 11 : *et lapides in ipsum proiiciunt.*
(*f*) *3 Soc.* 17 : *et dementiae deputabant vel imputabant.*
    1 Cel. 11 : *et dementiae imputabant.*
(*g*) *3 Soc.* 55 : *ut in angustia loci modicitate rumor insolens mentis silentium non per-turbaret.*
    1 Cel. 42 : *ne angustia loci modicitas mentis silentium perturbaret.*

Again, Celano has occasionally altered a sentence in order to include a phrase from the Bible. For example, in § 6 he copies from the *3 Socii* the words " *poenitebat eum pecasse tam graviter* " and then adds " *et offendisse oculos maiestatis* " from Isaiah iii. 8. Again, in § 10 he uses the phrase " *ut de manibus persequentium animam suam Dominus liberaret* ", which, though not an exact quotation, is reminiscent of the language of the Psalms. In the parallel passage the Three Companions have : " *ut Dominus liberaret eum de persecutione nociva* ". Or again, in § 11 he adds an expression from Ecclesiasticus vii. 9, whereas otherwise he is merely copying the *Legenda*. Perhaps the best example is in § 42, where Celano is speaking of the growth of the Order. The phrase in the *Leg. 3 Soc.* is " *augmentare videns beatus Franciscus fratres suos* ", but Celano brings it into line with Acts ii. 47, by writing : " *videns beatus Franciscus quod Dominus Deus quotidie augeret* (*numerum*) *in idipsum* ", where the expression " *in idipsum* " shows that Celano clearly had the words of the Bible in his mind.

Then, again, there are certain differences in the order of events narrated in the two legends. For example, the phrase " *ab ea itaque die coepit seipsum vilescere sibi* " is put by Celano in § 3 before there has been any real change in S. Francis's ideas. In the *Leg. 3 Soc.* it comes much more naturally in § 8 immediately after the account of the two visions which had persuaded Francis to take a very different view of himself and of life in general.

Further, the stories in the *Leg. 3 Soc.* are on the whole fuller and more natural than in *Celano*. Celano's account of the " conversion " of S. Francis is almost entirely concerned with devotional and mystical progress, and has very little to say about his growing humanitarianism. In the *Legenda* we begin by hearing of his generosity to the poor, including even the taking off of his shirt in secret to give to some beggar (§§ 8 and 9) ; then we go on to the story of his actually identifying himself with the poor at Rome on the steps of S. Peter's (§ 10) ; and so we are led up to the final conquest of himself in his service of the lepers (§ 11). Again, the story of Francis before the Bishop of Assisi is told in much more detail by the Three Companions than by Celano.[1] The account in the *Legenda* has, in fact, every appearance of coming from an eyewitness. It gives the words of Francis to the Bishop before his denudation (" *Domine, non tantum pecuniam, quae est de rebus suis, volo ei reddere gaudenti animo, sed etiam vestimenta* ") ; it describes his disappearance into the Bishop's palace from which he emerged with nothing on ; it mentions the small detail that Francis placed the money on the top of the bundle of clothes ; it gives his speech to the crowd : " *Audite omnes et intelligite : usque modo Petrum Bernardonis vocavi patrem meum, etc.*" ; it informs us that Francis was found to be wearing a hair-shirt under his fine clothes ; and it speaks of the mingled sorrow and anger of the father and of the indignation of the crowd against him. Celano, however, is content to tell the whole story in a few sentences :

Cumque perductus esset coram episcopo, nec moras patitur nec cunctatur de aliquo ; immo nec verba exspectat nec facit, sed continuo depositis et proiectis omnibus vestimentis restituit ea patri. Insuper et nec femoralia retinens totus coram omnibus denudatur. Episcopus vero animum ipsius attendens, fervoremque ac constantiam nimis admirans, protinus exsurrexit et inter brachia sua ipsum recolligens, pallio, quo indutus erat, contexit eum.

Lastly, there are one or two instances where a phrase in the *Vita Prima* betrays some confusion which is only explained by reference to the account in the *Legenda*. Compare, for example, the two accounts of the vision of the armour :

3 Soc. 5	1 Celano 4–5
Post paucos vero annos *quidam nobilis* de *civitate Assisii militaribus armis se praeparat*	Nam *nobilis quidam civitat*is *Assisii militaribus armis se* non mediocriter *praeparat,*

---

[1] Cf. *Leg. 3 Soc.* 19–20 and *1 Cel.* 15.

3 Soc. 5

1 Celano 4–5

3 Soc. 5	1 Celano 4–5
	et inanis gloriae ventu inflatus, *ad pecuniae vel honoris augenda lucra* iturum *in Apuliam* se spopondit. Quibus auditis Franciscus, quia levis animo erat et non modicum audax, *ad eundum conspirat cum illo,*
ut *ad pecuniae vel honoris lucra augenda in Apuliam* vadat. *Quo audito* Franciscus	
ad eundum cum illo aspirat, et ut a quodam comite, Gentili nomine, miles fiat, pannos pro posse praeparat pretiosiores concivi suo,	
	generis nobilitate impar sed magnanimitate superior,
pauperior divitiis sed profusior largitate. Nocte igitur quadam cum ad huiusmodi *consummanda tota se deliberatione dedisset, et ad iter agendum desiderio aestuaret*	*pauperior divitiis sed profusior largitate. Nocte igitur quadam cum ad* haec *consummanda tota se deliberatione dedisset, et* desiderio aestuans *ad iter agendum* maxime anhelaret, qui percusserat eum virga iustitiae *per visionem* nocturnam *visitat eum* in dulcedine gratiae ; et quia *gloriae cupidus* erat *gloriae fastigio* eum *allicit et exaltat.*
visitatur a Domino qui *eum* tanquam *gloriae cupidum*	
fastigio gloriae per visionem allicit et exaltat. Cum enim illa nocte dormiret apparuit ei quidam vocans eum ex nomine ac ducens ipsum in quoddam spatiosum et amoenum palatium *plenum militaribus armis scilicet* splendentibus *clipeis, ceterisque apparatibus* ad murum pendentibus, ad militiae decorem spectantibus.	Videbatur ei namque domum suam totam habere
	plenam
	militaribus armis sellis *scilicet, clypeis,* lanceis, et *caeteris apparatibus ;*
Qui cum *gaudens plurimum quid hoc esset secum tacitus miraretur*	*gaudensque plurimum quid hoc esset secum tacitus* mirabatur. Non enim consueverat talia in domo suo videre sed potius pannorum cumulos ad vendendum. Cumque ad subitum rerum eventum stuperet non modicum,
interrogavit cuius essent haec arma tanto splendore fulgentia et palatium sic amoenum. Et *responsum est* illi *haec omnia* cum palatio *sua* esse *militumque suorum.*	*responsum est* ei *omnia haec* arma *sua* fore *militumque suorum.*

3 Soc. 5	*1 Celano 4–5*
Expergefactus itaque *gaudenti animo mane surrexit,* seculariter cogitans tamquam qui nondum spiritum Dei plene gustaverat, se in hoc debere magnifice principari, atque *praesagium magnae prosperitatis reputans visionem iter* arripere deliberabat *in Apuliam* ut miles fieret a comite supradicto.	*Expergefactus* quoque *animo gaudenti mane surrexit,* et *praesagium magnae prosperitatis reputans visionem* prosperum futurum *iter* suum *in Apuliam* securatur.

In comparing these two accounts we notice that the Three Companions tell of the appearance in the vision of " a certain man ". But no one appears in Celano's account. This would not matter very greatly were it not for this fact : in the *Legenda* Francis asks of the man whose the armour is to be, and the man gives him an answer (" *responsum est illi* "). Celano has repeated the words " *responsum est* ", but in reply to no question put by Francis and on the lips of no person. Can we doubt that the *Legenda* here represents an earlier account than the *Vita Prima*, and that Celano, in trying to abbreviate his source, leaves out the appearance of the man and the direct question put by Francis, and yet repeats the words " *responsum est* " without realising that any explanation of this reply is necessary ?

To take another example ; § 6 of the *Vita Prima* opens with a couple of words which have always presented some difficulty. Celano has just been describing the first vision in which Francis had been told that the armour which he had seen was for him and his knights, so that he had risen up in the morning in great joy, confident that his expedition into Apulia would be crowned with success. Then, after a few words in which Celano compares Francis with David, he suddenly says, " *Immutatus quoque, sed mente non corpore, ire in Apuliam recusat* ", without giving any explanation of what changed his mind or why he now refused to go to Apulia. When we turn to the *Legenda Trium Sociorum* (§ 6) we find the solution ; for here we read of a second vision in which Francis was told to go back to his own land where he would receive further instructions. Francis obeyed, and the section ends with the words : " *Immutatusque iam mente in Apuliam ire recusat.* " This certainly suggests that Celano has taken the phrase from the *3 Socii* without realising that, bereft of the story of the second vision, it scarcely made sense.

The above considerations all point to one conclusion : that the narratives of the *Leg. 3 Soc.*, if not the actual sources used by Celano for his *Vita Prima*, yet represent an earlier tradition upon which he worked. This conclusion would, I believe, have been reached years ago if it had not been for the fact that critics had firmly in their minds the conviction that the *Leg. 3 Soc.* belonged to the year 1246 and the *Vita Prima* to 1229. In fact, Sabatier himself wrote of some of the parallel passages : [1] " si nous comparons ces passages de plus près, l'avantage est encore nettement en faveur de *3 Soc.* Celà est à ce point que si nous n'avions aucune indication sur les dates relatives de *1 Cel.* et de *3 Soc.* on serait amené à faire de *3 Soc.* l'original dont dépendrait *1 Cel.*" Of course Celano did not know the *Leg. 3 Soc.* in its present form ; but there does seem to be some reason for believing that the *Leg. 3 Soc.* is based on the written sources which Celano collected for his *Vita Prima* and left in the friars' library at Assisi after he had finished with them.

Any attempt to reconstruct the course of events must be largely conjectural, but it is at any rate possible that the story which lies behind these documents may be something like this. In May, 1228, Celano is commissioned to write the official Life of S. Francis. His own experience is limited, so that he must needs spend some time in collecting his material. He publishes his *Vita* in 1230 or 1231. By this time the convent is finished, and the library is beginning to be formed. Books were so rare and so much sought after by the friars that even small manuscripts which dealt with their founder would be treasured. There is, therefore, every reason to suppose that, when Celano had finished with the notes upon which he had been working, they were left in the brothers' library at Assisi, as we know happened with similar documents a few years later. [2] In 1244 was held the Chapter of Genoa, at which it was decided that a new Life of S. Francis should be written. Once more Celano is invited to be the biographer. He goes again to Assisi, finds there the old documents which he had left there fourteen years ago, together with a large pile of those which had recently been sent in. When he has finished, the sources are once more left in the book-cupboard. Then some years later an unknown scribe makes up his mind to write a life of S. Francis. He is definitely of the " Spiritual " party, and is a man of some literary style. Possibly he was invited to do so by John of Parma, a supporter of the *zelanti*, who was elected Minister General in 1247. The scribe uses the customary " scissors-and-paste " method, beginning on the documents which deal with the early years of S. Francis. These he copies down rather more faithfully than Celano had done. He probably also had access to a *Life of Brother Bernard* and to Leo's *Life of Brother Giles*. He also dipped into other Leo-matter, for he takes one story out of a collection which is now known as Section D of Delorme's Perugian MS. [3] But he does not

---

[1] Sabatier, *La Première Partie de la Vie de S. François*, in *Studi Medievali*, p. 39.
[2] Cf. the *Declaratio* of Ubertino da Casale in Sabatier, *Spec. Perf.*, p. cl.
[3] *Leg. 3 Soc.* 13 = *Per.* 72. See the following chapter for a discussion of the *Scripta Leonis*.

get very far with his work. With great thoroughness he writes his account of the early days down to about the year 1215 when the Order was divided into three parts. Here he breaks off. We do not know why. Perhaps he meant what he had written to be the first part of a much longer work of which the other parts are lost. Possibly some external reason prevented him from completing his work. At any rate, in the " fragment " which he managed to finish and which has come down to us he has given us a most vivid account of the youth of S. Francis and the early days of the Order. Some years later another writer finds this manuscript and adds a few chapters about Ugolino, and the way in which the Order was governed, and how the brothers were protected by the Curia. Later still, some scribe tries to complete the *Legenda* by adding an account of the Stigmatisation, death and canonisation of S. Francis and the Indulgence of the Portiuncula.

ADDITIONAL NOTE

A Lost Document

The theory that there was a dossier of written evidence behind even Celano's *Vita Prima* is borne out by reference to the *Legenda* of Julian of Speyer. This Legend, which was written about 1233, is little more than an abridgement of *1 Celano.* There is, however, one passage in which his account has just those characteristics of style which compel us to regard a narrative as primitive. It is the story of the final stage in the conversion of S. Francis and the coming of his first companions.

This account exists altogether in four different " states ": Julian's *Legenda*, §§ 15 to 17a, *Leg. 3 Soc.*, §§ 25 to 27a, *1 Celano*, §§ 21 to 23, and Bonaventura, *Leg. Maior*, iii, 1 to 3a. The historical sequence of these four documents which has usually been accepted is as follows : *1 Celano*, 1229 ; *Julian of Speyer*, about 1233 ; *Leg. 3 Soc.*, 1246 ; *Bonaventura*, 1260. The obvious conclusion, therefore, has been that Julian, the Three Companions and Bonaventura have all taken their information from Celano. Yet when we examine Julian's account of these incidents we find, in the first place, that it is far closer to that of the Three Companions than to *1 Celano.* So long as the *Leg. 3 Soc.* is regarded as a later document it is easy to imagine that in this section the author is copying from Julian instead of from Celano, though why he should have done so is not explained. Sabatier's theory that the *3 Socii* occasionally borrowed from Julian of Speyer in order that he might not be offended, is hardly satisfying.[1] But if, on the other hand, the *Leg. 3 Soc.* is to be accepted as the earliest document in our

[1] Cf. *Revue Historique*, 1901, p. 76.

possession, then we have to explain why Julian should suddenly desert his customary source, *1 Celano*, and turn for a few sentences to the *Legenda Trium Sociorum*.

The only way to answer this question is to examine in detail the various accounts to see whether it is possible to say which of the four represents the earliest tradition.

First, let us compare *Julian* with *Celano*. Here, let us remember, it is always assumed that Julian's account is definitely based upon that of Celano. Julian writes :

Beatus itaque Franciscus trium, ut dictum est, ecclesiarum opere consummato, habitum adhuc eremiticum tunc temporis habuit, baculumque manu gestans, pedibus calceatis et corrigia cinctus incessit. Audiens autem die quadam inter missarum solemnia ea quae Christus in Evangelio missis ad praedicandum discipulis loquitur, ne videlicet aurum vel argentum possideant, ne peram in via vel sacculum, ne virgam vel panem portent, ne calceamenta vel duas tunicas habeant ; intelligensque haec eadem postmodum plenius ab ipso presbytero, indicibili gaudio mox repletus : " Hoc " inquit, " est quod quaero ; hoc est quod totis praecordiis concupisco ". Igitur cunctis quae audierat tenaci memoriae commendatis, laetanter his adimplendis innititur, duplicibusque sine mora depositis, ex hoc iam virga, calceamentis, sacculoque vel pera non utitur. Fecit proinde tunicam plurimum contemptibilem et incultam, reiectaque corrigia, funiculo cinxit illam.

Omnem quoque sollicitudinem cordis apponens qualiter auditus novae gratiae verba perficeret, coepit instinctu divino evangelicae perfectionis annuntiator exsistere, coepit poenitentiae in publicum simpliciter verba proponere. Erant autem ipsius eloquia non inania nec risu digna, erant virtute Sancti Spiritus plena, erant medullas cordis penetrantia et in vehementem audientes stuporem provocantia. Sed et, sicuti postmodum ipse testatus est quod huiusmodi salutationem, Domino revelante, didicerat ut diceret : " Dominus det tibi pacem ". Sic in omni praedicatione sua, pacem annuntians, populum in sermonis exordio salutabat. Subito ergo spiritu prophetarum perfusus, iuxta sermonem propheticum annuntiabat pacem, praedicabat salutem ; factumque est ut salutaribus monitis foederaret plurimos verae paci qui discordes a Christo prius exstiterant a salute longinqui.

Innotescente igitur apud multos beati Francisci tam doctrinae simplicis veritate quam vitae, coeperunt post modicum viri quidam ipsius exemplo ad poenitentiam animari et eidem, relictis omnibus, habitu vitaque coniungi. Ut autem novis filiis sancti iam merita remunerari coeperunt, coepit et amplius ipse nova spiritus consolatione repleri, coepit et illorum diligentius invigilare saluti. Hinc paterno eos affectu demulcens et fovens, novis non destitit monitis informare, docens ipsos sanctae paupertatis et verae simplicitatis viam indeclinabiliter ambulare.

Celano writes as follows :

Factum est autem, cum iam dictam ecclesiam reparasset, conversionis eius annus tertius agebatur. Quo in tempore quasi heremiticum ferens habitum, accinctus corrigia et baculum manu gestans, calceatis pedibus incedebat. Sed cum die quadam evangelium, qualiter Dominus miserit discipulos suos ad praedicandum, in eadem ecclesia legeretur, et sanctus Dei assistens ibidem utcumque intellexisset verba evangelica, celebratis missarum solemniis, a sacerdote sibi exponi evangelium suppliciter postulavit. Qui cum ei cuncta per ordinem enarrasset audiens sanctus Franciscus Christi discipulos non debere aurum, sive argentum, seu pecuniam possidere, non peram, non sacculum, non panem, non virgam in via portare, non calceamenta, non duas tunicas habere, sed regnum

Dei et poenitentiam praedicare, continuo exsultans in spiritu Dei : " Hoc est " inquit, " quod volo, hoc est quod quaero, hoc totis medullis cordis facere concupisco " . . . Solvit protinus calceamenta de pedibus, baculum deponit e manibus, et tunica una contentus, pro corrigia funiculum immutavit. Parat sibi ex tunc tunicam crucis imaginem praeferentem, ut in ea propulset omnes daemoniacas phantasias ; parat asperrimam ut carnem in ea crucifigat cum vitiis et peccatis ; parat denique pauperrimam et incultam et quae a mundo nullatenus valeat concupisci. . . . Exinde cum magno fervore spiritus et gaudio mentis coepit omnibus poenitentiam praedicare, verbo simplici sed corde magnifico aedificans audientes. Erat verbum eius velut ignis ardens, penetrans intima cordis, et omnium mentes admiratione replebat . . . In omni praedicatione sua, priusquam convenientibus proponeret verbum Dei, pacem imprecebatur, dicens : " Dominus det vobis pacem ". Hanc viris et mulieribus, hanc obviis et obviantibus, semper devotissime nuntiabat. Propterea multi qui pacem oderant pariter et salutem, Domino co-operante, pacem amplexati sunt toto corde, facti et ipsi filii pacis et aemuli salutis aeternae.

If we put out of our minds for the moment the fact that we know for certain that Julian's *Legenda* was written four or five years later than Celano's *Vita Prima*, our study of these parallel passages would almost certainly lead us to suppose that *Julian* here represented an earlier version than *Celano*. For instance, in *Julian* the words of the Gospel are given in what is obviously their right place ; in *Celano* they are merely included in the explanation. Again, Celano alters one or two sentences in order to end with a *cursus* : e.g. where Julian writes " *reiectaque corrigia funiculo cinxit illam* " Celano has " *pro corrigia funiculum immutavit* ", an example of the *cursus velox*. Again, where Julian writes " *erant medullas cordis penetrantia et in vehementem audientes stuporem provocantia* ", which has no *cursus*, Celano writes " *penetrans intima cordis et omnium mentes admiratione replebat* ", a good example of the *cursus planus*. At the same time Julian is quite capable of writing a *cursus* ending when he wants to, e.g. " *exordio salutabat* ", " *invigilare saluti* ", etc. It is worth while also to compare Julian's account of the making of the first tunic (*fecit tunicam plurimum contemptibilem et incultam*) with Celano's " *parat sibi ex tunc tunicam crucis imaginem praeferentem ut in ea propulset omnes daemoniacas phantasias : parat asperrimam ut carnem in ea crucifigat cum vitiis et peccatis : parat denique pauperrimam et incultam* ", with its introduction of a phrase from Galatians v. 24. It should be noticed also that whereas Julian refers to that dangerous document, the Testament of S. Francis, Celano omits this reference. If therefore we did not know for certain that Julian's Legend was based on *Celano*, we should conclude from a study of these parallel passages that *Julian* was the source and *Celano* the copy.

Now let us compare the account in the *Leg. 3 Soc.* :

Beatus itaque Franciscus, ecclesiae Sancti Damiani perfecto iam opere, habitum eremiticum portabat, baculumque manu gestans, pedibus calceatis et cinctus corrigia incedebat. Audiens autem quadam die inter missarum solemnia ea quae Christus discipulis ad praedicandum missis loquebatur, ne scilicet aurum, vel argentum, nec sacculum vel peram, nec virgam portarent in via, nec calceamenta nec duas tunicas habeant, intelligensque haec postea clarius ab ipso presbytero indicibili repletus gaudio, " Hoc " inquit " est quod cupio totis viribus adimplere ". Igitur, cunctis quae audierat commissis memoriae, laetanter his adimplendis innititur, duplicibus sine mora dimissis, ex tunc iam virga, calceamentis, sacculo vel pera non utitur ; faciens autem sibi tunicam valde contemptibilem et incultam, reiecta corrigia pro cingulo funem sumpsit. Omnem quoque sollicitudinem cordis, novae gratiae verbis apponens, qualiter illa possit opere perficere, coepit instinctu divino evangelicae perfectionis annuntiator existere, poeni- tentiamque simpliciter in publicum praedicare. Erant autem verba eius non inania nec risu digna, sed virtute Spiritus Sancti plena, cordis medullas penetrantia, ita ut in stuporem vehementer converterent audientes.

Sicut autem postmodum ipse testatus est, huiusmodi salutationem, Domino revelante, didicerat, videlicet : " Dominus det tibi pacem ". Et ideo in omni praedicatione sua, pacem annuntians, populum in praedicationis exordio salutabat . . . Subito ergo vir Dei Franciscus spiritu prophetarum perfusus, iuxta sermonem propheticum statim post dictum suum praeconem annuntiabat pacem praedicabat salutem, eiusque salutaribus monitis plurimi verae paci foederabantur, qui discordes a Christo extiterant, a salute longinqui.

Innotescente autem apud multos beati Francisci tam simplicis doctrinae veritate quam vitae, coeperunt post duos annos a sua conversione viri quidam ipsius exemplo ad poenitentiam animari, et eidem, reiectis omnibus, habitu vitaque coniungi.

Again, a comparison of the texts points to *Julian* representing an earlier account than the *Leg. 3 Soc.* For instance, a bad ending like " *funiculo cinxit illam* " becomes " *pro cingulo funem sumpsit* ", a perfect example of the *cursus velox*. Again, a somewhat obscure phrase like " *et in vehementem audientes stuporem provocantia* " becomes " *ita ut in stuporem vehementer converterent audientes* ", thus at the same time avoiding the rather meaningless expression " *stupor vehemens* " and also ensuring a *cursus* ending. The *Leg. 3 Soc.* has also altered the vague " *post modicum* " to " *post duos annos a conversione sua* " and has improved upon one or two clumsy habits of style. Once more we are bound to admit that, on the whole, *Julian* appears in this passage to represent an earlier state of the narrative even than that of the Three Companions.

Finally we turn to the *Legenda Maior* of S. Bonaventura. About ninety per cent. of this Legend is taken from the works of Celano, and yet in this one instance he is clearly and certainly following *Julian* and not the *Vita Prima*. Bonaventura writes as follows :

Dum enim die quodam missam de apostolis devotus audiret, perlectum est evangelium illud in quo Christus discipulis ad praedicandum mittendis formam tribuit evangelicam in vivendo, ne videlicet possideant aurum vel argentum nec in zonis pecuniam, nec peram in via, nec duas tunicas habeant, nec calceamenta deferant necque virgam. Quod audiens et intelligens ac memoriae commendans, apostolicae paupertatis amicus indicibili mox perfusus laetitia, " Hoc est " inquit, " quod cupio, hoc quod totis praecordiis con- cupisco ". Solvit proinde calceamenta de pedibus, deponit baculum, peram et pecuniam exsecratur, unaque contentus tunicula, reiecta corrigia, pro cingulo funem sumit, omnem sollicitudinem cordis apponens, qualiter audita perficiat et apostolicae rectitudinis regulae per omnia se coaptet.

Coepit ex hoc vir Dei divino instinctu evangelicae perfectionis aemulator existere et ad poenitentiam ceteros invitare. Erant autem ipsius eloquia non inania nec risu digna, sed virtute Spiritus Sancti plena, erant medullas cordis penetrantia ut in vehementem stuporem audientes converterent. In omni praedicatione sua pacem annuntians dicendo : " Dominus det vobis pacem " populum in sermonis exordio salutabat. Hanc quippe salutationem, Domino revelante, didicerat, sicut ipse postmodum testabatur. Unde factum est ut iuxta sermonem propheticum et ipse spiritu prophetarum afflatus, annuntiaret pacem, praedicaret salutem ac salutaribus monitis foederaret plurimos verae paci qui discordes a Christo prius exstiterant a salute longinqui.

Innotescente itaque apud multos viri Dei tam doctrinae simplicis veritate quam vitae, coeperunt ipsius exemplo viri quidam ad poenitentiam animari et eidem, reiectis omnibus, habitu vitaque coniungi.

A comparison of the texts here will leave us in little doubt that Bonaventura is following *Julian*, whose narrative he copies almost verbatim.

Our study of the texts, then, compels us to admit that the account in *Julian*, though written there some five years after Celano had written his *Vita Prima*, is in fact the most primitive, and was deliberately used by Celano himself, by the compiler of the *Legenda Trium Sociorum* and by S. Bonaventura, in preference to any other source. There can only be one satisfactory explanation of this, which is that behind all our sources is a Lost Document, giving an account of the final stage in the conversion of S. Francis and of the coming of the first friars. This document was one of the written sources collected by Celano, and was certainly used by him. A few years later it was used by Julian of Speyer, whom we know to have been a compiler who adhered closely to his sources. As a result of this habit it is he who has given us the most faithful transcript of the lost document. Later the writer of the *Leg. 3 Soc.* and S. Bonaventura both had access to this primitive source.

As, therefore, Julian and Bonaventura both deserted Celano for this earlier document, we can only suppose that they regarded it as having a very high authority ; and, since it deals with an intimate moment in S. Francis's life, the probability is that it came from one of his closest friends. It is indeed at least possible that this Lost Document told not only the story of S. Francis's acceptance of the apostolic injunctions and of the coming of Bernard, Sylvester and Giles, but that it also went on to give an account of the journey which Francis and Giles made together to the Marches of Ancona and of the other early expeditions which were undertaken [1] If this were so it would be permissible to suggest the name of Brother Giles as the author. We have already accepted the fact that it must have been written by someone of great authority such as that in which Giles was always held ; and if it did, originally, include the story of the expedition to the Marches of Ancona, then the information must have come from either Giles or Francis himself. Further reasons for connecting it with Giles are (1) the fact

---

[1] Cf. *Leg. 3 Soc.* 33–40, all of which may come from this primitive source.

that at the moment when he quotes from this document Bonaventura says that he knows Giles personally ; and (2) that Wadding associates the salutation " *Dominus det tibi pacem* ", which is mentioned in this passage, with Brother Giles.[1]   Giles must have been one of the " faithful and approved witnesses " visited by Celano in collecting his material for the *Vita Prima*.   What more likely than that Giles wrote for him an account of the early events in which he himself played so important a part, and that this account was preserved among the friars' books at Assisi to be used afterwards by both Julian and Bonaventura, and to have been destroyed in 1266 when so much precious material perished ?

[1] Cf. Bonaventura, *Leg. Maior*, iii, 4 ; Wadding, *Annales, ad an.* 1209.

V

THE *SCRIPTA LEONIS ET SOCIORUM EIUS*

THOMAS OF CELANO published his *Vita S. Francisci* between 1229 and 1231, and for several years it remained the official biography of the Saint. There are, it is true, some shorter lives which were written during this period, but they all derive from *1 Celano* and give us no new information of any importance. Probably the earliest of them was the *Officium Rhythmicum* by Julian of Speyer, which was written in 1231-2 [1] and was followed a year or two later by the *Vita S. Francisci*, [2] which is little more than an abridgement of *1 Celano*. A little later John of Ceperano, a papal notary, wrote a Life which has unfortunately been lost, though a liturgical résumé of it, known as *Quasi stella matutina*, which took its name from the text of Gregory's sermon at the Canonisation of S. Francis, [3] has been preserved. [4] A more interesting experiment was the *Legenda Versificata* by Henry of Avranches, poet laureate to Henry III of England, which was finished about 1232 and dedicated to Gregory IX. [5] Besides these, there are certain minor liturgical works and *Legendae* by various writers, all of which belong to this period.

To us it must seem strange that the intimate friends of S. Francis— men like Leo, Bernard of Quintavalle and Pacifico, the *Rex Versuum*— did not write anything to supplement the narrative of Celano. Their minds must have been full of reminiscences of things which Francis had said, incidents of which they had been witnesses, wonderful works which they had seen and the memories of which they treasured. Sabatier would have us believe that Leo did indeed forestall even Celano by writing the *Speculum Perfectionis* as early as 1227; but it has been demonstrated over and over again that Sabatier was mistaken

[1] Published by the Quaracchi Fathers in *An. F.*, X, fasc. iv, No. 1.

[2] Published in *An. Boll.*, xxi, and re-edited in *An. F.*, X, iv, 1.

[3] *Ecclus.*, i, 6-7 : *Quasi stella matutina in medio nebulae, et quasi luna plena in diebus suis lucet ; et quasi sol refulgens, sic ille effulsit in templo Dei.*

[4] This was published by d'Alençon in 1899 under the title *Legenda brevis S. Francisci.* It is mentioned by Bernard of Bessa, cf. *An. F.*, III, p. 666.

[5] Published by Cristofani as *Il più antico poema della vita di San Francesco* in 1882, and now republished in *An. F.*, X, iv, 2. For a discussion of this work see Bihl in *A.F.H.*, xxii, and notes by d'Alencon in *Misc. Franc.*, iv, v and vi.

in this, and that the *Speculum* is an early fourteenth-century compilation.

The *Vita Prima* of Celano, then, with all its imperfections, held undisputed priority in giving to the world an account of the life and teaching of S. Francis until, in 1244, an attempt was made to supplement it out of the reminiscences of those who had known the Saint in his life. But before we come to a consideration of this further step we must trace the history and development of the Order during the years between 1228 and 1244 if we are rightly to understand both the necessity for a new *Life* and the form which it took.

During these sixteen years the dominant figure is that of Brother Elias. We have already seen something of his activity in securing a shrine which would serve as a centre for countless pilgrimages and bring perpetual fame and revenue to the town of Assisi. It was in order to have leisure to pursue this end that he stood down in 1227 and allowed the somewhat colourless John Parenti to be elected Minister General. But though Parenti might be the official governor of the Order, we notice that it was Elias who negotiated for the site of the new Basilica, and that it was he and not the Minister General who sent out the appeals for money for the building of the church and convent. But this was not the end of his activities.

In the year 1230 three very important events took place. The first was the Translation of the body of S. Francis from the little church of S. Giorgio to the new Basilica which was now ready to receive it. What exactly took place it is a little difficult for us now to understand. We have three sources of information : a Bull of Gregory's issued to the Bishops of Assisi and Spoleto,[1] a passage in the *Chronica XXIV Generalium*,[2] and the *Speculum Vitae*,[3] a somewhat later compilation ; but there are certain discrepancies in their various accounts. It appears that vast numbers were assembling at Assisi for this most important occasion, but that the Podestà, with the approval and assistance of Elias, secretly transferred the body to its new burial-place, thus not only depriving the crowds of a sight of the Stigmata which many of them had made long journeys to see, but also taking away the opportunity of making this the occasion for a great religious ceremony. The action of Elias and the Podestà caused great indignation, and Elias had to face an angry Chapter Meeting a few days later. Again, it is a little difficult to sort out the contradictory reports which have been preserved ; but it appears that after the opposition to Elias had spent itself and he had gone off to do penance, the Chapter fell to discussing the future of the Order, with special reference to the very urgent problem of the authority of the Testament of S. Francis

---

[1] Sbaralea, *Bull. Franc.*, I, p. 66.   [2] *An. F.*, III, p. 212.
[3] *Speculum Vitae*, f. 168a.

and the interpretation of Absolute Poverty as it was promulgated in the Rules which Francis had drawn up. The outcome of this meeting was an appeal to the Pope for guidance.

Gregory replied in the famous Bull, *Quo elongati*, of September 28th, 1230.[1] This Bull did more than anything else to shape the future policy of the Order and to lead it away from the strict and unflinching renunciation which S. Francis had enjoined, towards a manner of living much nearer to the practice of the monastic Orders. The first problem was that of the authority of the Testament. This, as we have seen, was the last appeal of S. Francis to the brothers to stand fast in the Poverty, Simplicity and Humility which he had so eagerly sought in his own life. Distressed beyond measure at the falling away of so many of the brothers from the high standard which he had set, he was determined to make this final effort to hold them together in the idealism for which he had contended. " *Haec est recordatio, admonitio et exhortatio et meum testamentum quod ego, frater Franciscus parvulus, facio vobis fratribus meis benedictis.*" But Elias and others were perfectly aware that an appeal is not the same thing as a command, and that even a last Will and Testament, touching and persuasive though it may be, has not the same authority as a papal Bull. The Testament of S. Francis did, however, present a very real difficulty ; for the legally-minded felt uncomfortable about its binding power, the companions of the Saint were inclined to treat it as of even greater authority than the *Regula Bullata*, while members of the relaxing party wanted to ignore it altogether. It was essential, therefore, that some authoritative statement about it should be issued.

Secondly, the whole future of the Order depended upon the interpretation of Absolute Poverty. The Rule of 1223, like its predecessors, said that the friars were to live " *sine proprio* ". But what did that mean ? They could not go about naked : they must have clothes. And if clothes, why not houses to live in and books to read ? No one can expropriate himself to the extent of having nothing at all : where, then, is the line to be drawn ? And again, the things which Francis condemned were money and possessions ; but this was not to say that the friars might not have the *use* of such things if they tended to the edification of themselves and of the Church, so long as they did not claim them as their property.

Gregory's task was no enviable one. On the one hand, he had the extremists who would hear of no departure from the strictest poverty, and who were content that the Order should continue as a band of homeless evangelists, " *idiotae et subditi omnibus* ". On the other hand, there were those who quite frankly hoped that the Order would develop on Benedictine or Dominican lines with the establishment of

[1] Sbaralea, *Bull. Franc.*, I, pp. 68–70.

large convents and the growth of scholarship. In between the extremists were probably the majority of the brethren who realised that some change and decay from the idealism of S. Francis was inevitable, but who yet cherished the hope that the Friars Minor would preserve their distinctive characteristics and remain the chief body-guard of Lady Poverty.

To these problems Gregory addressed himself in the Bull, *Quo elongati.* He decided, first, that the Testament of S. Francis could not be regarded as binding on the brothers because it had been drawn up by Francis alone without taking the advice of the Ministers, and because he had no power to commit his successor without his consent. Secondly, on the interpretation of the " *sine proprio* " clause in the Rule it is clear that the brothers must have houses to live in ; but as for furniture and books, the Rule will not allow them to *own* such things, though that is not to say that they may not have the *use* of them so long as they are officially and legally the property of someone else, such as the Cardinal-protector of the Order. Again, if the friars are in need of something, or have run into debt (!),[1] they may get some friend of the Order to pay for their necessities or to settle their accounts as a form of almsgiving, while gifts of money may always be deposited with an intermediary for future needs. Thus Gregory, in gentle and persuasive terms, and with many indications of the love and respect which he bore for the memory of S. Francis, quietly destroys the very foundations upon which Francis had built, and shatters his whole ideal.

This Bull was, of course, regarded as a triumph by the relaxing party ; and Elias felt that the opportunity had been given him to take things now into his own hands. At the Chapter Meeting of 1232 he persuaded a number of his supporters to carry him bodily into the midst of the brethren and demand his election as Minister General. A noisy scene seems to have followed, in the course of which John Parenti was observed to be quietly taking off his clothes. This was interpreted as a sign of resignation, and Elias was duly elected to succeed him. He immediately adopted a show of modesty in declaring that he was quite unworthy of so high a dignity, and that his poor health would not allow of his setting a good example to the others in the keeping of the Rule. To this the brothers replied that if he would only accept the position he should have a horse to ride and gold to eat if he wished. Elias appealed to the Pope, who ratified the election on the grounds that Elias had been a personal friend of S. Francis and was therefore a very suitable person to be Minister General.[2]

---

[1] " *Si rem necessariam velint fratres emere, vel solutionem facere pro iam empta.*"

[2] Cf. Lempp, *Élie de Cortone,* pp. 92–3 ; Scudder, *The Franciscan Adventure,* p. 89 ; Gratien, *Histoire de la Fondation, etc.,* p. 141 ; Jordano, *Chronica,* cap. 61 ; Eccleston, *De Adventu* (ed. Little), p. 79.

Elias held the office of Minister General from 1232 to 1239. During this time the principles enunciated in *Quo elongati* developed rapidly. The building, furnishing and decoration of the Basilica at Assisi went on apace,[1] more and more convents were being built in the towns, and the Order was growing enormously in public estimation, Elias receiving gifts from several of the crowned heads of Europe and enjoying an international reputation. Meanwhile encouragement was given to the friars to equip themselves more fully, by the study of theology, for the work of confuting heresy, and of preaching not only on the more elementary subjects of prayer and ethics, but on dogma and the sacraments.

Naturally the *zelanti* were appalled by all this ; but they seem to have kept very quiet, for the overthrow of Elias in 1239 was brought about not by them but by the moderates and the scholars. The chief causes of their opposition were the old ones of professional jealousy and dislike of interference. Elias seems to have had a domineering manner which they greatly resented,[2] and they naturally retaliated by finding fault with the opulence of his private life—living in a fine house at Cortona, keeping a stable, riding out attended by pages in livery, taking his meals apart like a Benedictine abbot, employing a first-class chef, and (most outrageous of all) was he not dabbling in alchemy ? [3] Still more exasperating was his method of government. In the seven years of his generalate he summoned no meeting of the Chapter General, preferring to act in a dictatorial and highly offensive way by using a host of " visitors " whom he sent round all the provinces, spying (as his critics would say) on the provincial Ministers. Again, he largely increased the number of the provinces and appointed almost exclusively laymen to positions of authority. Finally, his interminable exactions and levies for the building of the Basilica were a constant source of irritation, especially to those in the more remote provinces.

By the beginning of 1239 opposition to Elias was taking active form ; and, after various representations had been made to the Pope by disgruntled ministers, and a deputation led by Aymon of Faversham, a Chapter was at last summoned for Whitsuntide of that year. The meeting, like others before it, was a stormy one. All the indignation that had been bottled up for seven years, and to which a wiser man would have given vent long before, burst out. The Pope, seeing that

---

[1] The Upper Church had advanced sufficiently by 1236 to enable Giunta Pisano to begin work on the frescoes. Three years later the bells were hung in the campanile, to the great delight of Salimbene and others.

[2] Lempp, *Élie de Cortone*, pp. 118 and 119, n. 1.

[3] Most of this comes from Salimbene. Cf. *Chronica* in *Mon. Germ. Hist.* (*Scriptores*), xxxii, pp. 96 ff. Salimbene is not always very trustworthy, so cf. Lempp, *op. cit.*, pp. 121 ff. ; Gratien, *op. cit.*, p. 143, and *An. F.*, III, pp. 44 and 229.

he would have to take a firm hand, reprimanded the brothers for their very unfranciscan behaviour, compelled them to sit for a while in complete silence while they thought over their misdeeds, and then explained that he had allowed Elias to become Minister General because of his friendship with S. Francis, thinking that it was the wish of the Order as a whole. As, however, that was clearly no longer the case, he had no hesitation in relieving him of his office. The brothers replied by bursting into the *Te Deum*.

Having got rid of Elias, the brothers proceeded to elect Albert of Pisa as Minister General; but he survived for only eight months, and was succeeded in his turn by Aymon of Faversham, an Englishman. During the four years in which he held office further drastic changes were made in the government of the Order. By making the conditions of entry so severe that the recruiting of laymen practically ceased, and by prohibiting lay brothers from holding office, it may truly be said of him that " he put the seal on the transformation of the family of S. Francis from a spontaneous lay fellowship into an Order of clerks and priests ".[1]

As we look back over the years since the death of S. Francis we see that many and great changes have come over the Order. Instead of a band of vagrants, dependent upon the charity of their neighbours for their very existence and living in huts " of clay and wattles made " or in cells hewn out of the living rock, we see now something approaching a monastic Order, with its great Basilica and cloister at Assisi, its big churches and well-furnished convents in other cities, its libraries rapidly accumulating, and its standard of living everywhere being raised. Moreover, the express wishes of S. Francis that his brothers should have no concern with scholarship have been set aside, for Friars Minor are becoming more and more conspicuous at the great Universities such as Bologna, Paris and Oxford.[2] Perhaps John Parenti was partly responsible for this by his appointment of a *lector* from the schools of Paris to teach the brothers in the provinces of Germany.[3] It was certainly encouraged by the Pope, who had deliberately included books among those things of which the brothers might have the use when he had made his great declaration in 1230. Besides, he had always wanted to treat the friars as supplementary to the parochial clergy, many of whom were ignorant and totally unfitted to deal with the new learning which was beginning to spread outwards and downwards from the Universities.

All these developments could only be carried through, of course, if a certain liberty were taken with the wishes of S. Francis as expressed

[1] Scudder, *Franciscan Adventure*, p. 102; cf. Gratien, *La Fondation*, etc., pp. 111 and 153.
[2] Gratien, *La Fondation*, etc., p. 145.   [3] Jordano, *Chronica*, cap. 54.

in the Testament. That is why the Bull, *Quo elongati*, is so important. Before questions of poverty and privilege are discussed the Order must be clear as to the authority of the Testament. Hence, when Gregory wrote the words, " *ad mandatum illud vos dicimus non teneri* ", he was sealing the fate of the Order. Other interpretations such as that drawn up by the Four Masters of Theology in 1242 [1] and the Bull, *Ordinem Vestrum*,[2] of 1245, only carried the same policy a little further.

Throughout these years of change we hear little of the original friends of S. Francis. Scattered about in remote hermitages, they mourned the flouting of their master's wishes and the deterioration of the Order. Occasionally they appear on the stage, but our accounts of their performances are not always to be trusted. Angelo Clareno, writing his *Historia Septem Tribulationum* about 1320, has some stories to tell ; but he has so often been proved wrong that one does not know what to believe.[3] There is, of course, the notorious story of Leo coming to Assisi and breaking the marble vase which Elias had set up to receive money towards the building of the Basilica, and being afterwards flogged and banished by Elias ; but the authority for this is often disputed.[4] There is, however, a delightful story of Brother Giles being shown round the new convent at Assisi and remarking dryly : " All you want now is a few women. If you've given up poverty, why not give up chastity as well ? " [5] Bernard of Quintavalle was able to chaff Elias for the luxurious way in which he lived ; but behind the wit and the grace there was a sting which Elias felt deeply but dare not attack.[6]

Whether or not Clareno is right in his description of the persecution of the *zelanti* by Elias,[7] nothing can have pained them more than the course which events in the Order were taking. Yet it was not the *zelanti* who opposed Elias and brought about his downfall. In the spirit of their master they harboured no desire for revenge. All that they cared for was the memory of S. Francis. But to the majority of the friars, and even to some of those who held high office, Francis meant very little. They had never known him intimately : some had never even seen him. They knew that he was a saint, of course, and

[1] Published in an interesting collection of Franciscan documents called *Firmamentum Trium Ordinum Beatissimi Patris Francisci* (Paris, 1512), ff. xviib *et seqq.*

[2] Sbaralea, *Bull. Franc.*, I, pp. 401 f.

[3] Felice Tocco in his edition of *Le Due Prime Tribolazioni* (Rome, 1908) points out a number of glaring mistakes. Cf. pp. 103 ff.

[4] *An. F.*, III, p. 89.   [5] *Ibid.*, p. 90.

[6] Wadding, *Annales, ad an.* 1230 (Vol. ii, p. 241).

[7] According to the *Hist. VII Trib.*, Caesarius of Speyer was imprisoned and eventually clubbed to death, twelve friars were unfrocked and flogged, and Bernard was caught and imprisoned. Wadding repeats all this, *ad an.* 1239 (Vol. iii, p. 21).

that he had been stigmatised as an especial mark of his sanctity ; but
of the stories of his life and conversation what had they except the
narrative of Celano ?

So it came about that a desire gradually made itself felt among the
friars for a new Life of S. Francis ; and when the Chapter General
met at Genoa in 1244, under the presidency of Crescentius of Iesi,
the newly-appointed Minister General, this desire became a definite
request, and there went out from this meeting an invitation to all
the brothers to send in writing " *quidquid de vita, signis et prodigiis beati
Francisci scire veraciter possent* ".[1]   This invitation was eagerly accepted
by three men who had been intimate friends of the Saint : Leo,
Angelo and Rufino.   Gathered together at the hermitage of Greccio,
they saw that here was the chance for which they had waited so long.
Now they would give to the world a picture of S. Francis as they
had known him in his joys and in his sorrows ; now the world should
have a chance of knowing what his real wishes were : surely this
would bring the Order to its senses and ensure that the idealism of the
Saint should be more faithfully kept in the future.

For two whole years they worked away at the collection of tales
and reminiscences which they proposed to send in to Crescentius.
And when their work was done they included, with their packet of
" *rotuli et cedulae* ", an Introductory Letter in which they describe
their method of working.   " It has seemed good to us," they write,
" who, though unworthy, were with him for some time, to send to
you an account of some of the things which were done by him which
we either saw ourselves or have heard of from other holy brothers—
chiefly Brother Philip . . . Brother Illuminato da Arce, Brother
Masseo, Brother John the companion of the venerable Brother Giles
. . . and Brother Bernard of sacred memory—not content just to tell
of miracles, which shew but do not make holiness,[2] but rather to set
forth examples of his holy life and the intention of his holy will. . . .
And these things we write not in the manner of a Legend, seeing that
for a long time legends of his life and the miracles which God performed through him have been put together.   But rather, as from
a fair meadow we have plucked a few flowers which in our opinion
seemed the most beautiful, not following any consecutive story, but
leaving out many things which should follow one another since they
have already been so truthfully and so elegantly set forth in the said
legends." [3]

But when we turn to the so-called *Legenda Trium Sociorum*, which,

---

[1] *An. F.*, III, p. 262.

[2] They have taken this phrase from *1 Celano* 70, see *supra*, p. 63.

[3] *Leg. 3 Soc.*, Intro. Letter.   The " said legends " would be *1 Celano, Julian of Speyer,*
and probably some others which have since perished.

in the manuscripts, accompanies this letter, we recognise immediately
that it cannot possibly be the collection of disconnected stories put
together by Leo and his companions ; and, in spite of the attempts
which have been made to supplement the *Leg. 3 Soc.* in order to make it
fit in with the Introductory Letter, it is perfectly clear that the Letter
and the Legend which follow it are entirely independent of each other.
We have already made some suggestions as to how the *Leg. 3 Soc.*
came to be written. The question which we now have to examine is :
Is there any chance of discovering the real *Florilegium* which originally
accompanied the letter of the Three Companions ?

In order to answer this question we must turn to the five documents
which are all more or less based on the material sent in to Assisi in
1245–6. These are : (1) the *Vita Secunda* of Thomas of Celano,
published in 1247 and bearing the *Imprimatur* of the Minister General ;
(2) the *Speculum Perfectionis*, which exists in two " states ", a shorter
and earlier one which is to be found in the S. Isidore MS. No. 1/73,
which was published by Fr. Lemmens in his *Documenta Antiqua
Franciscana* in 1902, and the longer one which Sabatier edited in 1898
and again in 1926–7 ; (3) two small tracts, also from the S. Isidore
MS., called *Verba S. Francisci* and *Intentio Regulae* ; (4) the collection
known as *Legenda Antiqua S. Francisci* from the Perugian MS. No. 1046
which has been edited by Fr. Delorme ; and (5) the manuscript which
is now in the possession of Dr. Little and has been published in the
Collectanea Franciscana.[1]

Since all these documents are largely based on the material sent in
to Assisi in 1245–6, they have naturally much in common. A glance
at the admirable tables supplied by Dr. Little in his pamphlet " *Some
recently discovered Franciscan Documents* ", published by the British
Academy in 1926, will show that many stories are common to all the
five compilations, and that a great many appear in more than one
" state ". Much work has been done in comparing these various
narratives, but it still remains to indicate which can be regarded as
originals and which are later recensions. For we must remember that,
somewhere in Assisi, lay a mass of papers sent in by friars in response
to the general invitation of 1244 ; and that it was from these papers
that the various compilations were made. Fortunately for us, the
method of the medieval chronicler was very different from ours. He
was not concerned with telling the story in his own words, but was
often content to compile a *legenda* by simply copying out, sometimes
word for word, passages from the sources upon which he was working.

---

[1] In the following pages I shall use the abbreviations devised by Burkitt, viz. :
Sp. S. = *Spec. Perf.* ed. Sabatier ; *Sp. L.* = *Spec. Perf.* ed. Lemmens ; *Per.* = the
Perugian MS., and *Little* = Dr. Little's MS.

This " scissors-and-paste " method is of very great help to us when we come to compare these several narratives, for it means that we have often two or three versions of the same incident, from a comparison of which we can often determine which is the original account and which are later editions.

Our first task, then, is to examine closely every story told in these five documents, to take note of the position which it occupies in the manuscript, and to see whether it can be accepted as an " original " or not. In these five collections there are altogether 279 different stories or chapters, of which 116 appear only in one document, whereas the remaining 163 are told in two or more of the compilations. This does not necessarily mean that they appear in more than one " state " as some of them have been merely copied out verbatim by one scribe from another. Of the 116 which have no parallels elsewhere, 93 are in *2 Celano*, 4 in *Sp. S.*, one in *Sp. L.* and the rest in *Little*. The numbers are as follows : *2 Celano* 26, 27, 29, 30, 32, 33, 34, 42, 43, 46, 47, 52, 53, 54, 55, 66, 67, 68, 70, 71, 78, 79, 80, 82, 83, 93, 94, 95, 97, 98, 99, 102, 104, 107, 109, 112, 116, 117, 118, 121, 134, 135, 136, 137, 138, 139, 140, 142, 147, 149, 154, 156, 162, 163, 164, 167, 168, 169, 170, 172, 173, 174, 177, 178, 179, 180, 182, 183, 189, 191, 192, 193, 194, 197, 198, 199, 202, 203, 204, 205, 206, 207, 209, 210, 211, 212, 218, 219, 220, 221, 222, 223, 224 ; *Sp. S.* 78, 83, 84, 120 ; *Sp. L.* 45 ; and *Little* 94, 134–9, 141–3, 145, 146, 178, 180–3, 199. To these we must add 27 chapters of *2 Celano* which have obviously been transcribed by the compiler of *Per*. (viz. *2 Cel*. 56, 60, 65, 69, 86, 87, 88, 89, 103, 113, 114, 127, 148, 150, 153, 155, 157, 159, 161, 175, 184, 185, 186, 188, 195 and 208), thus bringing our number up to 143, and leaving us with 136 which appear in more than one version.

These 136 chapters are divided up as follows :

i. *Intentio Regulae* and its parallels	16 chapters.
ii. *Verba S. Francisci* and its parallels	6 chapters.
iii. *Per.* 21 and its parallels	1 chapter.
iv. *Per.* 42–97 and their parallels	65 chapters.
v. *Per.* 102–15b and their parallels	19 chapters.
vi. *Sp. L.* 6 and 8–19 and their parallels	13 chapters.
vii. *Sp. S.* 52, 79, 85 and their parallels	3 chapters.
viii. *Little* 153b–5, 187, 194–5, 197 and their parallels	7 chapters.
ix. *Sp. S.* 6, *Per.* 18, *2 Cel.* 106, 125 and 201, and *Little* 125 and their parallels	6 chapters.

i. *The Intentio Regulae.*
This little collection of intimate stories of S. Francis has been published by Fr. Lemmens in Vol. ii of his *Documenta Antiqua Franciscana*, from the S. 'Isidore MS. 1/73. The whole of it appears also in *Per.* (98–101) and in *Sp. S.*, though here in a totally different order. Most of it is also included in *Little* and *2 Cel.* Professor Burkitt has already shown convincing reasons for supposing this to be one of the " rolls " sent in by Brother Leo in 1246.

ii. *Verba S. Francisci.*

This comes from the same source as the *Intentio Regulae*. The parallels with the other documents are as follows :

Verba 1 =	Per. 14 =	2 Cel. —	= Sp. S. 12 =	Little 86
2	15	—	13	87
3	38	208	76	121
4	16	—	1	81
5	17	—	68	114
6	19	—	50	105

There is surely very little doubt that we have here another collection of stories compiled by one of the friars. The state in which we know it is probably not that in which it originally appeared, as a study of its contents and the parallels with other documents show that it has suffered at the hands of later scribes. For example, in the S. Isidore MS. the collection begins with the word "*item*", which suggests that the beginning is mutilated. Again, No. 3, the description of the Rule, appears to be an interpolation, taken from *2 Cel.* and inserted into the tract by the scribe of S. Isidore. It is not included in the quotations from the *Verba* in Angelo Clareno's *Expositio Regulae*. This chapter is so short and so aphoristic that it may well represent a solitary *dictum* of S. Francis which was widely known. Chapter 6 of the *Verba* is not in S. Isid. 1/73, but is taken by Lemmens from the quotations in *Clareno*. In the S. Isidore MS. three chapters from *Sp. S.* (52, 79 and 85) take its place. Dr. Little considers these as part of the original roll, but this is open to doubt. We shall see later some reasons for believing that these three chapters formed a small tract sent in by one of the brothers.

The evidence, in fact, points to the original *Verba* consisting of No. 1, 2, 4, 5 and 6. Not only is this the original sequence given by Clareno and attributed by him to Brother Leo, but it is also the order in *Per.* However, between Nos. 5 and 6 *Per.* inserts *2 Cel.* 146 (= *Per.* 18). Dr. Little suggests that Leo himself may have put this into his tract and regards it as a Celanese version of *Verba* 6, but I find this very hard to accept.

The suggestion which I would make is that the *Verba* is a Leo-paper, most likely in imperfect condition. It was probably not part of the *Scripta Leonis* to which the Introductory Letter of *Leg. 3 Soc.* refers, as it lacks the distinguishing marks of the rest of that document, and does not appear to have been known to Celano, who was the official biographer and therefore had access to all available material. It is quite likely that it was written by Leo and circulated long before 1246. The fact that *Per.* has inserted an extra chapter may be explained by his using a different copy from that known to Clareno, a copy into which someone had already inserted *2 Cel.* 146 because of the similarity between it and *Verba* 5.

iii. *Per. 21.*

This chapter comes at the end of section A of the Perugian MS. and is almost identical with *Sp. S.* 88 and similar to *Sp. L.* 34 and *Little* 186. When we examine the two versions closely it is not difficult to see which is the original. In *Per.* 21, after telling how Francis broke bread with the brothers in imitation of what Christ did on Maundy Thursday, we are told that it was not really a Thursday at all when this incident occurred, but some other day : "*hoc manifeste considerare possumus, quia, cum esset alia dies quam feria quinta, ipse dixit fratribus quod credebat feriam quintam esse*". This is a very natural and credible explanation. Francis made a mistake about the day, and when this was pointed out to him he said : "Oh, I thought it was Thursday to-day." But it is altogether too naïve for the scribe of *Sp. L.*, who writes : "*hoc manifeste considerare possumus, quia, cum esset alia dies quam feria quinta, ipse dixit fratribus reservari particulam unam de illo pane.*"

iv. *Per. 42–97.*

This long section must be divided up into five parts : 42–8, 49–58, 59–91, 92–5 and 96–7.

(a) *Per.* 42–8 appears twice in the S. Isidore MS., once in a collection known as *De Legenda Veteri b. Francisci* 1–7, and once as part of the *Speculum Perfectionis* (*Sp. L.* 24–7). The parallels are as follows :

Per. 42 = *Leg. Vet.* 1 = *Sp. L.* 24		
43	2	25a
44	3	25b
45	4	26
46	5	—
47	6	—
48	7	27

It appears, therefore, that we have here a little collection of stories which has survived as a complete whole. It was copied out by the scribe of *Per.* and by both the scribes who worked on the S. Isidore MS., one of whom wrote the first 78 folios, and the other the remaining 117. The question of the author of this tract will be discussed later.

(b) *Per.* 49–58 is again pretty closely followed by *Sp. L.* 28–33. A study of the contents shows us that *Per.* 55 is obviously an interpolation. After two stories about the Portiuncula, two about S. Francis's sojourn at Siena in the spring of 1226, and then two more about the Portiuncula, the scribe goes on to a story of the Marches of Ancona (*Per.* 55). Then he starts No. 56 with the words, " *in eodem loco S. Mariae* ", which obviously refers to the Portiuncula. It should be observed that neither *Per.* 55 nor 56 appears in *Sp. L.* An examination of this sequence of chapters shows them to be uniform in style, and that many of them are linked together by such phrases as " *in illis diebus* ", " *iisdem temporibus* ", or " *in eodem loco* ". We are probably therefore justified in regarding these ten chapters (with the exception of No. 55) as one of the *rotuli* sent in to Crescentius in 1246.

(c) *Per.* 59–91 forms the whole of section D of the Perugian MS. Burkitt has shown good grounds for accepting it not only as a complete whole, but also as one of the rolls sent in by Brother Leo. We shall return to this matter later.

(d) *Per.* 92–5. The parallels here are as follows :

Per. 92a = *Sp. L.* — = *Little* — = 2 *Cel.* 77			
92b	1	—	72–3
93	2	93	73
94	2–3	—	75
95	—	147	76

Is this another original sequence ? There seem to be reasons for accepting it as such, though there are signs that it has been revised. For example, it is difficult to know how it originally began. It will be noticed that both *Sp. L.* and *Little* omit *Per.* 92a. Is *Per* 92a therefore an addition to the original ? I think not ; for 92a begins with a most careful statement of time and place (*post reversionem de Senis et de Cella Cortonae venit b. Franciscus apud ecclesiam S. Mariae de Portiuncula et postea ivit ad manendum in loco Bagnariae super civitatem Nucerii* . . . etc.), whereas 92b begins : " *nam b. Franciscus* . . ." But why the scribe of *Sp. L.* should omit the first chapter of his source it is impossible to say, unless it was mutilated. A further proof of the integrity of *Per.* 92–5 is furnished by 2 *Celano*. At § 71 of the *Vita Secunda* Celano begins a section entitled " *De Petenda Eleemosyna* ". § 71 is editorial, 72 is a very much shortened form of *Per.* 92b, 73 is a Celanese version of *Per.* 93, 74 is taken from *Per.* 43 and is suggested by the thought of Christ's poverty in the previous chapter, 75–7 are Celanese versions of *Per.* 94, 95 and 92a, and 78 and 79 are stories for which there is no parallel in the other documents. Celano has therefore taken the sequence in *Per.* almost as it stands into his *Vita Secunda.*

(e) *Per.* 96 and 97. *Per.* 96 has quite clearly no connection with the preceding chapters. It is written in an entirely different style, much more literary and with the verb nearly always put at the end of the sentence. *Per.* 97 is in the style of the great section D of *Per.* It may have come from Brother Leo, but there is no real proof of this.

v. *Per. 102–15b.*

Up to *Per.* 105 we have a number of apparently disconnected chapters. *Per.* 102 is in a totally different style from the others, and tells how Francis used to impose a penance of so many *Paternosters* on the brothers who spoke idle or profane words. Neither in style nor in subject does it bear any resemblance to the writings of Brother Leo. *Per.* 103 is a long chapter, divided into four parts by Delorme, telling of how Francis decided to go on a missionary journey to France : how when they came to Arezzo, Sylvester was bidden to drive the devils out of the city ; and how, on reaching Florence, they found Ugolino there, who dissuaded them from going any further on their intended journey. *Per.* 104 tells how S. Francis said that he ought to be glad if he were mocked at by the Chapter for his ignorance and stupidity ; and *Per.* 105 is the story of how Francis tamed the cicada.

Per. 106 begins a series of chapters on Poverty and on the high ideals of S. Francis, and contains also an account of the state of the Order and the observance of the Rule. Nos. 106–10 and 112–15 run *pari passu* with *Sp. L.* 39–43 and 20–3. Whether or no the original source of this was two small tracts, represented by these two short series in *Sp. L.* with *Per.* 111 as an interpolation, it is impossible to say. What we can say with certainty is that there are many similarities of style between these chapters and the *Scripta Leonis,* some of which we shall examine later.

vi. *Sp. L. 6 and 8–19.*

The parallels with *Sp. L.* 6 are *Per.* 98b, *Sp. S.* 26c and *Little* 95. When we examine these we shall find that *Per.* 98b is composed of No. 3 of the *Intentio Regulae* with a short story inserted into it. This short story, which tells us how in the early days of the Order S. Francis sent one of the brothers out to greet everyone with the salutation, " *Dominus det tibi pacem* ", forms No. 6 of Lemmens' *Speculum.*

As for *Sp. L.* 8–19, this has every appearance of being a complete roll ; and Burkitt has already suggested that, like *Per.* D, it is one of the documents submitted by Leo in 1246.

vii. *Sp. S. 52, 79 and 85.*

These three chapters, though widely separated in the *Speculum Perfectionis,* are taken together because in the S. Isidore MS. they are attached to the *Verba S. Francisci* in place of No. 6 of that collection. When we examine their contents we find that they have one thing in common : each is a *list.* The first might be called " The Three Woes on the Brothers ", the second " The Four Privileges for the Friars ", and the third " In Praise of the Ten Good Friars ". They have every appearance of coming from one hand, from a man who had a mind for cataloguing. He was obviously one of the *zelanti,* for the brothers whom he selects for his praises were all, with one exception, members of that party, viz. Bernard, Leo, Angelo, Masseo, Giles, Rufino, Lucido, Roger and Juniper. The exception, John de Laudibus, was, according to Salimbene, a real terror to the Spirituals ; but this chapter deliberately suggests that he was not always like that, as it adds to his name the words : " *qui illo tempore* ".

In *Miscellanea Francesco Ehrle* (Vol. iii, p. 23) Burkitt has argued that the author of these three chapters may well be Brother Leo, since, in an earlier form of Chapter 85, preserved in the Antonio MS., a shorter version is preserved in which Leo's name is not mentioned. (Cf. *Archivum Franciscanum Historicum,* xii, pp. 321–401.) This, however, would not account for the mention of Leo by name in Chapter 52. Leo seems always to have been very reluctant to disclose his identity, even in the La Verna stories when he was so close to S. Francis.

On the whole I am inclined to believe that these three chapters were all written by some unknown friar with a particular but not uncommon type of mind. We can easily imagine him going his way among the hermitages of the brothers and saying : " Do you know the Three Woes which Christ pronounced on the brothers ? Ah, I see you don't. Then let me tell you " ; or " Do you know the Four Privileges which the Lord promised to the blessed Francis ? " And then one day his chance came of writing them down, and for some strange reason they got bound up with one of Brother Leo's rolls and so were included in the *Verba* by the scribe of S. Isidore.

viii. *Little 153b–5, 187, 194–5 and 197.*

These chapters are most important. Unlike almost everything else in *Little*, they appear in neither version of the *Speculum Perfectionis* nor in *Per.* (A few lines of *Little* 187 reappear in *Sp. L.* 34 and *Sp. S.* 47, but they are little more than an odd *dictum* of S. Francis and may quite well have come from some other source.) They were, however, known to Celano, who uses them all in the *Vita Secunda*.

Is it possible that we have here a little book which was known to Celano and to the scribe of *Little* but not to the compilers of *Sp. S., Sp. L.* and *Per.*? The external evidence certainly seems to point to this. When we look at the internal evidence the probability becomes even stronger. The stories are all written in the style of Brother Leo ; they contain such phrases as " *nos qui cum ipso fuimus* " (about which we shall have more to say later) ; and they are intimate stories of the Saint such as only a close friend could have written. 153b tells how S. Francis gave his tunic to a certain brother who seems to have been Leo himself ; 154 tells how Francis gave Leo the *cartula* on La Verna ; 155 is the account of how Francis wished to be stripped of his clothes shortly before his death ; 187 is the account of how Francis sent the brothers out to get him some parsley ; 194 tells of how Francis comforted the brother who was being bullied by his companion ; 195 is the story of the brother out of whom Francis drove the devils ; and 197 is the narrative of the pig which, having killed a lamb, sickened and died as a result of Francis having pronounced a curse upon it.

ix. *Sp. S. 6, Per. 18, 2 Cel. 106, 125 and 201, Little 125.*

Sp. S. 6 is the story of the ejection of the brothers from the house at Bologna. Another version occurs in *2 Cel.* 58. The style of *Sp. S.* is simpler than that of *Celano*, but Celano gives a detail, not in *Sp. S.*, to the effect that Francis was at the time on his way from Verona. The last sentence, " *et frater existens infirmus qui de ea domo tunc fuit eiectus testimonium perhibet de hiis et scripsit hoc* ", shows that we have here something very near to an original paper sent in by some brother with perhaps very vivid memories of the occasion. There is no means of saying whether *Celano* or *Sp. S.* is nearer to the original.

Per. 18 (= *2 Cel.* 146, *Little* 109, *Sp. S.* 54) has already been discussed in the notes on the *Verba S. Francisci.*

2 Cel. 106. The only other version of this story is *Little* 179. Neither version can be the original, which must have been written down by Brother Pacifico himself. Celano's version is written in his usual style, yet the account in *Little* omits several details of importance which must have stood in the original version. In the first part of the story Celano conceals the identity of the brother, referring to him simply as " *saecularis quidam* ", and explains that it was Francis who gave him the name of Pacifico. *Little*, on the other hand, and less naturally, calls him Pacifico from the beginning. Celano also gives us the information that the two men met at a monastery of poor nuns, whither Pacifico had gone on a visit to a relative. The fact that Bonaventura can tell us the name of the monastery—San Severino—suggests that he may have seen the original document. The only conclusion that one can come to is that neither *Celano* nor *Little* is an exact transcript of the original.

2 Cel. 125 has a certain affinity with *Per.* 115b, but is probably nothing more than a cento from a number of different sources, with a good deal of purely editorial matter included.

2 Cel. 201 is again a cento from various sources, some of which are represented by *Per.* 103a–b (= *Little* 189 and *Sp. S.* 65).

Little 125 is the story of S. Francis's prayer before the crucifix in San Damiano. If it is genuine it can only come from Francis himself. It seems more probable that it was a later tradition, and is perhaps of no great value. It appears also in *Fac secundum exemplar* (*Vat.* 4354).

Our task so far has been to get at the earliest versions of the various narratives which have come down to us. Some of them may be exact and literal copies of what was sent in to Assisi in 1245–6 ; others (especially those in *Celano*) have undoubtedly been largely rewritten and stylised. This may be regretted, but cannot, unless further documents come to light, be remedied. We may, however, admit that the majority of our " originals " are written in an extraordinarily simple and natural style, and are therefore probably very little changed from their first state.[1]

Our next task is a more difficult one, which is to see if we can find an author for at least some of these " originals ". To do this we must first summarise the external evidence which is at our disposal. To begin with, we know that in 1246 the Three Companions—Leo, Angelo and Rufino—sent in a collection of stories in response to the appeal issued by the Chapter of Genoa. They state in their letter that they have had the collaboration of several other brothers : Philip the Long, who, according to Celano, was the seventh to join the fraternity [2] ; Illuminato of Arce, near Rieti, who went with Francis to the East in 1219 ; Masseo of Marignano, one of the closest friends of the Saint ; John the companion of Giles, who gave much information which he had received from Giles himself ; and Bernard of Quintavalle, the first to attach himself to Francis as a disciple. With such names before us we should expect a very intimate account of the Saint, for these were the men who had most opportunity not only of knowing the details of his life, but also of appreciating his true intentions.

By August, 1246, Leo and his fellow-workers had finished their *Legenda* and sent it in. It was to be not a chronological " Life " of S. Francis, but a " Bundle of Memories " designed to illustrate his personality and ideals. This most precious of all Franciscan sources has, of course, long been lost ; but fortunately much, if not all, of it has been copied out by other scribes. The official historiographer, Thomas of Celano, certainly had the *Scripta Leonis* before him when he wrote his *Vita Secunda*, and we shall see later what use he made of it. But the question which concerns us at the moment is : What happened to the rolls and notes after Celano had finished with them ?

[1] See Appended Note A at end of this chapter.   [2] *1 Cel.* 25.

Here we turn to the famous *declaratio* of Ubertino da Casale.[1] In his *Arbor Vitae Crucifixae*, written in 1305, he not only quotes the sixteen chapters of the *Intentio Regulae* in full and in the order in which they appear in that tract, but he also gives us some very valuable information about his sources. Having told us, first, that he had obtained most of his information from Conrad of Offida, who was a personal friend of Brother Leo, he goes on to say that Leo wrote certain rolls : " *hoc ipsum in quibusdam rotulis manu sua conscriptis, quos commendavit in monasterio S. Clarae custodiendis ad futurorum memoriam, dicitur contineri. In illis, autem, multa scripsit sicut ex ore patris audiverat, in factis suis viderat ; in quibus magnalia continentur de stupendis sancti, et de futura corruptione regulae, et de futura renovatione ipsius, et de magnaliis circa regulae institutionem a Deo, et de intentione B. Francisci super observantiam regulae . . .*" Then he goes on to say : " *cum multo dolore audivi illos rotulos fuisse distractos, et forsitan perditos, maxime quosdam ex eis*". But he seems to have been mistaken, for a few years later he had these actual rolls before him, together with a book which he found in the brothers' library at Assisi. He now writes : " *(haec) solemniter conscripta (sunt) per manum fratris Leonis in libro qui habetur in armario fratrum de Assisio*" ; and " *haec omnia scripta sunt per manum fratris Leonis in libro qui est Assizii et in rotulis quos habemus*".[2] A little later, probably about 1320, Angelo Clareno, in writing his *Expositio Regulae*, quotes the *Verba S. Francisci* with the words : " *sicut frater Leo scribit*".[3] Meanwhile, in 1311, the compiler of the Perugian legend came to Assisi.[4] We know that he must have worked there, for he copies out several Bulls which were only to be found in the library of the Sacro Convento. What else did he find in the book-cupboard ? Was the precious manuscript of Brother Leo, the original " Legend of the Three Companions ", still there ? These are questions which can never be finally answered. Whatever the internal evidence, there must always remain an element of doubt ; but at least we can see in what direction that evidence points us.

My own belief is that the original legend of Leo, Angelo and Rufino, the legend to which the Introductory Letter of *Leg. 3 Soc.* refers, did, in fact, survive in the form of a number of rolls, one of which was used by Ubertino da Casale and by the scribe of the S. Isidore MS. 1/73 and is called *Intentio Regulae* ; and most, if not all, of which were seen and copied out by the compiler of the Perugian MS. But I would go further than that and suggest that the original *Scripta Leonis et Sociorum eius* consisted of the following :

---

[1] This *declaratio* has been often quoted, e.g. by Sabatier in *Spec. Perf.*, p. cxliii, and by Little in *Some recently discovered Franciscan documents*, p. 17.

[2] *A.L.K.G.*, iii, pp. 168 and 178.   [3] *Expositio Regulae*, ed. Livarius Oliger, p. 126.

[4] For a discussion of this date see below, p. 129.

L.S.F.A.   H

    a. Introductory Letter.
    b. Per. 42–58, mostly stories of the early years.
    c. Per. 92–95, miscellaneous stories.
    d. Per 103–105, miscellaneous stories.
    e. Per. 106–115, miscellaneous stories.
    f. Intentio Regulae, miscellaneous stories.
    g. Little 153b–5, 187, 194–5, 197, miscellaneous stories.
    h. Per. 59–91, mostly stories of the later years.
    i. Sp. L. 8–19, stories down to the day of Francis's death.

Turning now to the internal evidence, it is quite clear that the style of all these chapters is the same. The only exception is the Introductory Letter which is certainly more cultivated than the rest. But it is no unusual thing for an Introduction to be written in a different style from the remaining parts of a book, as may be seen in the Gospel according to S. Luke. In these *Scripta Leonis* a carefully written Introduction is followed by an easily-flowing narrative which is content to tell the stories in a simple and conversational style which anyone could read and enjoy.

Another point to be noticed about these chapters is the frequency with which the authors give some indication of the date and locality of the incidents which they are recording. Thus of the 116 chapters which make up the *Legenda*, 66 are traceable to a particular place—16 to the Portiuncula, 7 or 8 to the Bishop's palace at Assisi, 5 to Fonte Colombo, 5 to Rivo Torto, 4 to Rieti, 4 to Greccio, 2 to Rome, 4 to San Damiano, and 20 to various other places such as Poggio Bustone, Perugia, Cella di Cortona, La Verna, Siena, Arezzo, Florence, Borgo San Sepolcro, etc.[1] Of the same chapters, no less than 67 can be almost certainly dated, 23 belonging to the early days before 1215, 3 to 1217, 1 to 1218, 7 to 1220, 6 to 1223, 6 to 1224, 13 to 1225, 17 to 1226, while a further 14 obviously belong to the later years, though no actual date can be assigned.[2]

---

[1] The places either mentioned by name or indicated by the context are : *Portiuncula* (*Int.* 12, *Per.* 48a, 48b, 48c, 48d, 49, 53, 56, 57, 68, 89, 95, 103a, 104 and 105, *Sp. L.* 14 and possibly *Little* 187) ; *The Bishop's Palace at Assisi* (*Int.* 1 and 13, *Per.* 63 and 64, *Sp. L.* 8 and 9, *Little* 153b and possibly 194) ; *Fonte Colombo* (*Per.* 61, 81, 82, 83 and 90) ; *Rivo Torto* (*Per.* 42a, 45, 46, 88 and 94) ; *Rieti* (*Per.* 59, 85 and 91, *Sp. L.* 13) ; *Greccio* (*Per.* 66, 67, 69 and 114) ; *Rome* (*Per.* 112 and 115a) ; *S. Damiano* (*Per.* 77, 78, 79 and 80) ; *S. Fabriano* (*Per.* 60) ; *Celle di Cortona* (*Per.* 62) ; *Perugia* (*Per.* 70) ; *Assisi, or near it* (*Per.* 54, 72 and 74) ; *La Verna* (*Per.* 84b and 113 and *Little* 154) ; *Siena* (*Per.* 51 and 52) ; *The Valley of Spoleto* (*Per.* 58) ; *Between Siena and Assisi* (*Per.* 92a) ; *Arezzo* (*Per.* 103c) ; *Florence* (*Per.* 103d) ; *S. Eleutherius* (*Per.* 106) ; *Rocca Bricii* (*Per.* 109) ; *Borgo San Sepolcro* (*Per.* 110) ; *San Verecondo* (*Little* 197).

[2] The following chapters obviously belong to the early years, before about 1215 : *Int.* 3, *Per.* 42a, 42b, 43, 44, 45, 46, 48a, 48b, 48c, 49, 53, 54, 56, 57, 58, 72, 88, 92b, 94, 95 and 106, *Sp. L.* 12 ; to the year 1217 : *Per.* 103a and 103d and possibly 68 ; to the year 1218 : *Per.* 86 (?) ; to the year 1220 : *Int.* 5 and 9 (?), *Per.* 74 and 89, *Sp. L.* 14 (and perhaps *Per.* 48d and 104) ; to the year 1223 : *Int.* 6 and 16, *Per.* 75, 112, 115a

When we turn to consider details of style, we note first the characteristic phrase " *nos qui cum ipso fuimus* ", or words to that effect. Not only does it occur in the Introductory Letter, but it is to be found no less than eighteen times in the chapters which follow. It does not occur anywhere else in the early sources. The use of the expression in the *Scripta Leonis* is as follows : " *visum est nobis qui secum . . . fuimus* " (Intro. Letter), " *nos vero qui cum ipso fuimus* " (*Per*. 42b, 50 and *Int*. 16), " *nos vero qui fuimus cum beato Francisco* " (*Per*. 48b and *Sp. L*. 19), " *nos qui cum ipso fuimus* " (*Per*. 106, 89 and *Int*. 4), " *nos qui . . . ad diem mortis eius cum ipso fuimus* " (*Per*. 112), " *nos qui fuimus cum illo* " (*Per* 60, 84a, *Sp. L*. 15 and *Little* 187), " *nos qui fuimus cum ipso* " (*Per*. 76), " *nos qui fuimus cum beato Francisco* " (*Per*. 79 and 85), " *nos vero qui cum ipso eramus* " (*Per*. 83), and " *nos qui cum illo fuimus* " (*Per*. 84c).

Secondly, the authors are most insistent that what they are recording is the result of their own personal experience. Thus we get in the Introductory Letter the words " *pauca . . . quae per nos vidimus* " ; and then in *Per*. 60 : " *nos vidimus multa* " ; in *Per*. 76 : " *nos vidimus et audivimus* " ; in *Per*. 79 : " *nos oculis nostris vidimus* " ; in *Per*. 84a : " *sicut vidimus* " ; in *Per*. 89 : " *quae oculis nostris vidimus* " ; in *Sp. L*. 15 : " *hoc vidimus oculis nostris multoties* " ; in *Little* 187 : " *quae vidimus et cognovimus* ". With these we should compare *Per*. 57 : " *qui scripsit hoc vidit et testimonium perhibuit* " (probably a reference to one of the brothers mentioned in the Introductory Letter), *Per*. 72 : " *quem novimus et ab eo istud intelleximus* ", *Per*. 50 : " *multotiens audivimus* ", and *Int*. 4 : " *ab ore eius audivimus* ".

Hitherto everything suggests that the writers were in constant touch with S. Francis. The next phrase supports this theory. Over and over again we find the imperfect " *dicebat* ", and frequently the phrase " *unde* (or, *nam*) *saepe dicebat* " (*Per*. 69, 73, 86, 107b, *Int*. 9 and 16, *Sp. L*. 13). In *Per*. 94 and 113 it is varied by the expression " *multotiens dixit* " and in *Per*. 50 by " *multotiens dicens* ".

Again, S. Francis was constantly referring to the necessity of his setting a good example to the other brothers, the expression which he used being : " *oportet me esse formam et exemplum omnium fratrum* ". This phrase occurs in *Per*. 42b, 73, 93 and 106, while in *Per*. 49 it is applied to the Portiuncula : " *iste locus est forma et exemplum totius religionis* ".

Another characteristic expression in these chapters is that S. Francis

and 115b ; to the year 1224 : *Per*. 66, 67, 69 (?), 84b, and 113, *Little* 154 ; to the year 1225 : *Per*. 59, 60, 61, 77, 78, 79, 80, 81, 82, 83, 85, 90 and 91 ; to the year 1226 : *Int*. 1, 13 and 14, *Per*. 51, 52, 63 and 64, *Sp. L*. 8, 9, 10, 11, 17, 18 and 19, *Little* 153b and 187 (?) ; and to the later years generally : *Int*. 7, 8, 10, 11, 12, and 15, *Per*. 65, 73, 87, 107a, 107b, *Sp. L*. 15 and 16 and *Little* 155.

replied to someone " *cum magno fervore spiritus* ". It occurs in *Per.* 62, 92a, and 103d, *Int.* 5 and 11, *Sp. L.* 8 and 10.

Another thing of great interest to the authors was the frequency with which some prophecy of S. Francis was fulfilled " *ad litteram* ". Thus in *Per.* 69 we read : " *quomodo praedixerat . . . videntes ad litteram omnia impleta* " ; in *Per.* 70 : " *unde ad litteram de ipsis impletum fuit sicut praedixerat de eis beatus Franciscus* " ; in *Per.* 79 : " *cum praediceret . . . ad litteram fere fiebat* " ; in *Per.* 92a : " *ad litteram verum fuit sicut illis praedixerat* " ; in *Per.* 110 : " *ad litteram de puncto ad punctum* ", and in *Sp. L.* 17 : " *ad litteram de puncto ad punctum verum fuit quod de ipso praedixerat* " ; in *Little* 197 : " *ad litteram verum fuit sicut de ipsa praedixerat* ". With these we might compare *Int.* 6 : " *ad litteram sanctum evangelium observavit* ", and *Per.* 44 : " *ad litteram voluit observare formam sancti evangelii* ". The phrase recalls the famous scene at Fonte Colombo when we are told that Christ declared that the Rule was to be kept " *ad litteram, ad litteram, sine glossa, sine glossa, sine glossa* " (*Verba* 4).

We also find the authors most careful about details, especially topographical details. Here are a few examples out of many which could be quoted :

a. Int. 12 : " *iuxta cellam post domum in via* ".
b. Per. 46 : " *cella quae erat retro post domum* ".
c. Per. 51 : " *cella ubi post mortem eius oratorium pro ipsius reverentia fuit aedificatum* ".
d. Per. 62 : " *dum transiret per viam subtus quoddam castrum quod vocatur Limisianum prope locum fratrum de Pregio* ".
e. Per. 66 : " *cumque . . . separaret se a loco quantum iactus est lapidis* ".
f. Per. 69 : " *erat ibi cella una paupercula quae erat valde remota* ".
g. Per. 78 : " *cellula . . . quae erat facta ex storiis ex una parte illius domus* ".
h. Per. 114 : " *cella ultima post cellam maiorem* ".
i. Per. 105 : " *cella ultima iuxta sepem horti retro post domum* " (about which there could surely be no doubt !).

Besides topographical details, there are a great many other details introduced into the stories, from among which we give a few examples :

a. Per. 59 : this tells of the curfew at Rieti which was marked by the ringing of a bell three times.
b. Per. 64 : this tells us that the person who brought the food to the Bishop's palace at Assisi had " *tres magni squali* (a kind of fish) *bene parati et cuppi de gammaris* ".
c. Per. 61 : this tells us that the woman who brought the food to Fonte Colombo had a basket " *plenum de pulcro pane et piscibus et mastillis gymarorum, melle et uvis* ".
d. Per. 83 : this gives details of the cauterisation of S. Francis's head " *incipiens iuxta auriculam usque ad supercilium oculi . . .* ", and of the surgeon who " *perforavit ambas eius auriculas* ".
e. Per. 113 : this gives details most carefully of the dates when Francis and Leo were at La Verna.

f. Per. 114 : This gives a detail about the brother at Greccio to whom S. Francis handed his pillow and who " *accepit illud dextera manu et proiecit illud super spatulam suam a latere sinistro tenens illud cum dextera manu* ".

g. Little 155 : this describes S. Francis sitting naked on the ground " *tenens manum sinistram ad cicatricem lateris* ", where one would have expected the right hand, not the left, as the wound was on the right side.

Then again in these chapters we are given a great many details of the customs which S. Francis used to observe, the phrase " *nam mos erat beato Francisco* " occurring several times. For example :

a. Per.   52 : " *nam mos erat b. Francisco* " to bless not only those who already belonged to the Order, but all future brothers as well.

b. Per.   66 : how no one dared to go near S. Francis when he was praying, as he wished always to be left quite alone.

c. Per.   67 : " *consuetudo erat . . . sancti patris* " that if he were late for a meal the others were to begin without him, and not to wait.

d. Per.   68 : how the brothers always sat on the ground when eating at the Portiuncula, as this was the custom of S. Francis.

e. Per.   71 : " *nam mos erat b. Francisco* " to pray at once for anyone who desired his prayers so that he should not forget to do so.

f. Per.   84 : various customs of S. Francis.

g. Per.   86 : " *nam mos erat b. Francisco* " to give everything away.

h. Per. 103a : " *nam mos erat sanctissimi patris* " to get other brothers to pray for him when he had an important decision to make.

i. Sp. L. 11 : how S. Francis would allow no women to enter the cloister at the Portiuncula.

Naturally the majority of these marks of style come from *Per.*, as this collection has the greatest proportion of the chapters which we are examining. It might, therefore, be suggested that the style was the style of the scribe of *Per.*, not that of the original sources which lie behind it. But a glance at the following table will show that these marks of style are not those of any one scribe but of the *Scripta Leonis* as a whole.

	Intro. Letter	Per. 42–58	Per. 92–5	Per. 103–5	Per. 106–15	Int. Reg.	Little 153b, etc.	Per. 59–91	Sp. L. 8–19
i. " *Nos qui cum ipso fuimus* "	*	*			*	*	*	*	*
ii. " *Nos vidimus . . .* " etc. .	*	*				*	*	* .	*
iii. " *Saepe dicebat* " . . .			*		*	*		*	*
iv. " *Forma et exemplum* " .		*	*	*				*	
v. " *Cum magno fervore spiritus* "			*	*		*		*	*
vi. Fulfilment of Prophecy .			*		*	*	*	*	*
vii. Topographical details		*		*	*	*		*	
viii. Other details					*		*	*	
ix. Customs of S. Francis .			*	*				*	*

Turning now from details of style to the general subject-matter of these chapters, we find that they obviously all come from writers who were anxious, above all else, to declare the real wishes of S. Francis. The main *casus belli* between what came to be called the " Conventuals " and the " Spirituals " were these. First, what precisely was meant by Absolute Poverty ? This question would include two very important issues : the problem of Building, which had been greatly intensified by the erection of the Basilica at Assisi ; and the problem of Learning, which raised the question of whether or no a friar could legitimately possess any books. Secondly, What were to be the relations between the friars and the secular clergy ? We have already seen how difficult this was becoming in the years immediately following the death of S. Francis. It raised also the question of papal privileges, which S. Francis had declared so expressly to be contrary to his wishes, since the privileges sought by the friars were so often for protection against the secular clergy. Thirdly, How far was the Testament of S. Francis binding upon the brethren ? We have already seen how, in 1230, Ugolino had, in the Bull, *Quo elongati*, declared that the friars were not bound by the Testament. But this declaration would hardly satisfy the intimate friends of the Saint who saw in the Testament the ultimate wishes of their master.

As we read these chapters of the Three Companions we see how often these three problems appear. This is only natural when we recollect that in the Introductory Letter they expressly state that they have set out to declare " the intention of his holy will ". With regard, then, to the problem of Absolute Poverty, we find that the penury and hardships of the early days are carefully described, together with Francis's insistence that the brothers must not be ashamed to go begging for food. In *Per.* 43 and 92b we are told how Francis regarded begging as the noblest of occupations ; in *Per.* 93 we have the story of how, when he was staying in the palace of the Cardinal Ugolino, he slipped out one day before dinner in order to go and beg for a few scraps of food ; in *Per.* 94 a brother who would not go for alms is expelled from the Order ; in *Per.* 95 Francis welcomes the brother who returns from begging with a song of praise on his lips ; and in *Int.* 9 Francis declared that neither praying nor preaching must interfere with the duty of going for alms. The question of clothes is constantly referred to, and Francis's wish that the brothers should be content with the " one patched tunic " of the *Regula Primitiva* is mentioned several times (*Per.* 75, 86 and 106), while there are stories of Francis giving away his tunic either to another brother or to the poor (e.g. *Per.* 86 and 87 and *Little* 153b) and of his distress on finding anyone more shabbily dressed than himself (*Per.* 108). The question of the poverty of the buildings is constantly discussed. In *Per.* 48a Francis expresses his desire for a small church (*parva et paupercula ecclesia*) where the brothers could say their offices and around which they could build their mud huts (" *ex luto et viminibus* "). In *Per.* 48d we are told how Francis, moved with indignation at finding a stone building at the Portiuncula, climbed on to the roof and began to throw down the tiles with his own hands. *Per.* 49 tells a similar story of Francis's disgust on finding some new building in process at the Portiuncula. *Per.* 51a begins with the intention of S. Francis that all buildings should be of clay and wattles " *ad conservandam melius paupertatem et humilitatem* ", and *Per.* 51c tells how Francis abhorred large churches and would on no account allow the brothers to build or acquire them—a direct attack on the Basilica at Assisi and such churches as Santa Croce in Florence. The question of building occurs again in *Int.* 14 and 15, where the phrase " *ex luto et lignis* " is twice used.

The problem of books is dealt with mainly in the *Intentio Regulae*, where we are told of a certain novice who was anxious to possess a book, and how S. Francis would on no account allow it (*Int.* 5, 7, 10 and 11), while in *Per.* 89 we read how Francis bade Peter Catanii give a New Testament away to a poor woman when they had nothing else to give. The question of the poverty of their food is considered in *Per.* 42a–b and 67, and in *Per.* 45 we are informed that in the early days the friars refused to have any medical supplies. Then in *Per.* 50 we read how S. Francis refused to enter a certain cell because someone had referred to it as his ; in *Per.* 68 of how Ugolino marvelled at the poverty of the brothers and was thereby much edified (though not apparently enough to make him very sympathetic to Francis's wishes afterwards) ; in *Per.* 109 Francis discourses on the poverty and humility of Christ, and in *Per.* 112 Francis refuses to accept the hospitality of Ugolino at Rome in spite of its being winter time and most unsuitable for tramping (" *ineptum tempus ad ambulandum* "). Francis's adherence to absolute poverty is referred to again in *Int.* 13 and *Sp. L.* 12, while in *Per.* 52 he expresses his wish that the brothers should always love and serve " *dominam nostram sanctam paupertatem* ".

The problem of the relations between the friars and the clergy does not receive very much attention in these chapters, perhaps because Leo had already dealt with it in the *Verba*. But in *Per.* 51b we are told how Francis made the brothers honour and respect the clergy, and how he himself would always obey even the poorest priests, regarding them as his lords : " *pauperculos sacerdotes volo diligere et venerari et tenere eos pro meis dominis* ". Again, in *Per.* 52 Francis is made to declare his three main wishes, one of which was that the brothers should always be faithful and in subjection to the bishops and every priest of the Church (" *semper praelatis et omnibus clericis sanctae matris ecclesiae fideles et subiecti* ").

That much-debated document, the Testament of S. Francis, is

quoted six times in these chapters, in *Int.* 7, 14 and 15, and in *Per.* 48b, 51 and 103b. There is also much about the keeping of the Rule in its entirety, especially in *Per.* 107b, where Francis is made to say : " *ego iuravi et statui fratrum regulam observare, et fratres omnes similiter ad hoc se obligaverunt* ". *Int.* 4 and 6 deal with the question of those who refuse to obey the Rule.

It might be of interest, in conclusion, to see how Leo speaks of Brother Elias. By the time this document was composed Elias had left the Order and was living an outcast and excommunicate. Leo has no wish to exult over this, though he must have been glad when Elias's term of office came to an end. His references to Elias are, therefore, slight. In *Verba* 4 (which we believe to have been written a good deal earlier than the writings of the Three Companions, perhaps during the years of Elias's tyranny) Elias appears in a very unfavourable light as critic and opponent of S. Francis at the writing of the Rule at Fonte Colombo in 1223. Now, however, Leo is more merciful. Elias is mentioned only once by name, in *Per.* 81, where we are told that Francis would not allow the surgeon to begin the operation on his eyes until Elias had arrived. In *Per.* 77 and 85 he is referred to by his title of " *generalis minister* ", first as persuading Francis to undergo some treatment for his eyes ; and secondly as forbidding him to go on giving away his tunic unless he had special permission. In these references Elias appears as the friend and wise counsellor of the Saint, as indeed for a time he undoubtedly was. It was only after Francis's death that Elias became the declared enemy of those who wanted to be faithful to the high standards of the early days.

Leo, then, serves the cause of the Spirituals not by attacking the changes·in the Order, nor by abusing those who were responsible for them, but by quietly describing the character and intentions of S. Francis. If his stories were accepted by Crescentius, if they became known among the brethren, then surely a change must come over the Order. And if not, then there was always the hope that a future historian might find these rolls hidden away in some dark corner, and that the light of the true Franciscan ideal might then once more shine through the Order and recall men to the Poverty, Simplicity and Humility which Francis had lived and died to give to the world.

APPENDED NOTE A

" *Original* " *Chapters and Their Parallels in Other Documents*

Verba	= *Per.*	= *Little*	= *Sp. S.*	= *2 Cel.*	
1		14	86	12	—
2		15	87	13	—
4		16	81	1	—
5		17	114	68	—
6		19	105	50	—

		= Per.	= Little	= Sp. S.	= 2 Cel.
Sp. S.	52	= Per. 20	= Little 107	—	= 2 Cel. —
	79	—	124	—	—
	85	—	127	—	—
Per.	42a	= Leg. Vet. 1	= Little 160	= Sp. S. 27	= 2 Cel. 22
	42b	1	160	27	21
	43	2	90	18	74
	44	3	—	19	—
	45	4	161	28	176
	46	5	162	—	100
	47	6	163	106	124
	48a	7	140	55, 7	18, 19
	48b = Sp. L.	27	140	55, 7	18, 19
	48c	27	140	55, 7	18, 19
	48d	27	140	55, 7	18, 19
	49	28	165	8	—
	50	29	—	9	59
	51a	30a	166	10	146
	51b	30a	166	10	146
	51c	30a	166	10	146
	52	30b	—	87	—
	53	31a	110	56	—
	54	31b	111	57	190
	56	—	168	99	115
	57	32	169	58	—
	58	33	—	59, 60	122-3
	59	—	—	—	126
	60	—	—	104	—
	61	—	—	110	44
	62	—	—	—	38
	63	—	—	103	40
	64	—	—	111	—
	65	—	—	—	31
	66	—	—	—	45
	67	—	—	20	61
	68	—	—	21	63
	69	—	—	—	35-6
	70	—	—	105	37
	71	—	—	—	101
	72	—	—	91-2	11
	73	—	—	—	105
	74	—	—	61	—
	75	—	—	62	130-1
	76	—	—	63	132
	77	—	—	91, 100	—
	78	—	—	100, 119	213
	79	—	—	101	—
	80	—	—	90	—
	81	—	—	115a	—
	82	—	—	89	—
	83	—	—	115b	166
	84a	—	—	115c, 116	—
	84b	—	—	117	—
	84c	—	—	118	165

Per.	85	—	—	Sp. S. 33	2 Cel. 92
	86	—	—	34	181
	87	--	—	35	196 (end)
	88	--	—	36	—
	89	—	—	38	91
	90	—	—	—	(Mir. 18)
	91	—	—	—	41
	92a	—	--	22	72–3
	92b = Sp. L.	1	—	23	73
	93		2 = Little 93	23	73
	94	2–3	—	24	75
	95	—	147	25	76
	103a	37c	189a	65a	201
	103b	36, 37a	189b	65b	201
	103c	37b	189c	—	108
	103d	37d	189d	65c	—
	104	38	190	64	145
	105	—	191	—	171
	106	39	89	16	—
	107a	40	126	81	158
	107b	40	126	81	—
	108	41	192	17	84b
	109	42	193	37	85b
	110	43	196	66	—
	111	—	198	102	28b
	112	20	—	67	—
	113	21a	159	99	—
	114	21b	—	98	64
	115a	22a	—	94	96
	115b	22c, 23	131–3	95–7	125, 128, 129
Intentio Regulae	1 = Per.	98a = Little —	= Sp. S.	2 = 2 Cel.	—
	2	98b	95	26	—
	3	98b	95	26	cf. 71
	4	98c	--	2	—
	5	99	83	3	cf. 62
	6	99	83	3	—
	7	100a	118, 150	4, 72	163
	8	100b	118, 150	72	—
	9	100b	118, 150	72–3	164
	10	100c	150	4	195
	11	100d	151	4	195
	12	100e	152	4	195
	13	101a	184, cf. 166	71	—
	14	101b	185	11	—
	15	101b	185	11	—
	16	101b	185	11	—
Sp. L.	8 = Per.	4 = Little	153a = Sp.S. 109	= 2 Cel. 210	
	9	5	—	124	—
	10	6	156	123	—
	11	7	157	112	(Mir. 37–8)
	12	8	101	44	—
	13	9	102	45	141, 133
	14	10	158	39	143

Sp. L.	Per.	Little	Sp. S.	2 Cel.
Sp. L. 15	Per. 10	Little 158	Sp. S. 46	2 Cel. 151
16	10	158	40	144, 151
17	11	—	107	48
18	12	—	108	—
19	13	—	113–14	200
Little 153b	—	—	— = 2 Cel.	50
154	—	—	—	49
155	—	—	—	214–15
187	.—	—	.—	51
194	—	—	—	39
195	—	—	—	110
197	—	—	—	111
Sp. L. 6 = Sp. S.	26 = Little	95	—	
Per. 21	88	186 = Sp. L. 34		
55	—	167	— = 2 Cel.	81
96	121	148	4	217
97	122	149	5	217
102	82	188	35	160
2 Cel. 71 = Sp. S	26	—	—	—
146	54 = Little	109	— = Per.	18
152	48	103	—	—
156	cf. 70, 87	—	—	—
163	cf. 4, 72	—	—	—
164	72–3	150	—	100
187	cf. 80	—	—	—

APPENDED NOTE B

Synopsis of the Original " Scripta Leonis et Sociorum Eius "

1. *Leg. 3 Soc.* 1. Introductory Letter.
2. *Per.* 42a How S. F. ate with the brother who was dying of hunger.
3. ,, 42b The asceticism of the early days.
4. ,, 43 On going for alms.
5. ,, 44 No thought to be taken for the morrow.
6. ,, 45 How S. F. ate with a sick brother in the vineyard.
7. ,, 46 How the Bishop of Assisi was not fit to see S. F. at prayer.
8. ,, 47 How S. F. comforted the brother who was tempted.
9. ,, 48a How S. F. asked for the Portiuncula.
10. ,, 48b How S. F. loved the Portiuncula.
11. ,, 48c The same continued.
12. ,, 48d How S. F. threw down the tiles from the new building at the Portiuncula.
13. ,, 49 How the Portiuncula was to be the pattern for the whole Order.
14. ,, 50 How S. F. would have no cell described as his.
15. ,, 51a S. F. tells the brothers what sort of buildings he wishes them to have.
16. ,, 51b The same continued.
17. ,, 51c The same continued.
18. ,, 52 How S. F. blessed all the brothers.
19. ,, 53 How S. F. hated to see dirty churches.
20. ,, 54 The conversion of Brother John the Simple.
21. ,, 56 How S. F. was tempted and comforted by Christ.
22. ,, 57 How Br. James served the lepers, and how S. F. punished himself.

VI

CELANO'S *VITA SECUNDA* AND THE COMPILATIONS DEPENDENT UPON THE *SCRIPTA LEONIS*

I. 2 Celano

ACCORDING to the Introductory Letter, the *Scripta Leonis* were sent in to Assisi in August, 1246, just over two years later than the Chapter at Genoa which had invited the friars to send in their reminiscences. Besides these *rotuli* of Brother Leo and his companions there must have been a fair amount of other material, no doubt of widely different value. After an attempt by the Minister General, Crescentius of Jesi, himself to write a biography,[1] the task was entrusted to Thomas of Celano, who set out to produce, from the contributions which had been submitted, a new and acceptable life which would supplement what he had written nearly twenty years ago.

Celano divides his book into two parts which are wholly different. In the first part he gives an account of the early years of S. Francis to supplement, from the new material at his disposal, what he had already written in the *Vita Prima*. In the second part he gives us not so much a biography as a pen-portrait, a study of the character and ideals of the saint, dividing his information under various headings rather than following any chronological sequence.

The first part is comparatively short. After a preface, in which he states his intentions, he gives us twenty-three paragraphs in which he tells again the familiar story of the conversion of S. Francis and the beginnings of the Brotherhood. New information on these years has come to hand, and he thinks it right that it should be included in this new biography. As he himself writes : " This work contains first of all, certain wonderful events in the conversion of S. Francis which were not put into the legends composed some time ago concerning him, because they had not then come to the author's notice." [2]

---

[1] Bernard of Bessa says of Crescentius : " *opusculum quoddam in modum dialogi fecit* ", *An. F.*, III, p. 697. Cf. *Chron. XXIV Gen.* in *An. F.*, III, p. 263, Lemmens in *Doc. Ant. Franc.*, III, p. 19, and Sabatier in *Opuscules*, fasc. iii, p. 110.

[2] *2 Cel.* 2.

We have already seen reasons for supposing that the sources which Celano was using are more faithfully preserved in the *Legenda Trium Sociorum*.[1] If we are right in thinking that the *Leg. 3 Soc.* is based upon the sources of both *1* and *2 Celano*, we shall see at once that Celano's method of using a source has changed very considerably in the intervening years between the writing of the two *Legendae*. In the *Vita Prima* he follows the *3 Socii* very closely, only altering a phrase on a point of style or to bring in some Biblical expression. In the *Vita Secunda* he merely takes the main outline, borrowing an odd phrase here and there and only occasionally taking a complete sentence.

When we compare the first part of the *Vita Secunda* with the *Leg. 3 Soc.* we see that Celano has little to add from other sources. Apart from *2 Cel.* 18-19 and 21-2, which are based on the *Scripta Leonis*, the whole of this first part is parallel to the *Leg. 3 Soc.* There are only two occasions upon which Celano definitely adds something which is not in his source. One is the fact that after Francis had embraced the leper he discovered that the man had entirely disappeared from view, an addition which is easily explained by the supposition that the story had been embellished in being circulated among the friars, and had thereby acquired a more miraculous flavour. The other addition is in the form of an interpretation of the parable of the King and the Poor Woman in *2 Cel.* 16-17. The other amplifications are either such editorial matter as was dear to Celano, or scriptural and hagiographical allusions such as the comparison of Francis with, first, John the Baptist, then S. Martin, and finally S. Paul, in *2 Cel.* 3, 5 and 6. We can therefore say that, if we have *1 Celano*, the *Leg. 3 Soc.* and chapters 42 and 48 of *Per.* in front of us, we can ignore the first part of *2 Cel.* altogether and lose nothing of importance in the Franciscan legend.

In the second part of the *Vita Secunda* there are, according to the enumeration used by Edouard d'Alençon, 199 paragraphs, numbered 26 to 224 inclusive. Of these, 93 are peculiar to Celano,[2] appearing nowhere else in the documents which derive from the material sent in to Crescentius. To these 93 we must add a further 27 which occur in other documents but which are certainly copied from Celano. Four are doubtful in origin and have already been examined,[3] one seems to come from a source which is more accurately reported in *Sp. S.*,[4] and three come from passages in *Per.* which are not by Leo and his companions.[5] This leaves us with seventy-one chapters which

---

[1] See above, pp. 70-6.   [2] See p. 91 for the references.
[3] Viz. 106, 125 and 201 for which see p. 95, and 146 for which see p. 92.
[4] *2 Cel.* 58 = *Sp. S.* 6 (see p. 95).
[5] *Ibid.*, 160 (= *Per.* 102) ; 216 (= *Per.* 21) ; 217 (= *Per.* 96-7).

appear to be based on the *Scripta Leonis* as they were contained in the *rotuli* sent in by the Three Companions from Greccio.

But before we begin to examine Celano's use of this material we must spend a moment in considering his plan in this second part of the *Vita Secunda*. In part i. he has given a chronological account of the early years of S. Francis and of the Brotherhood : it is the beginning of a true biography. But in the second part he abandons the biographical method in order to give us a " character-study " of his hero. Just as the Three Companions " plucked as it were from a fair meadow a few flowers which in their opinion seemed the most beautiful ",[1] so Celano draws upon his sources for the material which he requires, taking now from one source, now from another, according to the particular characteristic or virtue of the saint which he wishes to illustrate.

He begins with a short Introduction (§ 26) describing the purpose of this second part as " both commending the saint himself and arousing our slumbering affection ", and then divides his work into twenty-three sections, as follows :

    i. On the spirit of Prophecy in S. Francis (28 chapters).
    ii. On S. Francis's Poverty (39 chapters).
    iii. On his Prayers (8 chapters).
    iv. On his Preaching (10 chapters).
    v. On his Teaching about Women (3 chapters).
    vi. On his Temptations (10 chapters).
    vii. On Spiritual Joy (5 chapters).
    viii. On Vainglory (5 chapters).
    ix. On the Concealment of the Stigmata (5 chapters).
    x. On Humility (11 chapters).
    xi. On Obedience (8 chapters).
    xii. On Idleness (4 chapters).
    xiii. On the Ministers of God's Word (2 chapters).
    xiv. On S. Francis and Nature (7 chapters).
    xv. On his Charity (10 chapters).
    xvi. On Slander (2 chapters).
    xvii. On the Minister General (5 chapters).
    xviii. On Simplicity (7 chapters).
    xix. On S. Francis's Special Devotions (8 chapters).
    xx. On the Poor Clares (4 chapters).
    xxi. On the Commendation of the Rule (2 chapters).
    xxii. On S. Francis's Sickness (4 chapters).
    xxiii. On the Death of S. Francis (7 chapters).

He concludes with a Prayer of the Saints' Companions (§§ 221–4).

In writing this work it is clear that Celano regarded himself as the mouthpiece of a large number of the friends and companions of S. Francis—all those, in fact, who had provided him with the material

---

[1] *Leg. 3 Soc.*, Intro. Letter.

for his *legenda*. In the Preface to the *Vita Secunda* he says that he has been asked to " write of the deeds and also the words of our glorious father Francis, because through long experience of them they were better known to us than to others by reason of our constant association with him and the mutual intimacy between us ".[1] The first person plural in this sentence can hardly be an editorial convention, for Celano himself had neither been in " constant association " nor in " mutual intimacy " with S. Francis. The Epilogue, which takes the form of a Prayer of the Saints' Companions to him, makes this more clear. After praying for the Minister General, to whom the work is dedicated, Celano inserts a prayer for himself as the writer of the book. " We beseech thee also," he writes, " O kindest father, with all our heart's affection, for this thy son who now and before has written thy praises. He, together with us, offers and dedicates to thee this little work which he has put together . . ."

Thus acknowledging his indebtedness to the more intimate friends of the saint, Celano proceeds to draw upon the information which they supplied. Of the 120 chapters which are peculiar to Celano, some 50 are merely editorial or composed of general teaching of S. Francis, leaving about seventy which seem to be dependent upon some earlier version, some scrap of parchment or some little bundle of memories sent in by the friars in response to the general appeal. These sources have vanished ; but, if we are right in our reconstruction of the collection sent in by Leo, Angelo and Rufino, we are in the happy position of having before our eyes, in the case of 71 other chapters, not only the version of Celano but also the original source which he has used.

When we examine and compare the style and method of Celano there are certain features which stand out. In the first place, Celano almost always contracts. It is unusual to find Celano's account longer than that of Leo, though he does from time to time introduce the narrative with some general observations or conclude it with a moral tag of his own. As a typical example of his method we might compare the following :

Per. 109	*2 Cel.* 85
Cum beatus Franciscus ivisset ad quoddam heremitorium fratrum prope Roccam Bricii occasione *praedica*ndi hominibus illius provinciae, accidit in illa *die* qua debebat ibidem praedicare	Alia sua *praedica*tionis *die*

---

[1] Cf. also *2 Cel.* 52 : " *scimus enim omnes qui vidimus* ".

Per. 109	*2 Cel.* 85
quod *quidam* homo *pauperculus et infirmitius venit ad* eum. Et cum videret ipsum coepit considerare paupertatem et infirmitatem eius ita quod motus pietate, visa paupertate et infirmitate eius,	*quidam pauperculus et infirmus venit ad* locum.
	Cuius duplex incommodum miseratus, inopiam scilicet et languorem,
coepit dicere *cum socio suo de* nuditate et infirmitate eius illi *compatien*do.	*coepit* *cum socio suo de* paupertate habere sermonem. Cumque patienti *compatien*s iam in affectum cordis illius transisset,
Et *dixit socius* eius *ad eum:* *Frater, verum est* quod iste satis *pauper* est, *sed forsitan in tota provincia non est voluntate ditior* illo. Et reprehendit illum beatus Franciscus quod non benedixisset, ita quod inde dixit suam *culpam.* Et ait ei beatus Franciscus : Vis inde poenitentiam facere quam dixero tibi ? Et respondit : Libenter. Et dixit ei : Vade *et exue te tunicam tuam et* vade nudus coram *paupere* et *proice* te ad *pedes* eius et dicas ei quo modo peccasti in ipso, quoniam detraxisti ei, et dicas ei ut oret pro te ut Deus tibi indulgeat. *Ivit* ergo ille et fecit omnia sicut dixerat ei beatus Franciscus ; quo facto elevavit se et induit se tunicam et reversus est ad beatum Franciscum. Et ait ad eum beatus Franciscus : Vis ut dicam tibi quomodo peccasti in illo, immo in Christo ? Et ait : *Cum vides pauperem,* debes considerare illum in cuius nomine venit, videlicet Christum, qui nostram paupertatem et infirmitatem assumere venit. Nam paupertas et infirmitas istius est quoddam *speculum* nobis per quod speculari et *considerare* cum pie-	*dixit socius* sancti *ad eum:* *Frater, verum est* ipsum *pauper*em esse, *sed forsitan in tota provincia non est ditior voluntate.* Increpat eum illico sanctus et *culpam* dicenti sic dixit : Festina cito *et exue te tunicam tuam et* ad *pauper*is *pedes proie*ctus culpabilem te proclama. Nec solum veniam poscas, immo eius orationem efflagita. Paruit et *ivit* satisfacere et rediit. Cui dixit sanctus : *Cum pauperem vides,* o frater, *speculum* tibi proponitur

Per. 109

tate debemus paupertatem et
infirmitatem Domini nostri
Iesu Christi,
quas in suo corpore pertulit
pro salvatione humani generis.

2 Cel. 85

Domini
et pauperis Matris eius.

In infirmis similiter *infirmi-*
tates quas pro nobis assumpsit
considera.
Eia semper mirrhae fasciculus
commorabatur Francisco, semper respicit in faciem Christi
sui, semper virum dolorem et
scientem infirmitates attrectat.

A comparison of these two accounts will show that Celano has here given most of the essential details of the story, the main exception being the name of the place where this incident occurred.

Celano, however, does not always use his material in the same way. Sometimes he copies his source very closely ; sometimes he makes considerable changes ; sometimes he merely gives the gist of the story ; sometimes he gives only a passing reference. As an example of Celano copying fairly closely we might compare *2 Cel.* 49 with *Little* 154.

Little 154

Socius beati Francisci cum
maneret cum illo *in monte*
Alvernae,
quando stetit ibi in carcere
*desider*abat *habere* aliquem (!)
recreabile scriptum manu sua
de verbis Domini

maxime quia erat tunc tribu-
latus maligna et *gravi temp-*
tatione
non carnis sed spiritus.

Et dixit ad eum *quadam die*
beatus Franciscus :
Da *mihi cartam et atra-*
mentum, quoniam volo scribere
quaedam *verba* Domini *et eius*
laudes quae meditatus sum in
corde meo.

2 Cel. 49

Dum
maneret sanctus   *in monte*
Alvernae cella reclusus, unus
de sociis magno *desiderio*
cupiebat *habere de verbis Domini*
recreabile scriptum manu
sancti Francisci breviter
adnotatum.

Gravem enim qua vexabatur *ten-*
tationem
non carnis sed spiritus
credebat ex hoc evadere, vel
certe levius ferre. Tali
desiderio languens pavebat rem
aperire patri sanctissimo, sed
cui homo non dixit spiritus
revelavit.
Quadam enim *die* vocat eum
beatus Franciscus, dicens :
Porta *mihi cartam et atra-*
mentum, quoniam verba Dei
et laudes eius scribere volo
     quae meditatus sum in
corde meo.

<table>
<tr><td>

Little 154

Ille vero dedit ei. Ivit
beatus Franciscus et *scripsit*
illa *verba* et illas *laudes* et
in fine scripsit suam *benedict-*
ionem illi, *dicens* ad eum :
Accipe hanc *cartam*
et custodias diligenter
usque ad diem mortis tuae.
Et plurimum admiratus et
laetatus est frater ille,
maxime quia sine rogamine et
dicto suo satisfecit sanctus
pater de voluntate Domini
desiderio suo. Nam post
mortem beati Francisci plura
miracula et magna Dominus
operatus est per illam
litteram in illis quibus
signati fuerunt in magnis
infirmitatibus suis cum
illa carta.

</td><td>

2 Cel. 49

Allatis protinus quae pet-
ierat, *scribit* manu propria
laudes Dei *et verba* quae
voluit, et ultimo *benedict-*
ionem fratris, *dicens* :
Accipe tibi *cartulam* istam
et usque ad diem mortis tuae
custodias diligenter.

Fugatur statim omnis illa
tentatio ;

                              servatur
littera, et in posterum
miranda effecit.

</td></tr>
</table>

As an example of Celano making considerable changes in the words
of Leo we might compare *2 Cel.* 81 with *Per.* 55. According to the
account in *Per.* Francis addresses the postulant in these words :

"Frater, si vis intrare religionem fratrum, oportet te primo omnia tua secundum per-
fectionem sancti evangelii pauperibus erogare et postea tuam voluntatem in omnibus
abnegare."

In Celano's version Francis is made to say :

"Si vis (Dei) pauperibus iungi, mundi pauperibus prius tua distribue ",

which is very neat but less like the actual words of S. Francis. And
when the would-be friar has gone and given away all his goods not
to poor but to his own relations, Francis says (in Leo's version) :

"Vade viam tuam, frater musca, quoniam tua erogasti consanguineis et vis vivere de
eleemosynis inter fratres ",

which in Celano becomes :

"Vade viam tuam, frater musca, quoniam nondum existi de domo et cognatione tua.
Consanguineis tuis tua dedisti et defraudisti pauperes, dignus non es pauperibus sanctis.
Incoepisti a carne, ruinosum fundamentum spirituali fabricae collocasti."

As an example of Celano's giving the general trend of a conversation
without attempting to adhere to his source, we might compare the
message of God to S. Francis as it is recorded by Leo and by Celano.
According to the former, Francis was subjected to an inquisition almost
as severe as that which was addressed to Job " out of the whirlwind " :

"Dic mihi (dictum fuit ei a Domino) quare contristaris tantum cum aliquis fratrum exit de religione et cum fratres non ambulant per viam quam tibi ostendi? Item dic mihi, quis plantavit fratrum religionem? Quis converti facit hominem ad faciendam poenitentiam in ea? Quis dat virtutem perseverandi in ea? Nonne ego? Ego non elegi te pro homine litterato et eloquente super familiam meam, sed simplicem te elegi, ut scire valeas, tam tu quam alii, quoniam ego vigilabo super gregem meum ; sed posui te signaculum ipsis, ut opera quae ego operor in te, ipsi in te debeant prospicere et ea operari. Qui ambulant per viam meam habent me et abundantius habebunt ; qui vero per viam meam ambulare nolunt, id quod videtur habere auferetur ab eis. Quapropter dico tibi ne tantum contristeris, sed age quod agis, operare quod operaris, quoniam in caritate perpetua plantavi fratrum religionem. Unde scias quod tantum diligo ipsam quod si aliquis fratrum reversus ad vomitum moriatur extra religionem, alium remittam in religione ut vice ipsius habeat coronam eius. Et ponatur quod non esset natus, faciam ipsum nasci. Et ut scias quoniam vitam et religionem fratrum spontanee diligo, ponatur quod in tota vita et religione fratrum non remanerent nisi tres fratres, in perpetuum non relinquam " (*Per.* 107a).

Celano has not only abridged this considerably, but he has no compunction in reporting what is quite a different speech, though a few phrases show that Leo's account is clearly before him. Celano gives the words of God to S. Francis as follows :

"Cur tu, homuncio, conturbaris? An ego te super religionem meam sic pastorem constitui, ut me principalem nescias esse patronem? Hominem *simplicem* ad hoc *te* constitui, *ut quae* in te fecero, caeteris imitanda, sequantur qui sequi voluerint. Ego vocavi, servabo et pascam, et in aliorum reparandum excidium alios subrogabo, ita ut si *natus non* fuerit *faciam ipsum nasci*. Non ergo turberis, sed tuam operare salutem, quoniam etsi ad numerum *trium* religio venerit, inconcussa semper meo munere permanebit " (*2 Cel.* 158).

As an example of Celano's giving a mere reference to some incident recorded by Leo the following will serve. When we compare *Per.* 45 with *2 Cel.* 176 we find that they both tell the same story, but that Celano is content to tell in 23 words what Leo writes in full. According to Leo,

Quodam tempore, cum esset beatus Franciscus apud eundem locum, *quidam* frater, spiritualis homo et antiquus in religione, manebat ibi, qui erat valde debilis et *infirmus*. Considerans igitur ipsum beatus Franciscus pietate motus est super eum. Sed quia fratres tunc infirmi et sani cum hilaritate et patientia paupertate pro abundantia utebantur, et in suis infirmitatibus medicinis non utebantur, sed magis quae erant contraria corpori libentius faciebant, dixit ad seipsum beatus Franciscus : " Si frater iste summo mane manducaret de uvis maturis, credo quod prodesset illi ". Et ideo surrexit quadam die summo mane secreto et vocavit fratrem illum et *duxit* illum *in vineam* quae est iuxta eamdem ecclesiam, et elegit quamdam vitem in qua erant bonae et sanae uvae ad manducandum. *Et sedens* cum illo fratre iuxta *vitem* coepit de uvis comedere, *ut* non verecundaretur solus *comedere* ; et manducantibus illis laudavit Dominum Deum frater ille, et illius misericordiae quam fecit propter eum sanctus pater toto tempore dum vixit cum magna devotione et lacrymarum effusione saepe recordatus est inter fratres.

Celano simply says :

Infirmum quendam, cui comedendarum uvarum desiderium inesse sciebat, semel *in vineam duxit, et sedens* sub *vite, ut comede*ndi audaciam daret, prior ipse comedit.

In contracting and abridging his sources Celano often leaves out details which, even if they are not of primary importance to the narrative, are yet of the greatest interest. Here are a few examples :

(*a*) *2 Cel.* 37 from *Per.* 70. Celano here omits the fact that the soldiers at Perugia scoffed at Francis because he was an Assisian, that the Church sided with the nobles against the people in the civil war at Perugia, and that in his preaching Francis was never afraid to speak out.

(*b*) *2 Cel.* 44 from *Per.* 61. Here Celano says nothing about the doctor being a rich man who, though often invited to a meal by the friars, had never consented to stay. He also omits the fact that the food which was miraculously supplied for the occasion was sent by a certain lady who lived in a castle seven miles away.

(*c*) *2 Cel.* 57 from *Per.* 48d. Here Celano omits five details—the careful description of the huts at the Portiuncula ; the fact that Francis was particularly worried about the effect which a stone building at the Portiuncula would have on future buildings ; that the Portiuncula was to be the " *forma et exemplum* " of the whole Order ; that Francis actually climbed on to the roof while the Chapter was in session, and that great crowds had assembled to see all the brothers.

(*d*) *2 Cel.* 119–20 from *Per.* 112. Here Celano omits a number of details, among them the following : that Francis was at the time of this incident on a visit to Ugolino, that it was winter and no time for going tramping, that Angelo Tancredi was with Cardinal Leo at the time, that it was Angelo who showed Francis the vaults, that Francis and his companion made certain plans as to how they were going to live in the vault, also a good deal of what Francis said about his setting a good example to the rest of the brothers, and that on leaving Rome he went to Fonte Colombo.

(*e*) *2 Cel.* 190 from *Per.* 54. Here Celano omits all the first part about Francis going about the country sweeping out dirty churches, and also most of the conversation between him and the parents of Brother John the Simple.[1]

(*f*) *2 Cel.* 213 from *Per.* 78. In this section Celano does not tell us that Francis had been blind for fifty days, nor that the mice ran all over him and even climbed on to the table and ate his food, nor that the cell in which Francis lay was built " *ex storiis ex una parte illius domus* ".

All these omissions may be accounted for by Celano's desire to save time and space. There are, however, certain omissions of names, whether of places or of people, which are less explicable. For example, in § 75 (= *Per.* 94) he omits the phrase " *in primordio religionis . . . apud Rigum Tortum* " (Rivo Torto) ; in § 96 (= *Per.* 115a) he suppresses

---

[1] On this chapter see Sabatier in *Spec. Perf.* (*B.S.F.S.*), ii, pp. 101–3.

the name of " *dominus Leo* ", who is presumably the Cardinal Leo of
Santa Croce mentioned in § 119 ; in § 108 (= *Per.* 103c) he conceals
Brother Sylvester's identity under the phrase " *quidam pauper* " ; in
§ 120 (= *Per.* 112) he makes no mention of Brother Angelo ; in
§ 122 (= *Per.* 58) he leaves out both the name of the companion of
S. Francis—Brother Pacifico—and also the name of the place to which
they were going—S. Pietro di Bovario. Again in § 126 (= *Per.* 59)
he omits both the name of the host, Tabaldo Saraceno, and the name
of the companion, who again was Angelo ; and in § 145 (= *Per.* 104)
he does not tell us that this incident occurred " at the Portiuncula,
at the approach of the Chapter Meeting "

It is certainly hard to account for these omissions. In the *Vita
Prima* Celano does of course say that he has suppressed the names
of the more intimate friends of the saint " to spare their modesty ",[1]
and it may be that a similar discretion is the cause of his keeping them
out of the *Vita Secunda.* At any rate, neither Leo, Angelo nor Giles is
anywhere mentioned by name in the *legendae* of Celano, though some of
the brothers, such as Bernard, Sylvester and Pacifico, sometimes appear.

On the other hand, there are some personal names and place names,
together with certain other details, which are introduced by Celano
into the narrative supplied by the Three Companions. These are as
follows : in § 31 (= *Per.* 65) we are told that the brother whom Leo
calls " *quidam frater spiritalis* " was in fact Brother Leonard, and that
the incident here recorded occurred when Francis was returning from
abroad—i.e. August, 1220 ; in § 37 (= *Per.* 70) he introduces the
narrative with the information that while at Greccio Francis had an
intuition of trouble at Perugia and decided to go there at once ; in
§ 39 (= *Little* 194) Celano tells us that this event took place at Assisi ;
in § 44 (= *Per.* 61) he changes the words " *socius suus* " to " *guardianus* ",
probably thereby indicating Elias ; in § 59 (= *Per.* 50) he tells us the
name of the " *quoddam heremitorium* ", which was Sarteano, about
2½ miles S.W. of Chiusi ; in § 77 (= *Per.* 92a) the " *quoddam castrum* "
of Brother Leo becomes " *villa quaedam pauperrima nomine Satrianum* ",
which is not to be confused with the above, but is a farm on the route
between Nocera and Assisi.[2] Again, in § 92 (= *Per.* 85) Celano tells
us that Francis was at the time in the Bishop's palace at Rieti and that
his Guardian claimed to be the owner of the cloak which Francis was
proposing to give away so that he could thus forbid him to dispose of
it ; in § 101 (= *Per.* 71) Celano adds the name of the abbot's
monastery—S. Justinus in the diocese of Perugia ; in § 131 (= *Per.* 75)
he gives the name of Podium (Poggio Bustone) to the monastery ; and
in § 151 (= *Sp. L.* 15) he brings in the name of Peter Catanii where
Leo has simply " *minister generalis* ".

[1] *1 Cel.* 102.   [2] Cf. Sabatier, *Spec. Perf.* (1898), pp. 21 and 45.

There are five possible explanations to account for these additions made by Celano to the sources upon which he was working. First, there is always the possibility that Celano had before him two narratives of the same event. The invitation issued by the Chapter of Genoa had been to all the friars who had any sort of story to tell, and there must constantly have been two or more accounts of the same incident. With more than one source before him Celano would be able to add little details, such as we have mentioned, to the information supplied by Leo and his companions. Secondly, there is no doubt that there was much oral tradition circulating among the friars, such as was collected afterwards in the *Actus*. Stories always gather round the name of an outstanding personality, and Celano must have been familiar with many of them. Thirdly, we must not forget that Celano himself had a certain amount of personal experience upon which to draw. In Chapter III we saw reasons for believing that he was in Italy from 1215 to 1221 and from 1223 onwards, and that although he may not have been one of the intimate friends of S. Francis he yet claimed, in the *Vita Prima*, to be writing " *ea quae ex ipsius ore audivi* " and " *prout potuimus recte scire* ". There is no doubt that Celano had some personal reminiscences upon which to draw, and he may therefore have been able sometimes to amplify the narratives of Brother Leo from his own memories. Fourthly, it is always assumed that Celano was present at the Canonisation of S. Francis in 1228, and indeed his description of that occasion gives every indication of being the report of an eye-witness. We also know that on that occasion certain events from the life of the saint, especially those of a miraculous nature, were read out, in which case Celano must have heard them. This seems to be the explanation of the two details given by Celano in § 31 (= *Per*. 65), for Leo himself tells us that this incident was recounted to the Pope and Cardinals at the time of the Canonisation. Fifthly, we ought not to exclude the possibility that Celano may have introduced certain details out of his own imagination. He certainly seems, in some of the stories, to amplify the words of Brother Leo by a number of additions for which he had no authority. For example, in § 100 (= *Per*. 46) he enlarges upon the discomfiture of the Bishop of Assisi by saying that he began to tremble, his limbs grew stiff and he lost the power of speech, though there is no warrant for this in the source which he was using ; in §§ 122-3 (= *Per*. 58) he makes a good deal more of the devils' assault upon S. Francis than the original would justify, while in § 124 (= *Per*. 47) he again enjoys the satisfaction of giving a more highly-coloured account of the temptations of one of the brothers and of his efforts to master them.[1]

---

[1] It is, of course, possible that such additions came from another source, but they have rather the appearance of being products of the imagination of Celano himself.

We have seen enough now to give us some impression of the way in which Celano dealt with his sources. Our next task is to find out something about his own ideas and the position which he himself had come to hold in the year 1247. When he wrote his *Vita Prima* he was careful to avoid too much reference to the problems which were even then beginning to trouble the Order. His purpose was to give a picture of a saint, not to weary his readers with the domestic troubles of the friars. But twenty years later things were very different. The fissures in the Order had become very much wider, the friars were grouping themselves around certain leaders and forming themselves into definite parties, and the points at issue were beginning to be disputed with a bitterness which was later to lead to a definite schism among the sons of Francis.

In his choice of Thomas of Celano, Crescentius probably thought that he had found a safe man. After all, his *Vita Prima* had been unimpeachable both in style and in subject-matter. Awkward questions had been tactfully avoided and the writer had kept himself to his main task, that of presenting a faithful portrait of the saint. But Celano's ideas as well as his style had undergone some modifications during the intervening years and the new Life which he now produced was a very different thing from the old one.

Celano states in his Introduction that he intends to set down in this new Life what were the real intentions of S. Francis [1]; and throughout the book he does not shrink from declaring most faithfully what S. Francis had said about the great problems which were uppermost in the thoughts of the friars. We have seen above that these problems were mainly three: What was meant by Absolute Poverty? What were to be the relations between the Friars and the Secular Clergy? and How were the Rule and Testament to be interpreted? [2] The problem of Absolute Poverty raised many vexed questions such as the type of building legitimate for the friars, the pursuit of learning and the consequent possession of books, the problem of whether the friars were to depend upon house-to-house begging or whether they might be supported by charitable friends, and the problem of their clothes. Again, the question of the relations between the friars and the clergy raised the subsidiary problem of papal concessions, the problem of lay preaching, as well as the whole question of Humility *versus* Privilege. Lastly, the question of the interpretation of the Rule and Testament was fraught with grave difficulties since the publication of the Bull, *Quo elongati*.

Celano has no fear of stating quite definitely what he believed to

---

[1] *2 Cel. 2: "Exprimere intendimus et vigilanti studio declarare quae sanctissimi patris tam in se quam in suis fuerit voluntas bona, beneplacens et perfecta."*

[2] See above, pp. 60, 84 and 102.

have been the wishes of S. Francis. On the subject of buildings he says : " he taught his brethren to make poor habitations (*habitacula paupercula*), of wood not of stone (*ligneas non lapideas*), and to build them as small houses on a humble plan " (*2 Cel.* 56). This recalls both the words of the Testament, which refers to " *habitacula paupercula* ",[1] and also the frequent mention of the phrase " *ex luto et viminibus* " on the lips of S. Francis.[2] Having stated the wishes of S. Francis, Celano gives two examples of his indignation against new buildings, the first example being taken from the *Scripta Leonis* and the second from an unknown source.[3] A little later on, in § 71, Celano refers to the pressing problem of the friars abandoning the smaller hermitages and going to live in the towns, by saying that Francis " wished the brethren to dwell not only in towns but in hermitages ". At the same time Celano sees the danger of the self-willed friar who, under a show of asceticism, is in fact a positive menace to the Order [4] ; while he admits that hermitages were not always conspicuous for sanctity, as many of those who live in them " turn the abode of contemplation into a place of idleness, and change the hermit-rule, which was devised for perfecting the soul, into a sink of pleasure ".[5]

On the subject of begging Celano has much to tell us of the *bona voluntas* of S. Francis. In § 14 he tells how Francis himself learned to go begging from door to door, and from § 71 to § 77 he devotes a whole section to this subject, each of his tales coming from the *Scripta Leonis.*[6] On the question of clothes he says (§ 55) that Francis " longed after Poverty with all his heart ", and gives, as a sign of this, the fact that " from the beginning of the Religion until his death he was rich in a single tunic (*tunica sola*) with the cord and breeches " [7] In spite of the *Regula Bullata* which said that novices might have two tunics and a large cape,[8] Celano tells us that Francis " execrated those in the Order who wore three garments " and that he would " under no circumstances allow the brethren to have more than two tunics " (*2 Cel.* 69). Later, in § 130, which comes from *Per.* 75, he tells us that the only covering which S. Francis had was " *unica tunica* ", and in § 215 Celano can say with pride that, by refusing to claim as his own even the poor and shabby clothes which he wore, Francis " rejoiced and exulted for gladness of heart, for he saw that he had kept faith with the Lady Poverty even to the end ". In § 80 Celano tells us that Francis made those who wished to enter the Order give up all their

---

[1] *Opuscula*, p. 80. [2] Cf. *Per.* 48a and *Intentio*, 14 and 15.
[3] *2 Cel.* 57 (= *Per.* 48d) and 58 (= *Sp. S.* 6). [4] See *2 Cel.* 32 and 156.
[5] *2 Cel.* 179.
[6] *Ibid.*. 72-7 (= *Per.* 92b, 93, 43, 94, 95 and 92a). *2 Cel.* 71 is editorial.
[7] Cf. the Testament : " *contenti eramus tunica una . . . cum cingulo et braccis* ".
[8] *Reg. II*, cap. ii, in *Opuscula*, p. 65.

possessions, keeping back nothing at all—an obvious reference to the words of the *Regula Primitiva*: "*vendat omnia sua et ea omnia pauperibus studeat erogare*"; while in the following paragraph he points out that "no one consecrates himself to God in order to enrich his kinsfolk". Francis's abhorrence of money is referred to many times, especially in §§ 65, 66, 68, 77 and 92, most of which are not based on Leo's writings; while in § 185, in the description of the perfect Minister General, Francis is made to say: "Let him be a man who will loathe money, the chief cause of corruption in our profession."

On the subject of books, which of course raises the wider problem of the friars' attitude towards learning, Celano is again very outspoken. In § 52, which is editorial, he contrasts the quiet and tranquillity of the early days with the troubles which came later, some of which he attributes to the "learning of dissemblers". Again, in the description of the ideal Minister General (from which, incidentally, we can learn a good deal about the wishes of S. Francis) the saint is made to say: "Let him not be a collector of books, nor much intent on reading, lest he be taking from his office what he is spending by anticipation on study" (§ 185); in § 194 Francis says that when a great clerk joined the Order he ought in some way to resign even his learning so that, having stript himself of such a possession, he may offer himself naked to Christ; and in § 195 he is reported to have said: "My brethren who are being led by curiosity after learning will find their hands empty in the day of retribution", and to have foretold that the time was not far distant when he knew that learning would be an occasion of falling.

To turn to the second great problem—that of the Relations between the Friars and the Clergy—we find that here again Celano declares the wishes of S. Francis without any hesitation. "Now although Francis wished his sons to be at peace with all men", he writes in § 146, "and to behave themselves as little ones (*parvulos*) towards everybody, still he taught by word, and showed them, by his example, that they should be specially humble towards the clergy. For he used to say: '. . . Be subject to them who bear rule (*praelatis*) that, so much as in you lies, no jealousy may spring up'." In § 148, where he is recording the interview between Francis, Dominic and Ugolino, he tells us that the Cardinal expressed a wish that some of the friars should be raised to high positions in the Church; to which Francis replied: "My lord, my brethren have been styled Lesser (*minores*) so that they may not presume to become Greater (*maiores*). Their calling teaches them to be in lowliness and to follow the footsteps of Christ's humility." In the following paragraph Celano bursts out into a tirade against the friars and their presumption and rivalry. A later chapter (§ 201) tells of Francis's reverence for the priests of the Church, informing us that he used often to say : " If I chanced to meet at the same time any saint coming from heaven and any poor priest, I would do honour to the priest first, and would sooner go to kiss his hands ; and I would say to the other : ' Oh, wait, S. Laurence, for this man's hands handle the Word of Life and possess something that is more than human.' " [1]   After this there could not be much doubt that Celano wished the brothers to adhere to the principles which S. Francis had stated in his Testament :

" *Dominus dedit mihi, et dat, tantam fidem in sacerdotibus . . . quod, si facerent mihi persecutionem, volo recurrere ad ipsos. Et si haberem tantam sapientiam quantam Salomon habuit . . . nolo praedicare ultra voluntatem ipsorum ; . . . et nolo in ipsis considerare peccatum quia Filium Dei discerno in ipsis, et domini mei sunt.*"

The third great problem was the Interpretation of the Rule and the Authority of the Testament. Celano does not mention the Testament in the *Vita Secunda*, though, as we have seen, he constantly refers to the problems with which it dealt and declares the wishes of S. Francis. For the Rule he has the greatest respect, devoting a whole section to Francis's commendation of it to the brothers. His remarks here are not copied from an earlier source, but appear to be his own. Speaking of the saint he says : " he was full of the most ardent zeal for the common Profession and Rule, and on such as should be zealous concerning it he bestowed a singular blessing. For this Rule he declared to be for his brethren the Book of Life, the Hope of Salvation, the Marrow of the Gospel, the Way of Perfection, the Key of Paradise and the Covenant of an Eternal Alliance." [2]   On another occasion Celano tells us of certain words which Francis wanted to include in the Rule, but was prevented by the fact that the Rule had been already sealed.

For those who would not obey the wishes of S. Francis Celano has the most profound contempt. In § 162 he gives us this account of them : " The practice of virtue is hateful to many of them who, by desiring to rest before they have toiled, prove themselves to be not sons of Francis but of Lucifer. . . . Still more do I wonder at the impudence of these men (to use blessed Francis's word), for whereas at home they could only have lived by their sweat ; now, without toiling, they are fed on the sweat of the poor. . . . They know their meal-times, and if ever they feel hungry they complain that the sun has gone to sleep. . . . Am I to believe, kind father, that these monsters of men are worthy of thy glory ? No, nor are they worthy of thy tunic." Celano ends by blaming those in authority. " This pestilence rages among the subjects because the Superiors are shutting their eyes to it,

[1] The point of this is that S. Laurence was a deacon.   [2] *2 Cel.* 208.

as if it were possible to escape the punishment of those whose vice they are tolerating." [1] Such is Celano's own feeling about it. He also tells us how it affected S. Francis himself. In § 145 he writes: " When he saw that some were panting after office, whom, in addition to other things, their mere eagerness for power rendered unworthy, he used to say that they were not Lesser Brethren, but that they had fallen from glory, having forgotten the vocation wherewith they had been called. And when some wretched men resented being removed from high office (since it was the honour not the burden of it which they sought) he would silence them by many discourses." Again, in § 157: " 'The best brethren', he would say, ' are put to confusion by the works of the bad brethren. . . . Wherefore they are piercing me with a cruel sword which they are plunging into my vitals all the day long.' . . . And he would say: ' The time will come when, through evil examples, the Religion beloved of God shall be so ill spoken of that it will be ashamed to shew itself in public.' " On a later occasion Celano writes: " On the little flock which he had drawn after him he looks with a loving sympathy full of misgiving, lest after losing the world they may perchance lose heaven also " (§ 174). But perhaps the most pathetic of all is the picture which Celano gives us of the sick man raising himself up painfully from his bed and crying out: " Who are they that have snatched the Religion of myself and the brethren out of my hands? If I get to the Chapter General then I will shew them what my will is." And when his companions asked him whether he would not change those Provincial Ministers who had so long abused their freedom, Francis answered: " No, let them live as they like, for the perdition of a few is a lesser loss than that of many." [2]

Before we leave the subject of Celano and the problems of his day we ought to examine his references to Brother Elias. It will be remembered that in the *Vita Prima* Celano speaks of Elias in such a way that Sabatier called the work " un vrai manifeste en sa faveur ".[3] At the time of writing Elias was at the height of his power and was in close touch with Ugolino, who commissioned Celano to write this Life. Though not actually holding the post of Minister General, Elias was exercising a far wider influence than the mild and emotional John Parenti, who was officially the head of the Order. But by the year 1247 Elias had had his day. His self-indulgence and autocratic ways had led to his downfall, and he was now living outside the Order and excommunicate. Whatever Celano may have thought of him, he would have to tread carefully in what he said of him in the new Life

---

[1] *2 Cel.* 193.

[2] *Ibid.*, 188. For other references to this subject see *2 Cel.* 23, 69, 70, 81, 149, 156, 158, 179 and 182.

[3] See above, p. 65.

of S. Francis. As we look through the *Vita Secunda* we observe that Elias is nowhere mentioned by name, though on one occasion Celano refers to him by his title of "*Vicarius sancti*", a post which he held from the death of Peter Catanii in March, 1221, until after the death of S. Francis.[1] This reference is in the story of Francis blessing the brothers on his death-bed. In the *Vita Prima* Celano has told in detail how Elias received a special blessing: in the *Vita Secunda* he simply says that Francis blessed all the brothers "*incipiens a vicario suo*". On another occasion Celano tells of one of the brothers who managed to catch a glimpse of the wound in S. Francis's side.[2] Reference to the *Vita Prima*, § 95, shows that this was Elias. But more interesting than Celano's attempts to disguise Elias is the description of the perfect Minister General which is given in §§ 184–6. This is not taken from Leo and we have no indication of its source. Nor can we say whether it reports an actual statement by S. Francis, or whether it represents the views of the brothers as to what sort of Minister General they would like. Certainly, in reading it, one cannot help being reminded of Elias and the picture which is given of him in the barren years of his second generalate. "After prayer," says Francis of the perfect Minister, "let him appear in public to be heckled by all, ready to give answer to all, and to provide for all with meekness"; but Elias never summoned the brethren for consultation and called no Chapter Meeting while he held office. "Let him be a man," continues the saint, "who will loathe money, the chief cause of corruption in our profession and perfection, and who, being the head of a poor Religion, and offering himself to be copied by the rest, will never make wrong use of treasure chests"; but Elias had spent much time in exacting money for the building of the Basilica, and, as we are told, had had one of his treasure chests broken by the indignant Brother Leo. "For such an one his habit and a little book should suffice as regards himself, and, as regards the brethren, a box of pens and a seal"; but had not Elias scandalised them all by the sumptuousness of his life—his grooms, his stable, his fine horse? "If through weakness or fatigue he should need more palatable food he should not eat it in private but in public," says S. Francis; but one of the charges against Elias was that he had taken his meals alone like a Benedictine abbot, and Brother Bernard had reproved him for so doing. In fact,

---

[1] *2 Cel.* 144 (from *Sp. L.* 16, which obviously belongs to the end of S. Francis's life). Celano does not like the title *minister generalis* and seeks to avoid it wherever possible. In transcribing the *Scripta Leonis* he changes *minister generalis* to *vicarius sancti* (*2 Cel.* 28, 91, 144 and 151). Celano has another word, *guardianus*; but this was used of someone quite apart from the *vicarius*. Cf. *2 Cel.* 151, where Francis asks Peter Catanii to appoint him a *guardianus*. The *guardianus* appears also in *2 Cel.* 215.

[2] *2 Cel.* 138.

the whole of this chapter in Celano reads like a subtle rebuke of the generalate of Elias and his dictatorial and self-indulgent ways.

Celano's *Vita Secunda*, then, is quite definitely written from the point of view of one who wished to see the ideals and wishes of S. Francis carried out to the letter. It was an attempt to make clear what the Order was meant to be like and to show how far it had deteriorated from its original poverty, humility and simplicity. As such it was probably a disappointment to Crescentius, whose sympathies lay entirely with the relaxing party. This perhaps explains why it never became very widely known,[1] and why, although it was the official biography, it was thought necessary to supersede it fifteen years later by the *Legenda Maior* of S. Bonaventura.

NOTE ON THE *TRACTATUS DE MIRACULIS*

The *Chronica XXIV Generalium* informs us that John of Parma, who was Minister General from 1247 to 1257, invited Thomas of Celano to complete his Life of S. Francis by recording some of the miracles, and that Celano complied.[2] Salimbene also tells us that Celano wrote " a very beautiful book about the miracles as well as about the life " of S. Francis.[3] In other words, the *Vita Secunda* was felt to be inadequate without some account of the miracles, and Celano accordingly completed it. Whether he originally intended his book to be in three parts, on the same plan as the *Vita Prima*, with the third section devoted mainly to miracle-stories, we do not know. At any rate a manuscript was discovered by the Capuchin, Père A. de Porrentruy in 1898 and published by van Ortroy in the *Analecta Bollandiana* in the following year, which is clearly Celano's *Tractatus de Miraculis*, though the Introductory Letter which once preceded it has disappeared.[4]

The Quaracchi Fathers have given reasons for supposing that the work was written between 1250 and 1253.[5] It contains altogether sixty-five extracts from Celano's earlier works—54 from *1 Cel.*, 10 from *2 Cel.* and 1 from the *Legenda ad Usum Chori*.[6] Apart from these extracts there are 133 paragraphs, not many of which are of any very great interest, being mainly conventional miracle-stories. The most important sections are those which deal with the Stigmata, where

---

[1] Only two Manuscripts and a few fragments have been preserved. Cf. *An. F.*, X, fasc. ii, p. ix. *2 Cel.*, however, was known to the scribes of *Sp. S.*, *Per.*, *Little* and *S. Isid.* 1/73, unless they are quoting from later excerpts.

[2] *Chron. XXIV Gen.* in *An. F.*, III, p. 267.

[3] Salimbene, *Chronica*, in *Mon. Germ. Hist.* (*Scriptores*), xxxii, p. 176.

[4] See *Traité de Miracles de S. François d'Assise* in *An. Boll.*, xviii.

[5] *An. F.*, X, fasc. iii, pp. iv–v.

[6] This is an abbreviation of the *Vita Prima* made by Celano himself for liturgical purposes. See d'Alençon, *Prolegomena*, p. xlvi.

Celano slightly alters his previous statements, and the account of the arrival of Jacoba de' Settesoli at the death-bed of the saint.[1]

As for Celano's sources for this treatise, no doubt most of his material was derived from the mass of information sent in in response to the invitation issued by the Chapter of Genoa. Celano gives surprisingly few miracles in the *Vita Secunda*; and it is probable that, as he sorted out the material at his disposal, he made a little bundle of the miracle-stories to which he could return later. There are, however, two instances in which he seems to be drawing upon his own recollections. In § 5, in the section in which he is describing the Stigmata, he writes : " *Vidimus ista qui ista dicimus, manibus contrectavimus quod manibus exaramus, lacrimosis oculis delinivimus quod labiis confitemur . . .*" This suggests that Celano may have been present when S. Francis died, or at any rate soon after.[2] Again, in § 9, after an account of a woman whose faith was strengthened by a miracle, Celano writes : " *Vidi maritatam hanc virtutibus plenam, vidi fateor . . .*" The fact that he does not say anything like this about any of the other stories makes it likely that his own reminiscences are very scanty, and perhaps confined to this one incident.

II. The Legenda Antiqua of Perugia

Thomas of Celano presumably wrote his *Vita Secunda* at Assisi whither the material had been sent by the friars. But what became of this material afterwards ? The answer is, no doubt, that much of it was dispersed or destroyed; but the researches which have been conducted in recent years point to the conclusion that a good deal of it was preserved in the friars' library at the Sacro Convento and at San Damiano.

In 1305 Ubertino da Casale, in writing his *Arbor Vitae Crucifixae*, quotes the whole of the *Intentio Regulae* just as we know it in Fr. Lemmens' *Documenta Antiqua Franciscana* from the *S. Isidore* MS. 1 /73. Moreover, Ubertino ends his quotation with the words " *huc usque verba sancti Leonis*". Ubertino was a disciple of Conrad of Offida, who died in 1306 and who had been a personal friend of Brother Leo himself. Ubertino therefore had good reason to know whether the words which he was quoting were in truth the words of Brother Leo or not.

---

[1] For a discussion of this see Sabatier, *Examen des récits concernant les visites de Jacqueline de Settesoli à S. François*, in *Opuscules*, fasc. xv.

[2] It is possible that Celano is here using the " editorial we " to describe what the brethren as a whole saw. If Celano had been present when S. Francis died it is probable that his account in the *Vita Prima* would have borne marks of being the words of an eye-witness, whereas his description of the Stigmata is almost entirely taken from the Letter sent out by Elias.

Some years later—perhaps as late as 1321 [1]—a kindred spirit to Ubertino, Angelo Clareno, was writing his *Expositio Regulae* and *Historia Septem Tribulationum*. His information about the life of S. Francis was probably gathered earlier than this, perhaps in 1305 when we know that he was in Perugia and may have met Ubertino.[2] If these two men did in fact meet on this occasion, then they must have discussed the affairs of the Order and the original intentions of S. Francis, and Ubertino may have put Angelo in the way of reading some of the tracts of Brother Leo. At any rate, Angelo quotes the *Verba S. Francisci* in full in his *Expositio Regulae*,[3] and gives a number of quotations from the *Intentio* in both of his books. This being so, it seems pretty well established that these two little works of Brother Leo, the *Verba* and the *Intentio*, were at Assisi during the early years of the fourteenth century.

Thither, about this time, came an unknown scribe with the purpose of making a great collection of Franciscan material. We can find little in his writing to indicate what sort of man he was. He is quite content to insert the wishes of S. Francis in the matter of the Friars not obtaining privileges from the Pope, yet he begins his work with a large collection of papal Bulls. It is from these Bulls that we get an idea of the date at which he was at work. The last Bull which he copies out is dated March 21st, 1310. The important Bull, *Exivi de Paradiso*, of May 6th, 1312, is not mentioned. It is therefore probable that he was working between these two dates.

Besides the collection of Bulls we have in this manuscript a fragment of the *Legenda Maior* of Bonaventura, and what is entitled the *Legenda Antiqua*. It is this last part which is of moment to our study, for it seems to be closely dependent upon the original writings of Brother Leo.

The beginning and end of this document are mutilated, what remains being divided by Fr. Delorme into 115 chapters.[4] Of these, some twenty-three are merely extracts from *2 Cel.*, mostly concerned with the fundamentals for which Francis stood—poverty in buildings, furniture and dress, readiness to distribute to the poor, the authority of the Rule, etc. ; [5] a few are dependent upon sources which are otherwise unknown ; [6] but the greater portion of the work seems to be nothing less than a faithful transcript of the *Scripta Leonis et Sociorum eius*.

---

[1] D. Douie, *The Heresy of the Fraticelli*, p. 74.   [2] *Ibid.*, p. 59.

[3] Ed. Livarius Oliger (Quaracchi), pp. 126–9.

[4] Cf. *La Legenda Antiqua S. Francisci du MS. 1046 de la Bibliothèque communale de Pérouse*, in *A.F.H.*, Vol. xv, fasc. 1–4. Delorme published the Legend *in extenso* in the second volume of a series known as *La France Franciscaine* (1926). It was a pity that in so doing he gave an entirely different enumeration to the chapters.

[5] The chapters of *2 Cel.* which the scribe of *Per.* uses are : 56, 60, 65, 69, 86–9, 103, 113–14, 127, 143–4, 148, 150, 153, 155, 157, 159, 161, 175, 184–6, 188, 195 and 208.

[6] Viz. *Per.* 18, 20, 21, 55, 96–7 and 102.

The only one of the *rotuli* of Brother Leo which the scribe of *Per.* does not seem to have known is the small tract represented by chapters 153b, etc., of MS. *Little.*[1]   If this conclusion is right, then the discovery of this manuscript at Perugia by Fr. Delorme has done more than anything else in recent years to increase our knowledge of the inter-relationships and comparative values of the sources for the Life of S. Francis.

III.   The Speculum Perfectionis

Had this study of Franciscan sources been written forty years ago it is probable that this section, on the *Speculum Perfectionis*, would have been the longest of them all, for there is no document among those which are concerned with the Life of S. Francis over which there has been so much controversy.   It is hard to believe that when Sabatier wrote his famous *Vie de S. François* in 1894 the *Speculum* was still undiscovered, though some of the chapters in it were known from a collection entitled *Speculum Vitae* and published in 1504.   The chief sources upon which Sabatier had to depend were the writings of S. Francis, the two Lives by Celano, *Bonaventura*, the *Legenda Trium Sociorum* and the *Fioretti.*   Convinced that the *Leg. 3 Soc.* could only be a fragment, and assuming that the major part of it had been deliberately suppressed by Crescentius, Sabatier instigated a search for the missing chapters.   Perhaps he did not find quite what he was looking for : what he did find was a number of manuscripts called *Speculum Perfectionis* and containing a remarkable collection of intimate stories of S. Francis, written with a freshness which seemed to carry the reader back to the inner circle of his companions.   Moreover, one of these manuscripts bore the extraordinary date of May 11th, 1228, or, according to our reckoning, 1227.   Here, then, was a discovery of the very first magnitude.   Hitherto the earliest known Life of S. Francis had been Celano's *Vita Prima*, which was dated February, 1229.   If Sabatier was right, then we must acknowledge the fact that Leo got in first with his study of S. Francis.   Sabatier confidently published the *Speculum* as the first volume of his *Collection d'Etudes et de Documents pour l'Histoire religieuse et littéraire du Moyen Age* with the sub-title of *Sancti Francisci Assisiensis Legenda Antiquissima, auctore Fratre Leone.*

Sabatier prefaced the text of his document with a two-hundred page Introduction which thrills with pride and enthusiasm.   He marshals his arguments with great skill, calling to his aid the evidence of Angelo Clareno and Ubertino de Casale, comparing the versions of Leo and

---

[1] See above, p. 95.   The little tract must have been taken elsewhere before the scribe of *Per.* came to Assisi.

Celano and proving convincingly that Celano is using the *Speculum* as his source, pointing to the obvious freshness and spontaneity of his manuscripts and to such tell-tale phrases as " *nos qui cum ipso fuimus* ", " *oculis vidimus* ", etc.

The world of *Franciscanisants* was taken by storm. A theory so startling needed close examination, and gradually the cold light of criticism began to show up the weak points in Sabatier's argument. The chief attack was launched at the date given in the *explicit* of the manuscripts which Sabatier was using. Another manuscript was found to bear the date not MCCXXVIII° but MCCCXVIII°, and A. G. Little and others were able to prove, by both internal and external evidence, that the *Speculum*, far from being *Legenda Antiquissima S. Francisci*, was, in fact, a compilation made by an unknown scribe in 1318. For a time controversy on this point raged ; but gradually those who had accepted Sabatier's theory either died or changed their views, and it would be difficult now to find a Franciscan scholar who believed that any of the chapters of the *Speculum* were written before the *Vita Prima* of Celano.

There does not seem, then, to be much doubt that the *Speculum Perfectionis* was put together in 1318. The scribe admits that he is dependent upon earlier sources, for he writes : " *Istud opus compilatum est per modum legendae ex quibusdam antiquis quae in diversis locis scripserunt et scribi fecerunt socii beati Francisci.*" [1] In the light of the conclusions which we have reached so far, can we determine what were his sources, the " *legendae quaedam antiquae* " to which he refers ?

As we turn over the pages of the *Speculum Perfectionis* we see that, like Celano's *Vita Secunda*, it is written, not as a chronological account of the life of S. Francis, but as a study of his character, divided under several headings. There are thirteen chapters bearing such titles as " *de perfectione paupertatis* ", " *de spiritu prophetiae* ", " *de amore ipsius ad creaturas et creaturarum ad ipsum* ", etc. In the edition published by Sabatier these thirteen sections contain altogether 124 chapters. When we compare these with our other documents we find that 115 of these are practically identical with a similar number of chapters in *Per.*, though arranged in an entirely different order. The fact, however, that the wording in the *Speculum* and *Per.* is so similar does not help us to decide which is the original and which the copy. In order to do that we must consider the following points. First, the external evidence of Angelo Clareno, Ubertino da Casale, the scribe of *S. Isidore* 1/73 and others shows that the sequence which they knew was that of *Per.* and not that of the *Speculum*. The tables on pp. 104–7

---

[1] *Spec. Perf.* (Sabatier), p. 250. This *incipit* caused Sabatier some anxiety and formed the subject of a separate treatise by him : *L'incipit et le premier chapitre du Spec. Perf.*, in *Opuscules*, fasc. xvi.

will illustrate this ; for if we compare, for example, the use of the *Intentio Regulae* in the various documents we can see at once that the order in *S. Isidore* 1/73 and *Per.* (which is also that used by Ubertino) must be the original, and the order in the *Speculum* a rearrangement. Secondly, it is perfectly clear that the *Speculum* has taken a number of chapters from *2 Cel.*[1] The style of Celano is unmistakable, and, in spite of all that Sabatier says to the contrary, there is really no shadow of doubt that Celano is here the original. There are altogether 23 chapters in *Sp. S.* which come from Celano. But *Per.* has also taken a number of chapters from *2 Cel.* When we compare the two we find that the chapters which *Sp. S.* takes from *2 Cel.* are the very ones which *Per.* has already borrowed. It therefore looks as if the scribe of *Sp. S.* did not go direct to *2 Cel.* for these chapters, but took them, with the rest of his material, from *Per.* Thirdly, we cannot prove that the *Speculum* is any earlier than 1318, whereas we have already seen that *Per.* was almost certainly written in 1311–12. The only possible conclusion from these facts is that no less than 115 of the 124 chapters of the *Speculum* are taken direct from *Per.*, though, of course, arranged in a totally different order.

This leaves us with nine chapters which must have come from some other source or sources. They are numbered 6, 47, 48, 78, 79, 83, 84, 85 and 120.

Nos. 79 and 85, together with No. 52, seem to have formed a little tract which was known to the scribe of *Per.* and to Celano. We have already considered it and its authorship in Chapter IV (pp. 94–5).

No. 120 is a version of the *Canticum Solis* from the writings of S. Francis.

No. 48 is parallel with *2 Cel.* 152 and is the only chapter borrowed from *2 Cel.* which is not also in *Per.* But this is easily explained. The beginning of *Per.* is mutilated and begins in the middle of the chapter which we know as *2 Cel.* 153. This becomes No. 49 of *Sp. S.* But the previous chapter in *Sp. S.* (No. 48) = *2 Cel.* 152. It seems quite clear that the copy of *Per.* used by the scribe of *Sp. S.* was not mutilated like our copy, but contained a whole chapter which has since disappeared. That chapter would be copied from *2 Cel.* 152.

No. 47 is a " saying " of S. Francis based on *Little* 187 which is by Brother Leo. It was probably well known among the friars and formed part of the oral tradition. It was known also to Celano, who uses similar words in *2 Cel.* 51.

No. 6 seems to be a faithful transcript of a fragment which was known also to Celano. See a discussion of this on p. 95.

No. 78 seems also to represent an original fragment which Celano made use of in Part i of the *Vita Secunda* (*2 Cel.* 24).

Nos. 83–4, which deal with the Portiuncula, are peculiar to the *Speculum*. They may possibly come from a document which was preserved at the Portiuncula where the scribe was working.

---

[1] They are, *Sp. S.* 5. 14, 15, 29, 30, 31, 32, 41, 42, 43, 48, 49, 51, 53, 69, 70, 74, 75, 76, 77, 80, 86 and 93.

To sum up, then: the *Speculum* was not written by Brother Leo in 1227, but is a compilation made by an unknown scribe at the Portiuncula in 1318. Apart from a few chapters which are based on other sources, practically everything is taken from what we know as the *Legenda Antiqua* of Perugia, which was compiled some six or seven years earlier. As this was itself based very largely on the writings of Brother Leo, Sabatier was perfectly right to see in the *Speculum* a work which clearly emanated from the circle of the Saint's intimate friends. It is only with Delorme's discovery at Perugia, and a careful comparison of the various texts, that we can now trace the parentage of this collection.

IV. The MS. S. Isidore 1/73 (= Lemmens)

Fr. Leonardus Lemmens published the most important parts of this manuscript in three pamphlets which he called *Documenta Antiqua Franciscana* (1901-2). The manuscript has been more recently examined by van Ortroy and Professor Burkitt. Its date is generally believed to be somewhere in the latter part of the fourteenth century. Burkitt suggests that there were two different scribes,[1] van Ortroy that there were three.[2] This, however, does not concern us as the parts with which we are concerned are mostly contained between ff. 19b and 58a, which are all by the same hand. There is, however, one short section in ff. 168-73 which is of importance.

Perhaps we may take this section first, as it may give us a clue to the origin of the whole collection. It is entitled " de Legenda Veteri Beati Francisci " and is mainly a copy of *Per.* 42-8 which it follows word for word. This fact proves that when this manuscript was compiled the writer either had access to the Perugian MS. or to some source behind it. But what about the earlier folios? So far as they are concerned, we find in them three passages of importance—the *Intentio Regulae*, the *Verba S. Francisci* and a collection of stories called *Speculum Perfectionis* which is a great deal shorter than, and in an entirely different order from, the collection of the same name edited by Sabatier. But when we examine this version of the *Speculum*, edited by Lemmens, we are bound to admit that the greater part of it is nothing more than a copy of passages from *Per.* Thus: *Sp. L.* 1-5 = *Per.* 92-7 (but omitting 95); *Sp. L.* 8-19 = *Per.* 4-13; *Sp. L.* 20-3 = *Per.* 112-15 (but omitting 113); *Sp. L.* 24-33 = *Per.* 42-58 (but omitting 44, 46, 47, 52, 55 and 56); *Sp. L.* 35-43 = *Per.* 102-10 (but omitting 105). On the other hand, the great section of *Per.*

---

[1] Cf. *La Légende de Pérouse et le MS. 1/73 de S. Isidore* in *Revue d'Histoire Franciscaine*, Vol. ii, No. 4 (1925).

[2] Cf. *An. Boll.*, Vol. xxi.

indicated by Delorme by the letter D, is entirely omitted by the *S. Isidore* MS. We cannot believe that the scribe of this manuscript, who was so ready to make use of the Leo-papers, can have entirely ignored this most important section had he known of its existence. We can only conclude that the scribe of the earlier folios of the *S. Isidore* MS. had before him, not the Perugian MS. itself, but either the original sources which lay behind it, or some copies from them which had somehow come his way. Of the *Scripta Leonis* the writer seems to have known the *Intentio Regulae*, the *Verba* (which was probably not included in the notes sent in by the Three Companions), *Per.* 42–58, *Per.* 92–5, *Per.* 103–5, *Per.* 106–15, and the section generally known as *Sp. L.* 8–19, but which might just as well be called *Per.* 4–13. He does not seem to have known either *Per.* 59–91 or *Little* 153b, etc. It ought also to be noted that the copies of the *Scripta Leonis* which the scribe of S. Isidore was using are not in their original form. I do not think that anyone could maintain that *Per.* 102 is by Brother Leo, though it has been attached to the section numbered 103–5, which bears every sign of being a Leo-paper. Again, *Per.* 96 is definitely not by Leo, yet it was inserted into, or added on to, part of the *Scripta Leonis*. In both of these instances *Sp. L.* has transcribed the non-Leo material with the authentic. What is the explanation of this ? Nothing can be said with any certainty, but the sort of explanation which suggests itself is that the great Perugian collection was copied out *in separate sections*, and that the compiler of *S. Isidore* 1/73 used sections A, C and E, but did not know B and D.[1]

There remain one or two chapters in Lemmens' *Speculum* which need a word of explanation. *Sp. L.* 6 and 34 have already been examined in Chapter IV, pp. 94 and 92 ; *Sp. L.* 7 is a doublet of *Intentio* 9 ; *Sp. L.* 45 comes from the Admonitions in the Writings of S. Francis (Nos. 11 and 22) ; and *Sp. L.* 44 is a doublet of *Verba* 6.

V.   MS. Little

In 1910 Dr. A. G. Little bought, at a sale of part of the Phillipps library, a manuscript of great interest to Franciscan scholars. He has described it fully in *Collectanea Franciscana*, I, published in 1914 by the British Society of Franciscan Studies.[2] The manuscript itself is of about the year 1400 and appears to have come originally from Venice. It contains much that is of importance in our study of the Franciscan sources and, as I believe, alone preserves one of Brother Leo's precious rolls.

---

[1] As section B is nothing more than extracts from *2 Cel.*, the scribe of *S. Isid* 1/73 may have ignored it as he had other plans for quoting from Celano.

[2] This was republished in a French translation in *Opuscules*, fasc. xviii. See also Dr. Little's notes in *Some recently discovered Franciscan documents*.

The parts which concern us now are in what Dr. Little calls section iii (ff. 104–41), and especially the chapters which he has numbered 147–98. In this section the scribe has obviously had various sources upon which to draw for his material, but the main source is *Per.* Thus, *Little* 147–52 follows *Per.* 95–100e (part of which, of course, is taken up with the *Intentio Regulae*); 153a, 156–8 follows *Per.* 4–10; 159 = *Per.* 113; 160–9 is a selection from *Per.* 42–58; 184–5 = *Per.* 101; 186 = *Per.* 21; while 188–98 follows *Per.* 102–11. *Little* 178, 180 and 183 belong to a later age. *Little* 170–7 runs parallel with certain chapters from Celano's *Tractatus de Miraculis*, though Dr. Little has pointed out that there is some doubt as to which is the original and which the copy.[1]

By far the most valuable part of this manuscript is a group of seven chapters, numbered 153b, 154, 155, 187, 194, 195 and 197, which appear to form one of the original rolls submitted by Brother Leo and his companions in 1246. Somehow or other this roll became separated from the rest, for it was not apparently known to the compiler of the Perugian MS., nor to the scribes of *S. Isidore* 1 /73. Perhaps it drifted away from Assisi and was preserved in some library where the scribe of *Little* had access to it. But whatever the truth about its history may be, there can be little doubt that, hidden away in it, is a faithful and accurate copy of one of the *rotuli* of Brother Leo.

[1] *Collectanea Franciscana* (*B.S.F.S.*), I, p. 16.

BONAVENTURA'S
LEGENDA MAIOR S. FRANCISCI

HENRY SCOTT HOLLAND, in an article on Fr. Stanton, says : " There are few moments more dramatic in our Religious History than the recovery in the slums by the Oxford Movement of what it had lost in the University.",[1] Precisely the opposite development took place in the Franciscan movement. In the early days the Friars were no more than wandering evangelists, living in the slums of cities or in caves and huts in the forests, sharing their food with lepers and their lodging with asses,[2] preaching everywhere the good tidings of salvation. Within fifty years of the death of S. Francis they had become a learned Order, their Minister General living at Paris, their leaders men of scholarly distinction, and their appeal an appeal as much to the mind as to the heart of their hearers. How this development took place, and how S. Bonaventura came in later years to be regarded as the " second founder " of the Order, we must consider shortly. But first of all we must see how the ideal of Absolute Poverty fared during the years between the Chapter of Genoa in 1244 and the Chapter of Narbonne in 1260.

While the Three Companions—Leo, Angelo and Rufino—were at work on the collection of reminiscences which they proposed to send in to Crescentius, and which was to show the real wishes of S. Francis, a further blow was struck at the ideals which he had proclaimed by the publication of the Bull, *Ordinem vestrum*, by Innocent IV in 1245.[3] As we have already seen, Gregory IX, with all the authority of one who was not only Pope but had also been a personal friend of the Poverello and Protector of the Order, had, by his declaration, *Quo elongati*, in 1230, set the standard which the Order was to follow in subsequent years. He had considered the very difficult question of the authority of the Testament of S. Francis and had declared that it was not binding on the brothers. Having made this important decision he was able to modify the Rule in such a way as to allow the Order to

---

[1] H. S. Holland, *A Bundle of Memories*, p. 95.
[2] As at Rivo Torto. *1 Cel.* 44.   [3] Sbaralea, *Bull. Franc.*, I, pp. 400–2.

develop along the lines which he had always had in mind. Innocent IV, fifteen years later, ignores the Testament altogether and addresses himself directly to the problem of Poverty which was still agitating the minds of the brethren.

His Bull is in the form of an Exposition on certain chapters of the Rule of 1223. In it he goes a good deal further than any of the previous expositors had ventured. He develops and extends the powers of the " *amici spirituales* " who were mentioned by S. Francis in the *Regula Bullata* [1] as people who could be called upon in moments of particular emergency to help with the care of sick brothers or with the provision of clothing. By adding to the words " *pro necessitatibus* " the words " *vel commodis* ",[2] Innocent not only went far beyond the intentions of S. Francis but also very considerably modified the poverty of the friars. What S. Francis had intended as an emergency measure he makes the general practice of the Order, and creates a body of well-disposed people to whom the friars can always resort not only for necessities but for the ordinary means of subsistence. Though the friars would remain dependent upon the charity of others, the sense of insecurity and the necessity of begging from door to door were now permanently removed. Henceforth the friars could settle down to enjoy the gifts which their generous friends bestowed upon them, without any need for the discomfort of mendicancy nor for the fatigue of manual labour. Moreover, the Bull also gives to the friars the right to enjoy the *usum* of any property given to them—whether houses, lands, furniture, books or utensils—though the *proprietas* shall go to the Pope, unless the donor expressly reserve it to himself.

These modifications in the Rule naturally made a very considerable difference to the daily life of the friars. Instead of being obliged to wander from town to town they could now settle where they pleased, for there were not wanting pious benefactors who were glad to bequeath property to the friars in exchange for their prayers. The tendency was, therefore, to abandon the remote hermitages and to settle more and more in the towns, where they began to provide themselves with the sort of buildings which we know that Francis himself would have been quick to demolish with his own hands. Meanwhile, books were multiplying, the standard of living was rising, and, if we are to trust Salimbene, some of the friars were trying to make life even more comfortable by adopting the monastic custom of employing servants to relieve them of the more menial duties of a convent.[3]

Naturally, not all the friars approved of these changes which were

---

[1] *Reg. Bull.* cap. iv.

[2] " *Ad ipsum* (i.e. the *nuncius*, or *amicus spiritualis*) *possunt etiam Fratres pro suis necessitatibus, vel commodis, licite habere recursum* . . . etc." Sbaralea, *Bull. Franc.*, I, p. 401.

[3] *Chronica* in *Mon. Germ. Hist.* (Scriptores), xxxii, p. 288.

taking place. We hear of the Provincial Minister of Venice refusing to accept the very substantial bequests of one Marco Ziani, who wished to liberate the brothers from the necessity of ever going begging again, until he was forced by Alexander IV to accept the offer at once, notwithstanding the constitutions of the Order.[1] Several of the brothers complained of the habit of seeking privileges—so directly opposed to the wishes of S. Francis—as also of the claim that the friars should be exempt from the jurisdiction of the secular clergy. But the movement had begun, and what was to be the end of it ? [2] The snowball which had been set in motion in 1220 when Francis was away in the Levant was becoming nothing less than an avalanche. Was anyone capable of stopping it ? We have seen how the *zelanti* were silenced by Elias and his immediate successors. Crescentius of Iesi, who held the office of Minister General from 1244 to 1248, was equally out of sympathy with them. Well advanced in years when he joined the Order, a lawyer and a doctor by profession, he was the sort of man who does not shrink from dealing strictly with those whose point of view, being different from his own, he is incapable of understanding. Soon after his election a number of hot-heads, goaded into action by the betrayal of their ideals in the Bull, *Ordinem vestrum*, appealed to the Pope against the Minister General. Crescentius acted quickly and effectively. Hearing of their dissension, he obtained permission from Innocent IV to deal with them, and, before their appeal had a chance of being considered, sent seventy-two of them into immediate exile.[3]

But in spite of his ability in removing recalcitrant brethren, Crescentius does not seem to have been *persona grata* with the Holy See, for in 1248 he was politely invited to resign, shortly afterwards to be rewarded with a bishopric. In his place was elected a very different man, John of Parma. We owe to Salimbene a delightful account of this truly delightful man,[4] who travelled on foot through one province after another, visiting the friaries and encouraging the brethren. Humble enough to wash vegetables with his inferiors, yet a scholar who had taught in the schools of Bologna and Paris, he was in many ways the ideal man for the delicate task of handling the affairs of the Order. No wonder Brother Giles exclaimed : " Well and opportunely have you come, Brother John ; but you have come too late." [5]

---

[1] Gratien, *Histoire de la Fondation*, etc., p. 181. The Bull of Alexander IV (May 14th, 1255) will be found in Sbaralea, *Bull. Franc.*, I, p. 755.

[2] As Père Gratien says : " *On se trouvait engagé sur une pente glissante où l'on était exposé au péril de trouver bientôt la Règle absolument impraticable* " (*op. cit.*, p. 227).

[3] *Hist. VII Trib.* in *A.L.K.G.*, ii, pp. 466–70. Cf. Gratien, *op. cit.*, p. 235, and Scudder, *Franciscan Adventure*, p. 115.

[4] Salimbene, *Chronica, op. cit.*, pp. 295–312.

[5] *Hist. VII Trib.* in *A.L.K.G.*, ii, p. 263.

John of Parma made a noble attempt, in his teaching as well as by the example of his life, to stem the flood which was threatening to swamp the ideals of S. Francis altogether. When pressed, at the Chapter General in 1249, to make certain new rules for the Order, he replied : " We do not want any new rules : let us try to keep those that we have got." [1] And, in opposition to the teaching of Gregory IX, he stood by the Testament of S. Francis which he claimed as the most authoritative of all the documents since it had been written by S. Francis after he had received the Stigmata.[2] No wonder that, to the *zelanti*, it seemed as if their deliverer had come ; no wonder that in the *Fioretti* it is John of Parma who figures as the perfect Friar Minor.[3] But, as Miss Scudder remarks,[4] " he was an intellectual man, and his mind worked on large lines. He sought and thought he found a philosophy of history by which the ideals of Francis were shown, not as a spasmodic Counsel of Perfection for the few, but as an harmonious and culminating phase in the sequence of man's spiritual history." In other words, he came under the influence of the Joachimite philosophy which was to be his undoing.

The philosophy of history expounded by the Calabrian Joachim of Fiore was just the sort of thing to appeal to the brothers of the strict observance, and therefore to John himself.[5] The Church was not long in recognising it as a heresy, and the famous exposition of the works of Joachim by Gherardo di San Donnino was bitterly denounced and its author driven into exile. It is difficult for us to realise how much this thought shook the Church : it was certainly largely responsible for the deposition of John of Parma, besides throwing considerable suspicion on the whole Order. In February, 1255, the Pope summoned a Chapter Meeting to be held at Rome at which he asked John of Parma to resign. Holding the opinions which he did, his continuance in office as Minister General could do the Order no good. John was willing enough to be released from office, but the brothers held him in such deep respect that at first they would not hear of his going. They gave in at last, at the same time forfeiting their rights of election by asking him to nominate his successor. " Father," they said, " you have made visitation of the Order ; you know how the brothers live, and what they are. Show us to whom this office should be entrusted ; show us who should succeed you." [6] John of Parma, without a

---

[1] " *Non multiplicemus constitutiones, sed servemus bene illas quas habemus* ", Salimbene, *op. cit.*, p. 301.

[2] Cf. *A.L.K.G.*, i, p. 275.   [3] *Fioretti*, cap. xlviii.

[4] *Franciscan Adventure*, p. 135.

See *Joachim of Flora and the Everlasting Gospel* by E. G. Gardner in *Franciscan Essays* (*B.S.F.S.*), I, pp. 50–70.

[6] Salimbene, *op. cit.*, pp. 309–10.

moment's hesitation, nominated as his successor a young man of thirty-six, Giovanni Fidanza, known to history as S. Bonaventura.

The problems which faced the young Minister General when he took over the affairs of the Order were of two different kinds—intellectual and practical. On the intellectual side he had not only to defend the Order against the suspicion of Joachimism, to which his predecessor had given countenance, but he had also to justify its very existence against the attacks made upon it by the secular Masters of the University of Paris under the leadership of William of S. Amour. The quarrel had been going on for some time. In 1252 the secular theologians at Paris had passed a statute restricting the activities of the mendicants, who, in the following year, were " solemnly expelled " and obliged to seek Papal intervention to secure their restoration.[1] The result was that the divisions between the masters and the friars became more acute, though the Franciscans, through the tactful intervention of John of Parma, whose sanctity all could appreciate, fared much better than the Dominicans. A few years later the Bishops joined with the Masters in attacking the friars on the illegality of their ministry and on their denial of their own principles.[2]

If the Order was to justify itself in the eyes of the world, it must needs take up this challenge, and it could probably have found no better advocate than Bonaventura. He had already lectured on the Sentences and established an orthodoxy which was unimpeachable, while his ability and sincerity were obvious to all.

On the practical side the difficulties were no less acute. By the time Bonaventura took over the administration of the Order a stage had been reached when the future of the Order must be finally decided. The relaxations, which had really begun with the *Regula Bullata* in 1223, had been carried on by successive Popes, Gregory IX in *Quo elongati* and Innocent IV in *Ordinem vestrum*. The result had been that the Order was approaching more and more to the monastic ideal, though without the disadvantage of the " *stabilitas loci* " which cut the monk off from the world. Was this to be the future of the Order ? Or was it possible to dispense with the privileges and relaxations which had been granted and go back to the old idealism and intransigeance of S. Francis himself ? Or was there a middle way which would preserve the distinctive characteristics of a mendicant Order and yet satisfy the rising generation of friars who had neither known S. Francis

---

[1] See Rashdall, *Universities of Europe* (New Edition), I, pp. 370–97. The statute of 1252 decreed that " no Religious not having a College at Paris should be admitted to the Society of Masters, and that each religious College should in future be content with one master and one school " (p. 377).

[2] Cf. Gratien, *op. cit.*, p. 216 : " *On ne s'attaquera plus seulement aux droits des réligieux exempts, mais à leur existence et à l'idéal franciscain lui-même.*"

personally, nor had read either the *Regula Primitiva* or the Testament ?
As Etienne Gilson points out, there were by now two quite different
interpretations of the Franciscan ideal, and each friar had to decide
for himself which of these he believed to be right. He could, like
John of Parma, ignore the papal relaxations and go back to the original
intentions of S. Francis himself ; or he could argue that the Rule of
1223 represented Francis's later wishes, that it had received official
sanction, and that the interpretations put upon it by successive popes
had the very highest authority behind them. " Doubtless in law,"
says Gilson, " these two interpretations of the Franciscan life were
not contradictory. But if logically they were not so, they were very
much so psychologically." [1]

In assessing the contribution which Bonaventura made to the development of the Order we must remember that he belongs essentially to
the second generation of Franciscans. He was only five years old
when S. Francis died ; as a young man he had been attracted to the
Order by its vitality and freedom ; but the fact remains that he never
really understood the Franciscan ideal. His natural home was Paris
and its lecture rooms, not the forests of La Verna or the rocky caves
of Greccio and Fonte Colombo. To Francis Poverty, Humility and
Simplicity were ends in themselves, to be courted and wooed with
the ardour of a lover ; and to find some new method of self-abasement
or self-denial was a source of unspeakable joy. Bonaventura was also
a lover of Poverty, Humility and Simplicity, but as means to an end :
and that end was Truth. The rising schools, and the pursuit of
Truth, had captivated the intellectual powers of the young Bonaventura,
and he could never forsake his first love. [2] In the Franciscan movement he saw a way of life which, by its combination of self-humiliation
and liberty, created the ideal atmosphere in which scholarship could
flourish. The alliance of Poverty and Learning was the ideal for
which he strove. It was a very lofty ideal, and one which probably
safeguarded the future of the Order in those difficult years. But it
was not the ideal for which Francis had lived and died ; and we can
understand Brother Giles's complaint : " Paris, Paris, thou hast
destroyed Assisi ! " [3]

When the Chapter General met at Narbonne in 1260 it entrusted
to the Minister General the delicate task of writing a new and official
life of S. Francis. The need for such a work was obvious. Apart
from minor legends, the only biography of the saint was to be found

[1] Gilson, *The Philosophy of S. Bonaventura* (Eng. tr.), p. 42.
[2] Bonaventura was the first Minister General to make his headquarters outside Italy.
Although an Italian himself, he had made Paris his home and he continued to live there
as much as possible.
[3] Cf. Scudder, *op. cit.*, p. 105.

in the two books by Thomas of Celano. As neither of these was complete in itself, the reader would need both if he was to get any adequate impression of S. Francis. Moreover, they had been written at very different times, with an interval of sixteen or seventeen years between them, during which Celano's ideas had changed a good deal. So long as the authoritative Life was a subject of controversy there could be little hope of peace in the Order. The need was for a new Life which would be acceptable to all as a just portrait of the Saint and which would yet gloss over those embarrassing moments in his career which had led to so much controversy among his followers. To carry out this extremely delicate task was the charge laid upon Bonaventura. There was probably no one else in the Order who could even have attempted it.

In his Prologue Bonaventura speaks of the sources upon which he has drawn. He gives the impression that he has depended entirely upon the evidence which he has personally collected from the primitive disciples. " Having to set forth the life of so holy a man," he writes, " that I might obtain more certain knowledge of all things relating to it, I went to the place where he was born and learned from many who had been familiar with him whilst he was yet on earth, the manner of his life and conversation and of his departure out of this world. I examined all these things with great diligence and conferred thereupon with some who, having been his chief disciples, had full knowledge of his marvellous sanctity." [1] He tells us that he has felt himself specially called upon to do this so that " the acts, words and virtues of his life . . . may not perish with the lives of those who lived and conversed with him on earth ". Nowhere does Bonaventura make any reference to any written sources, and the reader is led to believe that the Legenda is an entirely original work, based exclusively on the actual witness of those who had been the most intimate friends of S. Francis.

Yet when we examine the Legenda we find that it is actually little more than a transcription from the two Legendae of Celano. There are quotations from no less than 74 chapters of 1 Celano, 92 chapters of 2 Celano and 108 of the Tractatus de Miraculis.[2] In other words, about 85 per cent.[3] of Bonaventura's Legend is taken directly, and often verbally, from Celano, and supplies us with practically no new information.[4] The new material which Bonaventura supplies can be

---

[1] Bonaventura, Leg. Maior, Prologue.

[2] This makes a total of 263 chapters, allowing for 21 in the Tract. Mir., which are themselves quotations from 1 and 2 Cel.

[3] Goetz says " at least nine-tenths ", Quellen, p. 248.

[4] As we have seen in Chapter iii, Bonaventura seems to have borrowed a passage from a very early work which is now lost. See above, pp. 76–81.

summarised in a few words. He tells us that a certain simpleton of Assisi used to pay especial honour to Francis when he was a youth, that Francis had a vision of the Crucified prior to that in S. Damiano, that after his denudation before the Bishop he was provided with some old clothes belonging to a farm labourer, that Sylvester had a vision of Assisi surrounded by a dragon, that the Cardinal John of S. Paul persuaded Innocent III to trust S. Francis and give him licence to preach. He gives us a fuller and more detailed account of the visit to the Soldan in Egypt, he tells us that Francis once forgot his sermon when preaching before the Pope, that a good many people saw the Stigmata while Francis was living, and he records a number of new miracle stories. Of this new information which Bonaventura gives us, the story of the simpleton and of the labourer's clothes must have come from some townsman of Assisi, who may, of course, have been one of the brothers. The vision of the dragon probably came from Sylvester himself if he were still living.[1] The two stories of S. Francis before the Pope may have come from one of the original twelve brothers or from some member of the papal court known to Bonaventura. The account of the visit to the Soldan must have come from Illuminato, Francis's only companion on that journey, who in 1260 was Provincial Minister of Umbria with his headquarters probably at Assisi, of which city he became Bishop in 1273.[2] The information about the Stigmata and the miracles must have been supplied by various people. On the other hand, Leo, who lived until 1271, does not seem to have been consulted by Bonaventura, nor Giles at Perugia, although Bonaventura claims to have witnessed one of his celebrated ecstasies.[3]

With the three works of Celano, a few other written documents and his own notes of conversations with Illuminato and possibly Sylvester and one or two others, Bonaventura makes the selection which is to be henceforth the official *Life of S. Francis*. If the purpose of Celano in writing his *Vita Prima* was to present a picture of a saint for the edification of the world as a whole, Bonaventura set out to paint a portrait which would belong primarily to the Order. Celano, in pursuit of his object, omitted many incidents which we consider vital for a true understanding of S. Francis, but which were probably not essential for the purpose which he had in mind ; Bonaventura glosses over or suppresses many things for the sake of reconciling conflicting parties in the Order or to bring credit on the Order in the eyes of the world. He writes essentially as Minister General, a man

---

[1] There is nothing to say when he died, though in *3 Soc.* 31 he refers to himself as an old man. That was in 1209. Being an Assisian, he may have also supplied the two incidents just mentioned.

[2] Sabatier, *Spec. Perf.*, p. 306, n. 3.

[3] *Leg. Maj.*, iii, 4.

with a responsibility to fulfil and a writer whose every sentence must be considered in its bearing on the future of the Order.

We know that during Francis's lifetime there were many and great dangers and difficulties in the Order, and that Francis himself was often sorely troubled by the apostasy of the brethren. Celano suppresses most of this in his *Vita Prima* for reasons which we have already considered,[1] but in his *Vita Secunda* he tells us how deeply S. Francis felt the dissension of his disciples. In a number of stories [2] he shows us the troubled spirit of S. Francis yearning over his brethren, and we have that most moving picture of the sick man raising himself up on his couch and crying: " If I get to the Chapter General then I will shew them what my will is ! " Incidents such as this are very precious to us: but they were not precious to Bonaventura, for they could only bring a certain amount of discredit on the Order. It is not altogether surprising, therefore, to find that he omits them entirely, together with the only references in *1 Celano* to the future troubles. Indeed, as we read through Bonaventura's *Legenda* there is little or nothing to suggest that there was ever anything but perfect peace and quiet in the Order. The only reference to any false brethren is in viii. 3, quoting *2 Cel.* 156, which says: " they who by their evil deeds dishonour holy religion incurred the most heavy sentence of his male-diction ", where the Latin leaves us doubtful whether " *sacra religio* " refers to the Order or to the cause of religion in general.

But even though the troubles which existed during the lifetime of S. Francis might be exaggerated, no one could suppose that there was much harmony afterwards, or that the Order was anything but divided at the time when Bonaventura was writing. Controversy still raged over the problems of Absolute Poverty, the Relations of the Friars with the Clergy, the position of Learning in the Order, and the Authority of the Testament of S. Francis. Bonaventura could only keep silent on these matters at the risk of disfiguring his whole portrait, for they were all ultimately dependent upon the teaching and practice of S. Francis himself.

On the subject of Poverty Celano has much to tell us in both his *Legendae*. Bonaventura quotes a good deal of it, though he deliberately leaves out the description of the hardships of the early days lest the Order should seem to have deteriorated from its first idealism. He also omits the passage in which Francis says: " I tell you that many noble and wise men are to join our company who will think it an honour to beg for alms ",[3] and one wonders whether Bonaventura himself ever engaged in such occupation. Moreover, Bonaventura omits all mention of any regular service of the lepers as part of the duty of a

---

[1] See, above, pp. 64–5.

[2] Cf. *2 Cel.* 70, 157, 174, 188, etc.   [5] *1 Cel.* 74.

friar, though he tells us that Francis himself devoted some time to this work at the beginning of his conversion.

The problem of the Relations between the Friars and the Clergy had grown no easier with passing years. S. Francis's own wishes in this matter are well known : the friars were to be in complete submission to the parochial clergy and were not to officiate in any capacity in their parishes without their consent. In the early days, when most of the brothers were laymen, and when their particular message was to be delivered more by the example of their lives than by any spoken words, this regulation could be quite easily enforced. But by the time of Bonaventura all the leading friars were in priests' orders and naturally expected both to preach and to hear confessions in the parishes. To have given S. Francis's teaching in full on this subject would have engendered more controversy just at the moment when reconciliation was most necessary. So Bonaventura makes two general statements on this subject : that Francis taught the friars to pay especial honour to priests, and that he himself had great veneration for all the ministers of God's word,[1] while he omits the great chapter in *2 Celano* in which Francis urges the brothers at all costs to avoid stirring up the jealousy of the secular clergy.[2]

As for the problem of the Authority of the Testament of S. Francis, Bonaventura solves it by never mentioning it anywhere in his *Legenda*. Celano only mentions it once, where he quotes Francis's words about the lepers. In copying out this passage almost verbatim Bonaventura passes the quotation over in silence. As the passage is a good example of Bonaventura's method, it is worth printing it side by side with Celano.

1 Cel. 17	*Bon.* iv. 6
Deinde vero *totius humilitatis* sanctus *amator se transtulit ad leprosos, eratque cum eis diligentissime serviens omnibus propter Deum,* et *lava*ns *putredinem* omnem ab eis, *ulcerum* etiam *saniem extergebat,* sicut ipse in testamento suo loquitur dicens : Quia cum essem in peccatis nimis amarum mihi videbatur videre leprosos, et Dominus conduxit me inter illos et feci misericordiam cum illis.	*Exinde totius humilitatis amator se transtulit ad leprosos, eratque cum eis diligentissime serviens omnibus propter Deum.* Lavabat ipsorum pedes, ligabat *ulcera,* educebat plagarum *putredinem* et *saniem* abstergebat.

---

[1] *Leg. Maj.,* iv, 3, and viii, 1.   [2] *2 Cel.* 146.

The problem of the position of Learning in the Order was probably that which caused Bonaventura most uneasiness. There is not the slightest doubt that Francis was suspicious of learning and did not want his brothers to have anything to do with it. On the other hand, Bonaventura was by nature and by profession a scholar, to whom the strictures of his master must have caused considerable embarrassment. But he was able to satisfy himself that there were quite legitimate interpretations of the wishes of S. Francis which would allow a friar to devote much of his time to scholarship. His arguments seem to us to be very casuistic when the intentions of S. Francis are so clear, but they probably appeared quite honest to Bonaventura. Roughly speaking, the argument was this : Francis had been most insistent on the friars doing some form of work ; the output of the mind is by common consent of greater value than the output of the body ; therefore the highest function which a friar can perform is to labour with his mind.[1]

When we turn to the *Life of S. Francis* we find that Bonaventura makes two references to this problem of Learning. In vii. 2 he quotes these words of Francis : [2] " He who would attain to this height of perfection must lay aside not only worldly prudence but even all knowledge of letters, that thus, stripped of all things . . . he may cast himself naked into the arms of the Crucified." Again, in xi. 1 he tells how Francis, when asked whether he wished learned men who entered the Order to pursue their studies, replied : " I would not have them study in order to know how they ought to speak, but in order that they may do the things which they hear, and when they have done them, that they may set them before others." On the other hand, he omits the following important passages in *2 Celano* : how Francis did not read the Bible (§ 105); how he said : " Learning makes many men indocile, not suffering a certain stiffness of theirs to be bent by the discipline of humility " (§ 194) ; and again how he said : " My brethren who are being led by curiosity after learning will find their hands empty in the day of retribution " ; and that he knew that learning would prove to be an occasion of falling (§ 195).

Among the other significant omissions which we find in Bonaventura, when we compare his legend with the sources which we know to have been before him, are the following. He never mentions S. Dominic, and the story of how Francis impressed a Dominican by his skill in interpreting a passage of Scripture is altered so that instead of " *quidam de ordine Praedicatorum* " we read " *quidam religiosus vir* ".[3] The reason for this is that the rivalry between the Franciscans and Dominicans was so strong by the time when Bonaventura wrote that he no doubt

---

[1] For the full argument, see Gilson, *Philosophy of S. Bonaventura*, pp. 49-55.
[2] From *2 Cel.* 194.   [3] Cf. *2 Cel.* 103 and *Bon.* xi. 2.

considered it more prudent to say nothing about the rival Order nor its founder.[1]

Again there are certain homely details in *Celano* which Bonaventura considers either undignified or unsuitable for a work of hagiography. For example, Celano tells us that Francis became so carried away when preaching before the Pope that he began to dance, that he approved of Brother Barbaro chewing dung as a punishment for an unkind word which he had spoken, and that Francis used sometimes to pretend to play the fiddle. Bonaventura passes all these incidents over in silence. Again, we notice such little things as this : in *2 Cel.* 81 Francis replies to the postulant of Ancona " with a smile " (*irridens*). Bonaventura omits this one word in a passage which is otherwise copied out verbatim.[2] Again, in vi. 2, he tells a story which he has found in *1 Cel.* 52–3. According to Celano, Francis had been eating chicken when recovering from an illness. Bonaventura merely says vaguely that he had " relaxed the discipline of abstinence to a certain extent " but without saying how. Or again, in the story of the angelic lute, which Francis heard at Rieti, Celano, who takes the story from Leo, says that when Francis made his request for a little music his companion demurred on the grounds of impropriety, with which Francis acquiesced. In Bonaventura we are told that it was Francis's scruples, not those of his companion, which forbade him to ask for music (" *nec id honestatis decentia per ministerium fieri pateretur humanum* ").[3]

All these examples show how Bonaventura's mind was working. As Goetz says : " the saint must become ever more saintly ",[4] and little human touches, such as even Celano occasionally indulged in, must be omitted wherever possible. For the same reason Bonaventura quotes all the passages in Celano where S. Francis teaches the brothers to beware of familiarity with women, but suppresses his visits to S. Clare [5] and the arrival of his friend Jacoba de' Settesoli at his death-bed.[6] One other very significant omission in Bonaventura is the description of the perfect Minister General in *2 Cel.* 184–6, in which Francis is made to say : " For such an one his habit and a little book should suffice as regards himself, and as regards the brethren a box of pens and a seal. Let him not be a collector of books nor much intent on reading lest he be taking from his office what he is spending by anticipation in study."

---

[1] In 1255 the Ministers General of the two Orders had to issue a joint letter, " *de pace servanda* ", urging their members not to be so quarrelsome. Cf. *Monumenta Ordinis FF. Praed. Historica*, V, pp. 25–31.

[2] Cf. *2 Cel.* 81 and *Bon.* vii. 3.   [3] Cf. *2 Cel.* 126 and *Bon.* v. 11.

[4] Goetz, *Quellen*, p. 251 : " *der Heilige muss immer heiliger werden* ".

[5] E.g. *2 Cel.* 207.   [6] *Tract. Mir.* 37.

Among other indications of the attitude of mind in which Bonaventura composed his Legend are the following. He omits the phrase which occurs in Celano that Francis called the devils the "*castaldi Dei*", "God's officers";[1] also the incident in which two of the brothers were reprimanded by the Bishop of Fondi for their eccentricities;[2] also that the Bishop of Assisi was not worthy to go in and see S. Francis at prayer,[3] and that the Bishop of Tivoli collapsed on beholding a certain miracle wrought by the saint.[4] On the other hand, he adds to the story of the Christmas Crib at Greccio the information that permission was first obtained from the Pope for this innovation,[5] and to the account of a certain miracle that it was only performed after the patient had given up his heretical opinions.[6]

All these examples will show that Bonaventura's work was written with a definite purpose. It was important that the world should have an authoritative portrait of S. Francis, but it was equally important that the conflict of loyalties in the Order should be healed. The Order had progressed during the last forty years, and was now, by its association with the Universities, playing a part in the world which, even though it might be different from what Francis had originally intended, was yet an important and valuable one. That was the thing that mattered : that was the work to which all the energy of the Order must be directed : no useful purpose would be served by reminding people of certain things which S. Francis had said half a century before that development had taken place. A religious Order, like the Church itself, is a living organism which must grow and develop ; it is no good thinking that you can undo what has been done, nor stem the tide of progress. In all this Bonaventura was right, and his Legend must be regarded as a brilliant piece of work if we constantly bear in mind the circumstances in which it came to be written. Here we see S. Francis the humble imitator of Christ, the Saint, the wonder-worker, the founder of the most excellent community in the world. Let this be the official portrait : let men read here if they would know what S. Francis was like : let us forget or do away with other interpretations and make a fresh start.[7] So Bonaventura thought. Yet if we had no other source than this for the *Life of S. Francis* every one of us must admit that we should be immeasurably the poorer.

---

[1] *2 Cel.* 120: *Bon.* vi, 10.   [2] *2 Cel.* 156.   [3] *Ibid.* 100.
[4] *Tract. Mir.* 93 : *Bon. Mir.* v, 4.
[5] *Bon.* x, 7.   [6] *Bon. Mir.* v, 4.
[7] In 1266 a decree was passed by the Chapter that all previous manuscripts should be destroyed. Cf. Sabatier, *Vie de S. François*, p. lxxxv, n. 1. It has been suggested, by van Ortroy and others, that this decree referred only to Liturgical works, but the text as quoted by Little in *E.H.R.*, 1898, p. 705, makes it quite clear that it refers to all previous legendae : "*Praecipit generale capitulum per obedientiam quod omnes legendae de b. Francisco olim factae deleantur, et ubi extra ordinem inveniri poterunt ipsas fratres studeant amoveri.*"

NOTE: BONAVENTURA AND HIS SOURCES

Bon. i. 1. *1 Cel.* 1, 17. *3 Soc.* 6.
2. *1 Cel.* 2 and 5.
3. *1 Cel.* 5. *2 Cel.* 6. *3 Soc.*
5–6.
4. *1 Cel.* 6. Cf. *Julian* 3.
5. *2 Cel.* 9 and 11.
6. *1 Cel.* 17.
ii. 1. *1 Cel.* 8–9. *2 Cel.* 10.
2. *1 Cel.* 10–12.
3. *1 Cel.* 13–14.
4. *1 Cel.* 15. *2 Cel.* 12.
5. *1 Cel.* 16.
6. *1 Cel.* 16–17. Cf. *Julian* 11.
7.
8. *1 Cel.* 21. *2 Cel.* 20.
iii. 1. *Julian* 15. Cf. *1 Cel.* 22.
2. *Julian* 16.
3. *Julian* 17. Cf. *3 Soc.* 27,
2 Cel. 15.
4. *1 Cel.* 25.
5. *2 Cel.* 109. *3 Soc.* 30.
6. *1 Cel.* 26–7.
7. *1 Cel.* 29–30. *Julian* 20.
8. *1 Cel.* 32–3. *Julian* 21.
3 Soc. 53.
9. *2 Cel.* 16.
10. *2 Cel.* 17.
iv. 1. *1 Cel.* 34.
2. *1 Cel.* 35. *Julian* 23.
3. *1 Cel.* 42 and 45. *Julian* 27.
4. *1 Cel.* 47.
5. Cf. *1 Cel.* 44.
6.
7. *1 Cel.* 39–40.
8.
9. *2 Cel.* 106.
10. *1 Cel.* 48.
11. *2 Cel.* 209.
v. 1. *1 Cel.* 51.
2. Cf. *1 Cel.* 64.
3.
4. *2 Cel.* 116–17.
5. *2 Cel.* 112–14.
6.
7. Cf. *2 Cel.* 22.
8.
9. *2 Cel.* 166. *Tract. Mir.* 14.
10. *Tract. Mir.* 17.
11. *2 Cel.* 126.
12.

Bon. vi. 1. *1 Cel.* 53.
2. *1 Cel.* 52–3.
3. *2 Cel.* 133–4.
4. *2 Cel.* 151–2.
5. *2 Cel.* 145 and 148.
6. *2 Cel.* 123.
7. *2 Cel.* 202.
8. *2 Cel.* 147.
9. *2 Cel.* 108.
10. *2 Cel.* 119.
11. *2 Cel.* 154.
vii. 1. *2 Cel.* 55.
2. *2 Cel.* 56–9 and 194.
3. *2 Cel.* 81.
4. *2 Cel.* 67.
5. *2 Cel.* 68.
6. *2 Cel.* 93 and 84.
7. *2 Cel.* 72–3.
8. *2 Cel.* 71.
9.
10. *2 Cel.* 77.
11.
12. *2 Cel.* 46.
13.
viii. 1.
2. *2 Cel.* 164.
3. *2 Cel.* 155–8.
4. *2 Cel.* 182.
5. *2 Cel.* 85–7 and *1 Cel.* 76.
6. *2 Cel.* 111 and *1 Cel.* 77.
7. *Tract. Mir.* 31.
8. *1 Cel.* 60–1. *2 Cel.* 167.
Tract. Mir. 29–30, 23–4.
9. *2 Cel.* 171. *Tract. Mir.* 27.
Cf. *1 Cel.* 59.
10. *2 Cel.* 170 and 168. *Tract.
Mir.* 26 and 25.
11. *2 Cel.* 35–6.
ix. 1.
2. *2 Cel.* 201.
3. *2 Cel.* 198 and 197.
4.
5. *1 Cel.* 55.
6. *1 Cel.* 56.
7. *1 Cel.* 57.
8.
9.
x. 1. *2 Cel.* 94. Cf. *1 Cel.* 71.
2. *2 Cel.* 95 and 98.
3. Cf. *2 Cel.* 122.

Bon. x. 4.   *2 Cel.* 99 and 94.
    5.   *2 Cel.* 100–1.
    6.   *2 Cel.* 96–7. Cf. *1 Cel.* 82.
    7.   *1 Cel.* 84–6.
  xi. 1.   *2 Cel.* 102.
    2.   *2 Cel.* 103 and 102.
    3.   *2 Cel.* 30.
    4.   *Tract. Mir.* 41.
    5.   *2 Cel.* 41.
    6.   *2 Cel.* 38.
    7.
    8.   *2 Cel.* 31.
    9.   *1 Cel.* 49–50. *2 Cel.* 49.
   10.   *2 Cel.* 48.
   11.   *2 Cel.* 34.
   12.   *2 Cel.* 45.
   13.   *2 Cel.* 39.
   14.
  xii. 1.
    2.
    3.   *1 Cel.* 58. *Tract. Mir.* 20.
    4.   *1 Cel.* 59. *Tract. Mir.* 21.
    5.   *Tract. Mir.* 22.
    6.
    7.   *1 Cel.* 23 and 73.
    8.   *1 Cel.* 36.

Bon. xii. 9.   *1 Cel.* 65–6. *Tract. Mir.*
          175–6, 174 and 178.
   10.   *1 Cel.* 67 and 69–70. *Tract.*
          Mir. 177, 124, 121, 155–6.
   11.   *1 Cel.* 68, 63b and 64.
          Tract. Mir. 195, 108 and
          19.
   12.
 xiii. 1.   *1 Cel.* 91 and 94.
    2.   *1 Cel.* 92.
    3.   *1 Cel.* 94–5. Cf. *3 Soc.* 69.
    4.
    5.
    6.   *Tract. Mir.* 18.
    7.   Cf. *Tract. Mir.* 19.
    8.   Cf. *1 Cel.* 95. *2 Cel.* 136
        and 138.
    9.
   10.
 xiv. 1.   *1 Cel.* 103.
    2.   *1 Cel.* 107.
    3.   *2 Cel.* 214.
    4.   *2 Cel.* 215–17.
    5.   *2 Cel.* 216. *1 Cel.* 108–10.
    6.   *1 Cel.* 110. *2 Cel.* 217–18,
        and 220. *Tract. Mir.* 32.

Bon. xv is an account of the Canonisation of S. Francis. Parts of it, especially in §5, are copied from *1 Cel.* 116 and 118.

Bon. Mir. i. 1.   *Tract. Mir.* 2.
    2.
    3.   *Tract. Mir.* 10.
    4.   *Tract. Mir.* 8–9.
    5.   Cf. *Tract. Mir.* 11–13.
    6.   *Tract. Mir.* 6–7.
  ii. 1.   *Tract. Mir.* 40.
    2.   *Tract. Mir.* 46.
    3.   *Tract. Mir.* 43.
    4.   *Tract. Mir.* 42.
    5.   *Tract. Mir.* 44.
    6.   *Tract. Mir.* 45.
    7.   *Tract. Mir.* 47.
    8.   *Tract. Mir.* 48.
  iii. 1.   *Tract. Mir.* 49.
    2.   *Tract. Mir.* 50.
    3.   *Tract. Mir.* 51.
    4.
    5.   *Tract. Mir.* 54.
    6.   *Tract. Mir.* 57.
    7.   *Tract. Mir.* 58.
    8.   *Tract. Mir.* 59.
    9.   *Tract. Mir.* 56.
   10.   *Tract. Mir.* 61.

Bon. Mir. iii. 11.
   12.   *Tract. Mir.* 187.
 iv. 1.   *Tract. Mir.* 81.
    2.   *Tract. Mir.* 82.
    3.   *Tract. Mir.* 83.
    4.   *Tract. Mir.* 86, and cf.
        84.
    5.   *Tract. Mir.* 85.
  v. 1.   *Tract. Mir.* 88.
    2.   *Tract. Mir.* 89.
    3.   *Tract. Mir.* 91.
    4.   *Tract. Mir.* 93.
    5.   *Tract. Mir.* 94.
  vi. 1.   *Tract. Mir.* 95.
    2.   *Tract. Mir.* 96.
    3.   *Tract. Mir.* 97, and cf.
        99.
    4.   *Tract. Mir.* 98.
    5.   *Tract. Mir.* 106.
 vii. 1.   *Tract. Mir.* 116.
    2.   *Tract. Mir.* 118.
    3.   *Tract. Mir.* 119.
    4.   *Tract. Mir.* 120.
    5.   *Tract. Mir.* 122.

Bon. Mir. vii. 6. *Tract. Mir.* 123.
7. *Tract. Mir.* 117.
viii. 1. *Tract. Mir.* 125.
2. *Tract. Mir.* 109.
3. *Tract. Mir.* 152, and cf. 153.
4. *Tract. Mir.* 150, and cf. *1 Cel.* 137, and *Tract. Mir.* 151.
5. *Tract. Mir.* 147, and 146.
6. *Tract. Mir.* 148, and 149.
7. *Tract. Mir.* 181.

Bon. Mir. ix. 1.
2. *Tract. Mir.* 100, and cf. 101–3.
3. *Tract. Mir.* 129.
4. *Tract. Mir.* 128.
x. 1. *Tract. Mir.* 16.
2. *Tract. Mir.* 189–92.
3. *Tract. Mir.* 183, and cf. 184–6.
4. *Tract. Mir.* 182.
5. *Tract. Mir.* 158.
6. *Tract. Mir.* 159.
7. Cf. *Tract. Mir.* 159.
8.
9.

THE LAST FLOWERING OF THE FRANCISCAN LEGEND

WITH the completion of Bonaventura's *Life of S. Francis* about the year 1262 it might seem that the canon of the Franciscan Legend would be closed. The *Legenda Maior* was not just a casual work put out by one of the friars, but was the official biography, written by a man who was not only Minister General of the Order but also by far the most distinguished Franciscan of his day, or indeed for many years to come. It was, moreover, meant to be conclusive, to sum up the work of previous writers and to set the seal upon the official portrait of the saint. There had been controversy enough in the Order over what Francis actually said and did : now there should be before the brothers a standard biography, avoiding all extremes and seeking to do justice to both sides. The subsequent edict to destroy all previous legends was part of the same policy of standardisation.

To the majority of the brothers, no doubt, Bonaventura's Life seemed perfectly adequate. The number of those who had actually known S. Francis was growing small, for he had been dead now for close on forty years. The young men who joined the Order were probably conscious of the fact that there had been difficulties and disagreements, and that there were still a few who obstinately flew in the face of authority and insisted upon living alone in hermitages, refusing to come into line with the rest of the Order and with the developments which were taking place both in its constitution and in its work. But these men were rebels, if not schismatics, and the tradition which they treasured was probably quite unknown to the new generation of friars which was growing up. To the novice of 1265 there were two documents upon which his knowledge both of S. Francis and of the Order was based, the *Legenda Maior* of Bonaventura and the Rule of 1223. He may have been conscious of an earlier Rule, but what did it matter since it was never ratified by the Pope and was obviously abandoned when the *Regula Bullata* was promulgated ? Of the inner history of the writing of that second Rule he would learn nothing from the pages of Bonaventura. As for the Testament of S. Francis, it is doubtful whether he would even be aware of its existence. Certainly he would not regard it as a document of any real authority.

So the Order went its way as the years passed by and the number of those who had had any personal contact with the Saint grew less. It has been necessary in these pages to show how a good deal of the idealism of the Saint was gradually abandoned by the Order, and to trace the disappearance from the official portrait of many features which seem to us the most valuable. But we must not think of this development as a betrayal of all that S. Francis stood for. The problem as to whether the absolute Poverty of Francis and his first disciples could ever have become the standard for an Order of world-wide extent is one which will never be solved. It is easy for students who themselves have never had to face the problem of complete renunciation to lament all that occurred from 1221 onwards, and it is perhaps not unnatural that writers who themselves belong to the Order of S. Francis should have been more lenient towards the relaxing party than those who see the problem only on paper. To adapt a manner of living which was primarily intended for a small group, each carefully tested, and each individually under the inspiration of a man of consummate genius, to a vast international fellowship which was almost certain to take into its numbers some who were not altogether in sympathy with its ideals, was something which neither the inspiration of S. Francis nor the ingenuity of the Church could altogether accomplish. But even though the Friars Minor of 1265 were a different type from those of 1215, the fact remains that some of the finest spiritual work, and some of the greatest reforms of the thirteenth century, were due to these men.

The beginning of the break-up of Feudalism and the growth of the towns had created an entirely new problem for the Church and one which the parochial machinery was hardly capable of solving. Into the already overcrowded cities newcomers were continually forcing their way, many of them attracted from the country districts by the hope of freedom and prosperity. Within the city walls rich and poor lived together in conditions which we should nowadays regard as quite intolerable. The medieval town had few of the advantages and public services which we associate with municipal life to-day. The rich were, no doubt, able to provide more or less for their own needs, but the poor were huddled together in conditions of indescribable poverty and squalor. It was therefore in the midst of these people that the friars built their churches, and to them that they ministered.[1] Dressed in

[1] The evidence of the early records does not altogether bear out some of the statements in Brewer's otherwise admirable Introduction to the *Monumenta Franciscana*, I. Cf. Dr. Little's *Studies in English Franciscan History*, pp. 10-14. Our chief authority for the early history of the Grey Friars in England is Eccleston's *Chronica de Adventu Fratrum*

clothes no better than those of the poorest artisan, barefoot even in an English winter so that their bleeding feet, cut by the ice, left the print of blood on the snow, content with a tiny lodging and with the poorest of food, the Franciscan went his way among the people, preaching, no less by his life than by his words, the Christian message of love. Truly it might be said that the poor had the Gospel preached to them. No doubt there were bad convents where Lady Poverty was feared rather than loved, and no doubt there were bad friars who preached and ministered with an eye to material rewards; but the greater abuses which brought the Order into such contempt with writers like Chaucer and Langland, and with reformers such as Wyclif, were of later growth.[1] If we can trust contemporary chroniclers, the early settlements were poor enough, even though the buildings might be of stone and not of wood, and even though the friars might have beds to sleep on, a spare habit or a blanket for cold nights, and a few books with which to say the Offices.

Meanwhile, at the Universities, the friars were doing a valuable work by bringing a new atmosphere into the schools. At the time of the Franciscan revival the pursuit of learning had become opportunist and material. The most popular faculty was that of law, for the well-trained lawyer has generally been able to feather his own nest. But if the friar went to the University he went either for the sheer love of knowledge, like Bonaventura, Roger Bacon and many another, or he went in order to equip himself as a preacher, knowing that much of his preaching would be to the poor and ignorant. His presence at the University, therefore, encouraged the study and the dissemination of pure theology as opposed to the teaching of the Canonists and Logicians.[2] Meanwhile his manner of living, whether he be master or scholar, was simple enough to foster that alliance of scholarship with poverty which was so valuable a feature of medieval life.

The towns and the Universities, therefore, absorbed most of the Grey Friars into their atmosphere of progress and vitality, the friars themselves having much to offer in both spheres. Yet there remained always a minority to whom both of these developments were anathema. Indeed, to them, every official movement in the Order since 1221

Minorum in Angliam. This has been printed in *Mon. Franc,* I (1858) and *An. F.,* I (1885), but the definitive edition is that of Dr. Little in *Collection d'Études,* Paris, 1909. There are translations by Fr. Cuthbert (1903) and Miss Gurney Salter (1926).

[1] The friar of Chaucer's Prologue, a "wanton and a merrye" whose "absolucioun" could be so "plesaunt" if the penitent were liberal enough, and the mendicants of Piers Plowman "preching the peple for profyt of heore wombes" or bellies, are not attractive creatures, and have no spiritual kinship with the early companions of S. Francis. See Little's chapter on "The Failure of Mendicancy" in *Studies in English Franciscan History.*

[2] Brewer in *Monumenta Franciscana,* I, Intro., p. 1 (=50).

had been something of a betrayal of the high standards of S. Francis himself.   First had come the *Regula Bullata* of 1223, then the building of the Basilica at Assisi, then the Bull *Quo elongati* in 1230, followed fifteen years later by worse concessions in *Ordinem vestrum*, and now the official *Legenda Maior* of S. Bonaventura with its conventionalised portrait of the Poverello which they found so unreal.   It is easy to understand their attitude, and it is easy also to see how unpopular they must have been.   The few veterans of the little group which had shared the rigours of Rivo Torto were treated with the respect which was obviously their due, though they themselves seem to have kept very quiet after submitting their reminiscences in 1246.[1]   Like the more active of the *zelanti* they lived mostly as solitaries, or in some small community hidden away in a lonely part of the Apennines.   Among them all there was a comradeship which supported them in their trials and which was later to result in a belated flowering of the Franciscan legend which is one of the most enchanting things which we possess.

Among the " Spirituals " there were three main groups : one in Provence under the leadership of Jean Pierre Olivi, one in Tuscany under Ubertino da Casale, and one in the Marches of Ancona led by Angelo Clareno.   Of these three it is the last which is most interesting to us, partly because we have so vivid an account of their life and struggles in the fifth book of Clareno's *Historia Septem Tribulationum*,[2] and partly because it was among them that the traditions of the early days were most faithfully treasured.   " In the Marches of Ancona," writes Father Cuthbert, " the brothers of the strict observance were numerous and venturesome."   Their extremist views and insubordination to authority soon brought them into trouble.   We read of men who were cruelly imprisoned in solitary confinement, deprived of the Sacraments and forbidden the use of books ; others were exiled.   It is true that a brief respite was granted to them during the pontificate of Celestine V.   He was a man whose sympathies were entirely with the " Spirituals " ; and under his rule they were granted a number of privileges, including that of calling themselves " the poor hermits of Pope Celestine " and of being free from the control of the Order. But the reign of this holy but most inefficient of Popes was a short and unhappy one, and his successors were men of a very different stamp. More and more then were the " Spirituals " separated from the rest of the Order, driven in on themselves and turned into fanatics who cared only for their own interpretation of the Franciscan ideal.[3]

In their struggles for what they believed to be right, and in their

---

[1] Angelo is said to have died in 1258, Giles died in 1261, Masseo probably about the same time, Leo and Rufino lived on until 1271.

[2] Published by Fr. Ehrle in *A.L.K.G.*, ii, pp. 287–327.

[3] *A.L.K.G.*, ii, p. 309.

sufferings for conscience sake, there were two things which brought courage to these outcasts, and enabled them to carry on. One was the sense of having been entrusted with a mission, which was, to keep glowing the fast-cooling embers of the original Franciscan ideals of Poverty, Humility and Simplicity. It was in order to encourage one another in this project that they cherished among themselves the stories of the early days which they had received from the companions of S. Francis, who, though they gave little outward indication of their thoughts, were yet naturally sympathetic towards the idealists. Some of these stories were no doubt apocryphal, many were strangely distorted as they passed from mouth to mouth; but the tradition was handed down from the first generation of friars to men like Conrad of Offida, James of Massa, James of Fallerone, and from them to Angelo Clareno, John of La Verna, Ugolino of Monte S. Maria and many others. The other factor in their lives which brought them courage in the hard battle which they were fighting was a personal mysticism which not only strengthened them individually but also gave them some status in the eyes of the world. The visions of John of La Verna and James of Massa were of the kind which the medieval mind treated with respect, and " men took knowledge of them that they had been with Jesus ".

We have seen that to the majority of the brothers the *Legenda Maior* of S. Bonaventura seemed a perfectly adequate portrait of the saint. Yet there were some who felt that certain omissions in that Legend ought to be rectified, and the Chapter General of Padua in 1277 even went so far as to initiate a search for any available information about S. Francis which could still be collected.[1] What the result of this appeal was we do not know, but the lack of further biographies suggests that the response was disappointing. The only one whom we know of as having written a book which definitely set out to supplement Bonaventura was his own secretary and travelling companion, Bernard of Bessa.

His *Liber de Laudibus Beati Francisci*,[2] published about 1278, is frankly disappointing. Like the so-called *Legenda Trium Sociorum*, it starts bravely enough with an account of the conversion of S. Francis and the early days of the Order, and then seems to go to pieces in the middle. It begins with a lengthy prologue in which Bernard refers to the earlier sources from which he has drawn much of his material— Celano's *Vita Prima*, the lost document of John of Ceperano known as

---

[1] See Glassberger's *Chronicle* in *An. F.*, II, pp. 89–90 : *iniungébatur omnibus ministris . . . quod inquirant de operibus beati Francisci et aliorum sanctorum fratrum quaecumque memoria digna, prout in suis provinciis contigerunt, eidem Generali sub certis verbis et testimoniis rescribenda.*

[2] Published in *An. F.*, III, pp. 666–92.

Quasi stella matutina, Julian of Speyer and *Bonaventura.* Yet there
are two works from which he has quoted extensively and of which he
makes no mention at all. One of these is the *Vita Secunda* of Celano,
and the other the *Legenda Trium Sociorum.*[1] There is no satisfactory
explanation of this silence. Meanwhile, apart from the recognised
sources, Bernard says that certain new facts have come to light which
ought to be put on record. But these facts are almost entirely concerned with the second generation of friars and have little to tell us
about Francis himself.

The book is divided into nine chapters of which the first tells us of
the conversion of S. Francis and of the early disciples. Its main
interest is in giving us some information not only about the well-known
friars such as Leo, Angelo, Bernard, Giles and Rufino, but also about
several others whose names are not mentioned in the other Legends,
men like Soldanerius, another Leo who became Archbishop of Milan,
Augustine, Christopher and Stephen who had been a Benedictine
abbot until he discovered that he wanted to become a friar.[2] The
next five chapters are merely stories of S. Francis and the early days
taken from *1* and *2 Celano* and the *Legenda Trium Sociorum.* The
seventh chapter is headed " *De Tribus Ordinibus* " and is composed
of a number of stories of how various men of distinction entered the
Franciscan Order, many of them having previously been members of
other Orders. The chapter is very unevenly divided, being almost
entirely concerned with the friars themselves, while the Poor Clares
and the Third Order are cursorily dismissed in a few lines. From this
Bernard goes immediately to tell of the death and translation of the
Saint and rounds off his narrative with a series of miracles, all taken
from other sources. The value of the book is in the stories it tells
of some of the early friars ; as a new *Life* of S. Francis it has little to
add to our previous knowledge, while its omission of many of the most

---

[1] That the *Leg. 3 Soc.* is the source of *Bernard of Bessa* and not the opposite, as van
Ortroy would have us believe, is fairly clear. The following parallel passages are typical :

<table>
<tr><td>*Leg. 3 Soc.* 35</td><td>*Bernard of Bessa,* cap. iv</td></tr>
</table>

*Episcop*us vero civitatis *Assisii,* ad quem pro
consilio frequenter ibat vir Dei, benigne
ipsum recipiens, *dixit* ei : Dura mihi
videtur et *aspera vita* vestra, *nihil* scilicet *in
saeculo possidere.* Cui sanctus ait : Domine,
*si possessiones aliquas haberemus, nobis essent
necessaria arma ad protec*tionem nostram.
Nam *inde oriuntur quaestiones et lites,* solet-
que ex hoc amor *Dei et proximi* multipliciter
impediri, et ideo nolumus in hoc saeculo
possidere aliquid temporale.

Episcopo *Assisii dicente sibi,*
quod
multum
videbatur sibi *aspera vita* ista, *nihil in* hoc
saeculo possidere ; respondit :
*Si possessiones aliquas haberemus, arma ad
protegendum necessaria nobis essent,* quia
quaestiones et lites plurimae *inde oriuntur,*
de quibus *Dei* ac *proximi* solet dilectio
impediri.

[2] " *Voluit minorari.*" Cf. *An. F.,* III, p. 669.

significant events of the Saint's life, such as the journey to the East
and the impression of the Stigmata, is surprising in a book which
purports to be written in praise of S. Francis.

Apart from the *Liber de Laudibus* we know of no other work which
might be regarded as supplementary to Bonaventura. There was,
however, a tradition treasured among the friars of the Marches of
Ancona which, before long, was to be written down and published
to the world. But before we come to that we ought to glance at a work
of some interest known as the *Anonymus Perusinus.* This work, which
was known to the compilers of the *Acta Sanctorum*, was republished by
van Ortroy in the *Miscellanea Francescana* in 1902.[1] The author
confesses that he was only a disciple of the disciples of S. Francis and
declares that he has received from them information about the deeds
of the Saint himself and of the early brethren which he has now recorded
according to the direction of the Holy Spirit.[2] Again, as in the case
of Bernard of Bessa, our hopes are raised, only to be dashed by the
discovery that what the nameless Perugian gives us is merely a rescript
of the *Legenda Trium Sociorum.* There are, it is true, one or two
details given which are not in his source, but they are of no great
importance. Following the usual practice of medieval biographers, he
has copied out large passages of his source almost verbatim, while as
for the *acta* of S. Francis which he promises us, there is no mention
of them at all. The author, who no doubt belonged to the second
generation of the friars, must have gone to Assisi and have found there
the papers which we know as *Leg. 3 Soc.* and upon which Celano had
already worked. From them he compiles a *Legenda* which, as a new
edition of an earlier work, is not without merit, but which can hardly
be regarded as an original biography. The following example will
show his method :

Leg. 3 Soc. 41–2	*Anon. Perus.* 35
Quando autem se invicem *revid-ebant* tanta iucunditate replebantur et gaudio, ac si *nihil recordarentur* eorum quae fuerant passi ab iniquis.	Quando autem se *revid-ebant* tanta iucunditate et spirituali *gaudio replebantur,* quod *nihil recordabantur*
	adversitatis et maximae pau-pertatis quam patiebantur.
Solliciti erant quotidie orare et laborare manibus	*Solliciti erant quotidie* in *oratione et labore* manuum

[1] *La Leggenda Latina di San Francesco secondo l'Anonimo Perugino* in *Misc. Franc.,* ix, pp. 33–48.

[2] " *Ego qui acta eorum vidi, verba audivi, quorum etiam discipulus fui, aliqua de actibus Beatissimi Fratris nostri Francisci et aliquorum fratrum qui venerunt in principio Religionis narravi et compilavi prout mens mea divinitus fuit docta."* *Misc. Franc.,* ix, p. 36.

Leg. 3 Soc. 41-2

suis, ut omnem otiositatem,
animae inimicam, a se penitus
effugarent.
Surgebant in media nocte
solliciti et

                        orabant
devotissime cum immensis
lacrimis et suspiris, amore
intimo se invicem diligebant
et serviebat unus alteri
ac nutriebat eum, sicut mater
                filium unicum
ac dilectum.

Anon. Perus. 35

suarum, ut omnem otiositatem,
animae inimicam, a se penitus
effugarent.   Noctibus vero
similiter solliciti surgere
media nocte iuxta illud pro-
phetae : media nocte surgebam
ad confitendum tibi ; orabant
cum devotione multa et
lacrimis frequenter. Amore
intimo se invicem diligebant
serviebat quoque et nutriebat
unus alterum,   sicut mater
servit et nutrit filium suum.

The *Anonymus Perusinus* was probably written about the same time as Bernard of Bessa's *Liber de Laudibus*, that is to say, about 1275-80. For the next thirty years there is silence. Neither of the two works which we have just been considering made any appreciable impression on the Order, and the *Legenda Maior* of Bonaventura held the field. All the original companions of S. Francis were dead,[1] and many of the books which contained their writings had been destroyed. We feel that the great effort to present an adequate portrait of the Saint is now over, having in its time absorbed the energies of some great men. The rugged and homely narratives of Leo and his companions have been smoothed out by the rather sententious phrases of Celano and the dignified language of Bonaventura, just as the unhaloed portrait of *Frater Franciscus* at the Sacro Speco and the insignificant little figure of the Cimabue fresco in the Lower Church at Assisi have given place to the more conventional, fatherly saint of Giotto and Simone Martini. But in the Marches of Ancona a tradition was lingering which was soon to find expression in one of the most exquisite of all Franciscan documents, the *Actus S. Francisci* and its Italian translation known as the *Fioretti di San Francesco*. The *Actus* is not a biography of S. Francis but a large collection of stories, some directly concerned with the Saint himself, some concerned with the second or even the third generation of his followers. There is no manuscript known to us which contains all the chapters, and it is possible that there never was such a thing, but it is as if from the common stock various selections had been made. Thus in the manuscript used by Sabatier in his critical edition of the *Actus*[2] there are only sixty-six chapters, but he adds four from the Vatican MS. 4354, which obviously belong to the same collection,

---

[1] Wadding says that Masseo lived until 1280, but he has probably confused him with another friar of the same name.

[2] Cf. *Actus Beati Francisci et Sociorum Eius* in *Collection d'Études et de Documents*, Tome iv (1902).

and prints a Latin version of five out of the remaining six chapters of the *Fioretti*. Since Sabatier's book was published a much better text of the whole of these chapters has been found by Dr. Little in the manuscript called by his name and published in the *Collectanea Franciscana*, I. Putting all these together we get a total of 76 chapters, but it does not follow that this represents the whole of the original collection.

A cursory study of the *Actus* is enough to convince us that it is obviously founded upon at least two earlier sources. There are, in the collection, stories of two quite different types, the first being incidents from the life of S. Francis and his friends, the second tales of the friars of the Marches of the second and third generations. Not only are they concerned with quite separate groups of people, they are also written from two very different standpoints. So far as the first type are concerned, the emphasis is on Poverty and Humility, whereas in the others the tone is far more that of mysticism and the supernatural. As Sabatier says : " In spite of the similarity of style two very different hands have worked on the *Actus* . . . One of the most striking characteristics of the first is the intensity of life which runs through it. The saints are real saints already on the way to heaven, but they are still on earth : we see them and hear the sound of their voices. But as soon as we reach the friars of the Marches we find ourselves face to face with different beings : they have each a name, but we feel that these names are only a concession to our intellectual weakness, for they have all the same expression, the same voice, the same visions. They are no longer here, on earth, by our side, but we see them bathed in mysterious light, eternally rapt in contemplation." [1]

The separation of the two sources is not a very difficult task. The chapters in Sabatier's edition which are concerned with Francis and the early disciples are as follows : 1–8, 10–15, 17–21, 23–46, 59, 62–4, 67, 71–2. These tell us many stories of the early days, and introduce us to such familiar figures as Leo, Bernard, Giles, Masseo, Rufino, Angelo, Sylvester and S. Clare. As we read them we realise that they clearly reflect the point of view of the " Spirituals ", for they never tire of telling us of Francis's devotion to Poverty and Simplicity, and they quote from the Rule of 1221 and even from that forbidden document the Testament of S. Francis.[2] They have hard words to tell of Brother Elias, who figures very badly in these chapters, and of his betrayal of S. Francis's wishes in the matter of food. We notice, also, that the writer is one who is familiar with Assisi and its neighbourhood since he mentions the smaller places like Bettona (cap. 15), Bevagna and

---

[1] *Actus*, Préface, pp. iv–v.

[2] There are references to the Rule in caps. 3, 4, 13, 17 and 28, and to the Testament, though it is not mentioned by name, in 28.

Cannara (cap. 16), and Subasio (cap. 31), while there is an almost certain reference to the Carceri in chapter 2. Moreover, the writer obviously has his eyes on the past as he constantly uses such expressions as " in principio Ordinis" or " vivente Beato Francisco" (caps. 3, 4, 8, 14 and 19). He is also familiar with some of the earlier legends, quoting from 1 and 2 Celano, Bonaventura and Bernard of Bessa. He seems also to have read some of the works of S. Francis apart from the Rule and Testament.

When we turn to our second source we find a very different type of story. The original document would probably have begun with what is now chapter 53 of the Actus. This chapter opens with the following words :

The province of the Marches of Ancona was adorned as it were with certain notable stars, to wit with holy Friars Minor, who above and below (that is to say in the sight of God and of their neighbours) shone with radiant virtues, and whose memory is indeed holy and blessed.

Then the writer begins to tell of Lucido, Bentivoglia of San Severino, Peter of Monticulo and Conrad of Offida. In the other chapters of this source there are stories of Anthony of Padua, John of La Verna, James of Massa, James of Fallerone, John of Penna and many others who flourished about the end of the thirteenth century. This second source was incorporated into the Actus as chapters 48–9, 50–8, 60–1, 68–9 and 74–6.[1] In these chapters it is noticeable that there is practically no mention of S. Francis at all, and no reference to other known Franciscan literature.

If we take out of the Actus, as we know it, these two sources, the first containing fifty chapters and the second eighteen, we are still left with those numbered 9, 16, 22, 47, 65, 66, 70 and 73. Of these, 22, 66 and 70 must be registered as " doubtful " as there is nothing to show to which source they should be assigned. Again, chapter 65 appears to have been an interpolation, as it occurs again in the Speculum Perfectionis and the Verba Conradi.[2] The four remaining chapters are of peculiar interest, in that they throw some light on the very obscure problem of the authorship of at any rate part of the Actus.

Chapter 9 is the story of the gift of La Verna by Orlando da Chiusi and of S. Francis's retreat there in 1224. The whole experience, including the impression of the Stigmata, is, of course, one of the most important in the whole of the Franciscan legend. But as we read the

---

[1] Chapters 48–9 (about S. Anthony) and 60–1 might have come from either source, but their position in the compilation known as Fac secundum exemplar points to their belonging to the later source.

[2] Speculum Perfectionis (ed. Sabatier), pp. 140 ff., and cf. Verba Conradi, 4 in Opuscules, fasc. vi, pp. 376 f.

M

story here we find that the experiences of S. Francis himself are hardly mentioned, and that the Stigmata themselves are dismissed in a few words. What the writer is concerned to tell is not what was done by S. Francis but by Brother Leo. The end of the chapter explains this, as we find there these words : " This story Brother James of Massa had from the mouth of Brother Leo, and Brother Ugolino of Monte S. Maria from the mouth of the said Brother James, and I, who have written it, from the mouth of Brother Ugolino, a man worthy to be trusted in every way." In other words, this story claims to come from Leo himself, who is here simply describing his own experiences.

Chapter 16 is the story of how S. Francis consulted Clare and Sylvester on the problem of his own work, whether he was to go on as a popular evangelist, or whether he should give more time to contemplation. The account is similar to that in the *Legenda Maior*, xii. 1–2, which, as we have already suggested, was probably told to S. Bonaventura by Sylvester himself. The account in *Actus* adds the important detail that the messenger whom Francis employed was Brother Masseo, who gave an account of it afterwards to James of Massa.

Chapter 47 is only very short, recording a conversation between Giles and James of Massa.

Chapter 73 (= *Little* 48) is a story of Brother Simon, one of the early disciples. It begins with the characteristic phrase " *in principio nostri Ordinis* ", goes on with the words " *sicut audivi ab illis qui diu secum morati sunt* ", and then, speaking of James of Massa's friendship with Simon, says " *ut narravit mihi ille qui secum fuit* ". The chapter ends with the words : " *ego, frater Hugolinus de Monte Sanctae Mariae steti ibidem* (i.e. at Brunforte) *tribus annis, et vidi certitudinaliter dictum miraculum notum tam secularibus quam fratribus totius custodiae* ".

In two of these chapters occurs the name of Ugolino of Monte S. Maria, who is described as the author of chapter 73, and a friend of the writer of chapter 9. Moreover, he makes it clear that he is himself relying upon the testimony, whether written or oral, of Brother James of Massa. Now, although it is impossible to show any proof, it seems to me that a reasonably strong case can be made out for thinking of James of Massa as the author of the source which lies behind the earlier chapters of the *Actus*.

Though himself a layman,[1] James of Massa was a well-read and intelligent man, of whom Wadding writes : " *mirum in modum data est ei cum scientia intelligentia scripturarum et praescientia futurorum.*" [2] We know also that he wrote a history of the gift of La Verna by Orlando

---

[1] *Actus*, cap. 47 and 57.
[2] Wadding, *Annales Minorum*, ad an. 1256. T. IV, p. 11.

da Chiusi to S. Francis.[1]   References to him in the chapters which
we have been considering tell us that he was a personal friend of Leo,
Masseo, Giles, Simon and Clare, that the account of the experiences
on La Verna came to him from Leo himself, and that he had the story
of Francis's consultations with Clare and Sylvester from Masseo.[2]
We know also, from *Actus* 76, that James was a keen "Spiritual",
for in the great dream which is there recorded, the ideal Franciscan,
who climbs to the top of the tree, is John of Parma, the friend of the
zelanti.[3]   It should be noticed, also, that James is nowhere mentioned
in the fifty chapters which we have selected to form our first source.
To associate James of Massa with this source may be conjecture, but
at least we can say that his name is definitely given as the transmitter
of certain stories, and that only someone who was in direct and close
touch with the early disciples could have produced the sort of narrative
which is here given.

As a possible reconstruction I would suggest that James of Massa
either wrote these chapters himself or dictated them to Ugolino of
Monte S. Maria.   If we look up Ugolino in Wadding we read that he
was " *vir pius, et candidus author ; scripsit Historiam quam Floretum
praenotavit, in qua narrat vitam et gesta sancti Francisci ac Sociorum
eius, usque ad pontificatum Alexandri IV* ".[4]   What was this *Floretum* ?
Some think that it was the whole of the *Actus*, but it seems to me much
more probable that it was the collection of stories told to him by James
of Massa to which he has himself added three to tell us about Brother
James himself.[5]   To these a later scribe has added a further chapter
(*Actus*, 9), as is made clear from the text.   It is also reasonable to
suppose that this very chapter is the *Historia acceptionis loci Montis
Alvernae* which, according to Bartholomew of Pisa, was written by
James of Massa, and which a later scribe felt ought to be added to
the collection of stories which Ugolino had already had from James.
Ugolino seems to have died about the year 1300,[6] in which case he
may have been working with James of Massa either about 1265 with
a view to supplementing Bonaventura's *Legenda*, or after 1266 when
the older legends were destroyed and an attempt might be made to
write something quickly before the tradition was lost.[7]

---

[1] Wadding, *Scriptores*, p. 125. Sbaralea in the *Supplementum* to this work quotes from
Bartholomew of Pisa : " *de quo* (i.e. *loco Massae) fuit frater Jacobus qui historiam acceptionis loci montis Alvernae habuit a fratre Leone, et de miris factis in dicto monte, et de stig-
matibus sacris*." Cf. *Liber de Conformitatibus*, xi. 2 in *An. F.*, IV, p. 514.

[2] *Actus*, 9, 16, 47 and 73.   [3] See *Fioretti*, 48.

[4] Wadding, *Scriptores*, s.v. Hugolinus de S. Maria in Monte.

[5] Viz. *Actus*, 16, 47 and 73.

[6] Bughetti, *Alcune Idee Fondamentali sui Fioretti*, in *A.F.H.*, xix (1926), p. 325.

[7] If the note at the end of *Actus* 73 is trustworthy, Ugolino was writing about an incident
which took place at least fifty years before, and at which James of Massa was present.

Meanwhile, about the end of the thirteenth century, another Ugolino, whose surname is unknown, wrote down a number of stories about the friars of the Marches of Ancona. He refers to himself by name as a friend of John of Penna,[1] and also speaks in the first person in four other chapters where he appears as a friend of John of La Verna.[2] Eventually, and probably between 1322 and 1328, these two sources were put together to form a collection known as *Actus Beati Francisci et Sociorum Eius.* Together they form 76 chapters, but we have already seen that no known manuscript contains them all. We are therefore at liberty to ask whether the original collection was any longer. There is, of course, no reply to this ; but there are two small collections which, both in style and in subject-matter, are closely akin to the *Actus,* and may have once belonged to the collection from which the *Actus* is a selection. One of these is the tract known as *Verba Conradi* and the other the *Legenda Vetus.*

One of the brothers who is referred to in the Actus is Conrad of Offida, a friend of Brother Leo[3] and a " Spiritual "[4] whose ascetic zeal and devotion to poverty provoked Angelo Clareno to describe him in glowing terms.[5] He died at Bastia on December 12th, 1306.[6] Whether he was actually the author or merely the inspiration of the book called *Verba Conradi* is a matter of small importance ; the point is that these tales claim to come from a member of the second generation who was known to be a friend of Brother Leo.[7] In fact, the chapters might almost be called " *Verba Fratris Leonis* ", for they are nearly all concerned with Leo. The first begins with the words : " *Beatus Conradus de Offida audivit a beato fratre Leone socio beati patris nostri Francisci . . .* ", the second : " *Beatus Conradus audivit a fratre Leone . . .* ", the third : " *Semel frater Leo . . . misit quamdam litteram fratri Conrado in qua . . .* ", the fifth : " *Quadam vice sanctus*

Another argument in favour of an early date for this source is that the early years of the fourteenth century were such stormy ones for the " Spirituals " that it is unlikely that they could have produced anything so calm as these chapters.

[1] *Actus,* 69 : " *omnia praedicta retulit mihi Hugolino ipse frater Johannes.*"

[2] *Actus,* 51, 52, 54 and 58. It is possible that this Ugolino was Ugolino Brunforte, a well-known " Spiritual ". See Sabatier, *Actus,* p. xx.

[3] *Actus,* 65.

[4] *Actus,* 50 : " *mirabilis zelator evangelicae regulae Patris nostri S. Francisci, sanctus frater Conradus de Offida.*"

[5] Cf. *A.L.K.G.,* ii, p. 311 : " *LV annis et amplius una tantum tunica de veteri et vili panno, repeciata de sacco et aliis peciis contentus, nudis pedibus semper incedens, praeter tunicam et cordam nunquam in vita sua aliquid habere voluit ; nuda humus paleis strata vel storicis vel tabula lectus eius erat, ab oratione, vigiliis et ieiuniis continuis nunquam cessans . . .* etc.*"

[6] Sabatier, *Spec. Perf.,* p. 140, n. 1.

[7] The Collection was printed by Sabatier in *Opuscules,* fasc. vi, from the MS. S. Isidore 1/25.

frater Conradus audivit a fratre Leone . . . ", the sixth : " *Alia quadam vice dixit beatus Franciscus fratri Leoni* ", the seventh and eighth both refer to Leo, the tenth begins : " *Dicebat sanctus pater Franciscus sicut frater Leo scribit* ", and the eleventh : " *Retulit sanctus frater Conradus, sicut habuit a fratre Leone qui fuit socius et confessor beati Francisci et ab ore ipsius audierat* ". The collection as we have it is not, however, in its original state, as it contains some repetitions and interpolations from other sources.[1] But if the stories here told are substantially true, and if they can indeed claim to come from Leo through the writings of his friend Conrad of Offida, then they are worthy of a prominent place among the sources for the life of S. Francis.

The other tract which may be considered here is a small collection of seven chapters from the compilation known as *Fac secundum exemplar.* This document was well known among Franciscans in the Middle Ages and is contained in a number of codices scattered among the libraries of Europe.[2] According to Sabatier, this collection from various Franciscan sources was made about 1322, perhaps by Fabianus of Hungary,[3] taking its name from the words in Exodus xxv. 40 : " *Inspice et fac secundum exemplar quod tibi in monte monstratum est.*" The Preface to this collection says that it was formed from the following sources : a book belonging to Archbishop Frederick of Riga (1304–41), the (or a) *Legenda Vetus* which was read in the friars' refectory at Avignon, some writings of the companions of the Saint, and a work containing certain wonderful things about S. Anthony, John of La Verna and others. When we study the compilation we find that it is composed of a number of chapters from the *Speculum Perfectionis* (or possibly from *Per.*), a good deal of the *Actus,* seven chapters on the observance of the Rule which are not found elsewhere, some writings of S. Francis, sayings of Giles and some of the other brothers, and testimonies concerning the Indulgence of the Portiuncula. The problem which has vexed a number of those who have studied this work is how to make the contents of the book fit in with the plan laid down in the Preface. Sabatier suggests that the book of Archbishop Frederick was the *Speculum Perfectionis* ; that the seven chapters on the observance of the Rule formed the *Legenda Vetus*, or part of it ; that the writings of the companions of S. Francis are represented by the first sixteen chapters of the *Actus*—that is, about half of what we

---

[1] E.g. *Verba Conradi* 3 is akin to *Actus* 65 ; for *V.C.* 5 cf. *Actus* 59 ; *V.C.* 10 has a quotation from *2 Cel.* ; *V.C.* 11 is nearly the same as *Actus* 65 ; *V.C.* 12 contains a long quotation from the *Expositio Regulae* (ed. Oliger, pp. 44 ff.), and *V.C.* 13 = *2 Cel.* 207 and 205.

[2] The most important manuscripts are *Vat.* 4354 described by Sabatier in *Spec. Perf.*, pp. clxxvi–clxxxvi, and Liegnitz, *SS. Peter and Paul*, MS. 12, described by Sabatier in *Opuscules*, fasc. ii.

[3] Sabatier, *Spec. Perf.*, p. clxxxiii.

have called the first source of that work—and that the " wonderful things about S. Anthony, John of La Verna and others " means the later chapters of the *Actus*.

Whatever may be the true explanation, the seven chapters " *de legenda veteri* " are of considerable importance for our purpose.[1] They may well have formed part of some ancient exposition of the Rule which the friars of Avignon were accustomed to read during their meals to enforce upon them the duty of obedience.[2] They are written from a strictly " Spiritual " point of view, and, as we should expect, refer to some of the great problems which troubled the Order during the thirteenth century. The first chapter, which has some affinity with *Verba S. Francisci*, 5, tells of the growing laxity of the Order in receiving money, deserting the poor places in order to build themselves large houses in the towns, and in seeking privileges from the Pope. There seems to be a reference to Crescentius of Iesi, who waged war on the " Spirituals ", in the phrase " *non pastorem sed exterminatorem mittet eis Christus* ". This chapter purports to be based on the personal testimony of Brothers Leo, Bernard and Angelo. The second chapter, to which reference has already been made,[3] is perhaps the most interesting of all, for it tells us, on the evidence of Brother Leo, that in the first draft of the Rule of 1223, Francis made provision for those who wished to observe the regulations literally, even though their ministers might forbid them to do so ; but that the Pope persuaded him to alter these words.[4] The third chapter again tells of S. Francis's wish that the Rule should be kept " *ad litteram, sine glossa* ", and the fifth contains some observations on the subject of learning. The remaining three chapters are not of very great importance.

Whether or no the *Verba Conradi* and the *Legenda Vetus* were really part of the original collection known as *Actus Beati Francisci*, they certainly all belong to the same tradition, the tradition which emanates from the brothers of the Marches of Ancona who were striving, in face of great and sustained opposition, to keep alive the original idealism

---

[1] Published by Sabatier in *Opuscules*, fasc. iii. They occur also in MS. *Little*, Nos. 134–40 ; cf. *Collectanea Franciscana* (*B.S.F.S.*), I, pp. 72 f.

[2] " *Quaedam vero sumpta et reportata sunt de Legenda Veteri ipsius sancti, quam generalis minister, me praesente et aliquoties legente, fecit sibi et fratribus legi ad mensam in Avinione, ad ostendendum eam esse veram, utilem, authenticam atque bonam.*" *Opuscules*, fasc. iii, p. 80, from the Preface to *Fac secundum exemplar*.

[3] See p. 33.

[4] According to the *Legenda Vetus* Francis wrote : " *Ministri vero teneantur eisdem fratribus per obedientiam postulata benigne et liberaliter concedere, quod si facere nollent ipsi fratres habeant licentiam et obedientiam eam litteraliter observandi,*" whereas the Rule says : " *Ministri vero caritative et benigne eos recipiant et tantam familiaritatem habeant circa ipsos ut dicere possint eis et facere sicut domini servis suis* " (*Reg. Bull.*, cap. x).

of S. Francis and to observe the Rule as he had wished " *ad litteram et sine glossa* ". They looked back to Leo, Angelo and Rufino as those who had most claim to know the mind of the Saint, and they treasured the stories which had come down to them through Conrad of Offida, James of Massa and others who were their disciples and personal friends.

The *Actus* seems to have been compiled somewhere between 1322 and 1328.[1] Some years later fifty-three of its chapters were translated into Italian and published as *Fioretti di San Francesco*. To these fifty-three chapters were added five *Considerazioni sulle sacre stimmate*, and, in some manuscripts, the *Lives* of Juniper and Giles. This book, though in some ways the least reliable of our sources, has done more than any other to present a portrait of S. Francis to the modern world. This is due partly to the charm of the stories, partly to the quaintness of the old Italian in which they are told, and partly, in this country, to the delightful translation into the English of Malory by T. W. Arnold in 1898.[2] The original translator was a Tuscan, probably a native of Florence, and a Franciscan. Various names have been suggested, such as John of Marignolli (or S. Lorenzo), Bishop of Bisignano,[3] who died in 1359; but there is no real evidence of his identity.

Besides being a translator, the producer of this work was something of an author, as the five " Considerations on the Stigmata " show. These are based on certain chapters of the *Actus*[4] and some stories from *Celano* and *Bonaventura*, though the writer has made considerable alterations. A good deal of his material also comes from traditions which had lingered on at La Verna. The result of his labours is a fascinating narrative which Dr. Edmund Gardner calls " the most beautiful and convincing piece of Franciscan literature that we possess ".[5]

Yet when we try to assess the historical value of the collection of stories represented by the *Actus-Fioretti* we are faced with a difficult problem. Many of the narratives in the earlier chapters are similar to stories which had already been told by Celano and S. Bonaventura, but the author of the *Actus*, or of the source upon which it is based, has added a good deal to the more simple accounts of his predecessors. For example, in the story of the call of Bernard of Quintavalle, Celano

---

[1] Bughetti considers it much earlier, but in its present form it can hardly be earlier than 1322, as John of La Verna, who died that year, is spoken of as if he were no longer living. *A.F.H.*, xix, p. 326, n. 1.

[2] There are other versions, notably one by Professor Okey, and a not very successful translation into English verse by James Rhoades.

[3] Bughetti in *A.F.H.*, xix, p. 326.

[4] *Actus* 9, 18, 34, 38 and 39.

[5] E. G. Gardner, " The Little Flowers of S. Francis ", in *Essays in Commemoration*, p. 125.

tells us how Francis came to Bernard's house to spend the night, and how in the morning Bernard announced his intention of renouncing everything that he had.[1] The story in *Actus* is substantially the same, but adds the delightful details about Bernard and Francis both pretending to be asleep, in order that one might watch and the other pray in secret. How are we to regard this addition? Is it a fabrication for the sake of adding colour and interest to the narrative; or is it a fact known among the inner circle of the disciples and transmitted by them to James of Massa or whoever is responsible for the story in its present form? Again, the celebrated story of the preaching to the birds comes originally from *1 Cel.* 58, but is considerably amplified in *Actus* 16. Or again, the story of how Rufino saw and touched the scar in S. Francis's side comes from *1 Cel.* 95, and is spoken of again in *2 Cel.* 138, but in *Actus* 34 is told with much more detail. In the story of S. Francis before the Soldan in *Actus* 27 we read a strange account of how a woman invited Francis to lie with her and how he led her instead to a great fire, saying: " Come with me, and I will show you the most beautiful bed." With these words Francis threw off his clothes and lay down in the flames, inviting the woman to join him.[2] The rest of the chapter is based on *Bonaventura*, where we read of Francis suggesting that the relative truth of his faith and that of the Saracen hierarchy should be tested by their all submitting to an ordeal by fire. It seems probable, therefore, that in the *Actus* narrative this incident of Bonaventura's has been remodelled to form the curious account of the woman who tried to lure S. Francis from the path of virtue.

Although there are some modifications of earlier stories which strike us as fanciful it must not be too readily assumed that all the improvements upon the earlier narratives are necessarily unhistorical. If the *Actus* is indeed based upon the reminiscences of the first disciples, handed down either orally or in writing to the second generation of friars, then we may here have a source of great value and importance. And the quality of the narratives themselves is, in many instances, so high that we can hardly doubt that there is at least a kernel of truth in them. The Francis of these stories is the Francis whom we have learnt to love in the *Legenda Trium Sociorum*, the *Regula Primitiva* and the Testament, and is far removed from the more conventional figure of Bonaventura. The atmosphere, too, is that of the early days when Poverty was still the absorbing interest of the friars, and when the gaiety and excitement of their great experiment had not been overshadowed by organisation and officialdom. What could be more convincing than Masseo's jealousy of Francis's popularity, the story

---

[1] *1 Cel.* 24, *2 Cel.* 15, *3 Soc.* 27.
[2] The passage containing this account is not in the *Fioretti*.

of the wolf of Gubbio, Bernard's false snores, and Masseo's indignation at being made to turn round and round in the road like a top? And what, in the whole of the Franciscan legend, could be regarded as more beautiful and authentic than the chapter on Perfect Joy?[1] There are, it is true, mistakes in the *Actus* narrative, and there are miraculous events the historical truth of which may be open to doubt; but the fact remains that in this late flowering of the Franciscan legend we have something which strikes us as genuine, a tradition treasured and loved among those who were daily exposing themselves to indignities and persecutions in order to keep alive the flame which had been handed down to them from those who had had most opportunity of knowing the mind of S. Francis.

[1] This chapter is founded upon the 5th of the *Admonitions* of S. Francis.

INDEX